A residential building in the suburb Grbavica in Sarajevo, damaged in the shelling and crossfire during the 1992–1996 siege.
  People still live here.
  (Image credit: Tatjana Takševa 2017)

Unforgetting and the Politics of Representation

Based on interviews and conversations in the Bosnian Federation with women survivors of war rape, children born of armed conflict, leaders of NGOs who work with survivors, and people who lived through the war and who experienced it in different ways, this book challenges one-dimensional representations of the Yugoslav war and subsequent peacebuilding processes. Relying on feminist ethnography and autoethnography, this volume offers systematic engagement with the politics of representation of Bosnia and survivors of war in post-war journalism and scholarship.

Through rich and varied individual experiences of wartime violence and recovery that go beyond simple "us" vs "them" narratives of ethnic identity and intolerance, the book shows how public and private, individual and collective discourses actively shape one another and contribute to complex forms of engagement in recovery, healing, and rebuilding. The author draws upon archival material to undermine the fetishization of ethnicity as a determining category that often underpins journalistic and scholarly accounts of post-war Bosnia. By retracing and repairing separations between individual and collective remembrance, and by complicating linear and monolithic conception of this process, the narratives in the book actively contest reductionist and instrumentalist accounts of the civil war in Bosnia.

The book will appeal to scholars across the social sciences with interest in memory, peacebuilding, national identity, gendered violence, and processes of reconciliation.

Tatjana Takševa is Professor of Women and Gender Studies and Chair of the Department of English Language and Literature at Saint Mary's University, Canada. Born and raised in the former Yugoslavia, she holds a Ph.D. from the University of Toronto (2003), and is the author of numerous essays on feminist theory, nation building and the maternal, and co-editor of *Mothering Under Fire: Mothers and Mothering in Conflict Zones* (2015) and *Motherhood and Migration* (forthcoming 2026).

Unforgetting and the Politics of Representation

Voices from Contemporary Bosnia and Herzegovina

Tatjana Takševa

LONDON AND NEW YORK

First published 2025
by Routledge
4 Park Square, Milton Park, Abingdon, Oxon OX14 4RN

and by Routledge
605 Third Avenue, New York, NY 10158

Routledge is an imprint of the Taylor & Francis Group, an informa business

© 2025 Tatjana Takševa

The right of Tatjana Takševa to be identified as author of this work has been asserted in accordance with sections 77 and 78 of the Copyright, Designs and Patents Act 1988.

All rights reserved. No part of this book may be reprinted or reproduced or utilized in any form or by any electronic, mechanical, or other means, now known or hereafter invented, including photocopying and recording, or in any information storage or retrieval system, without permission in writing from the publishers.

Trademark notice: Product or corporate names may be trademarks or registered trademarks, and are used only for identification and explanation without intent to infringe.

British Library Cataloguing-in-Publication Data
A catalog record for this book is available from the British Library

ISBN: 978-1-032-02991-7 (hbk)
ISBN: 978-1-032-02992-4 (pbk)
ISBN: 978-1-003-18616-8 (ebk)

DOI: 10.4324/9781003186168

Typeset in Times New Roman
by SPi Technologies India Pvt Ltd (Straive)

Contents

About the Author	*ix*
Acknowledgments	*x*
Introduction: Pathways to Bosnia	1

PART I — 25

1 Why Stories Matter	27
2 Ecologies of Peace	36
3 Bosnia Beyond Balkanism	48
4 Sarajevo the Beautiful	58
5 Growing Up Under Siege	83

PART II — 89

6 Unforgetting the Children Born Because of War	91
7 What Does It Mean to Be a Child Born Because of War?	113

PART III — 133

8 The Space of Dialogue: Women Who Lived Through Violence	135

viii Contents

9 The Vulnerable and the Brave, in Their Own Words   143

10 Esma D., a Bosnian Woman Fighter   186

Conclusion: The Logic of Home: Transnational
Fieldnotes on Peace   196

Index   *208*

About the Author

Tatjana Takševa is Professor of Women and Gender Studies and Chair of the Department of English Language and Literature at Saint Mary's University, Canada. Born and raised in the former Yugoslavia, she holds a Ph.D. from the University of Toronto (2003), and is the author of numerous essays on feminist theory, nation building and the maternal, and co-editor of *Mothering Under Fire: Mothers* and *Mothering in Conflict Zones* (2015) and *Motherhood and Migration* (forthcoming 2026).

Acknowledgments

This book really belongs to the people who spoke with me about their lives and experiences and who put their trust in my ability to do justice to their words and their perspectives.. I am deeply grateful for the time they spent with me both back in 2017 when most of these conversations took place, and since then, as I have remained in touch with many of them in various ways. They have inspired me in more ways than I can name, both through the equanimity with which they have carried their pain, and with the resilience, strength, and courage they show every single day. In my own wanderings through historical time and multiple cultural and political spaces, they have taught me about the meaning of home and peace. "S.W.," Ajna, Lejla, Alen, Merima, both Selmas, Vahdeta, Sabina, S.Š., Alma, Munira, Azra, Esma, Sena, L.O.—I hope the book lives up to your expectations. All errors and omissions remain mine.

Duška Andrić, a fierce defender of human rights and a committed advocate for women and children who lived through violence during war, initially saw some value in my approach to the subject matter and put me in touch with some of the women and children born because of war. For this I remain very grateful. Beyond this, I have cherished the time we spent together that summer in Zenica and felt nourished by our conversations.

I am very grateful to Amra Delić for taking interest in my work and for sharing her master's thesis with me, in which she examines the quality of life and long-term psychological consequences in women with experience of war rape in Bosnia and Herzegovina. I benefited from having the opportunity to speak with her on several occasions and our correspondence, learning about her efforts in helping establish and develop the Association Forgotten Children of War in Sarajevo: Amra, you are a powerhouse, and you continue to be a true inspiration!

I owe much gratitude to Ajna Jusić, a 'child of war,' a passionate and brave feminist, whose activist work I have had the privilege of seeing develop since we first met in 2017, and whose personal and professional commitment to other children born of war, their mothers, and all women who survived sexualized violence remain a beacon of hope for me and others who work in this subject area.

Acknowledgments xi

I learned a great deal about everyday acts of peacebuilding from my conversations with Sabiha Husić, Munira Šubašić, Alisa Muratčauš, Lejla Sedić, Belma Zulčić, Mirha Pojskić, and Branka Agić. Their passionate and long-lasting commitment to improving the health and well-being of all people who survived war-related violence in Bosnia and Herzegovina through patient and inclusive practice is a true model of meaningful, intersectional feminist support.

The academic and feminist perspective reflected in the book has benefited from and has been sustained through several gatherings over the last five years. The two-day closed-door workshop organized by the Institute for Human Security at the Fletcher School of Law and Diplomacy at Tufts University in 2018 on the theme "Challenging Conceptions: Children born of wartime rape and sexual exploitation" was a unique, informal, and intense interaction among a group of 15 or so colleagues that facilitated agenda setting and meaningful exchange around the topic of children born of wartime rape and exploitation, their families, and communities. The two symposia of the Canadian Research Network for Women, Peace, and Security provided immensely rewarding, intellectually stimulating, and personally fulfilling feminist spaces for knowledge sharing among researchers, activists, and community members. In 2022, about 30 of us from many disciplines and walks of life came together in Montreal to interrogate existing definitions of peace and security in relation to gender. In 2023, I had the pleasure of hosting the event in Halifax, where we were engaged in developing the theme of "Reimagining Peace and Peacebuilding" in the context of the women, peace, and security agenda. I acknowledge the role that these storying knowledge circles of committed people played in helping me complete the book. In 2024, Flavia Guerrini from the Institut für Erziehungswissenschaft / CGI—Center für Interdisziplinäre Geschlechterforschung at the University of Innsbruck, who herself has recently published *Vom feind ein kind: Nachkommen alieter Soldaten erzählen* (Mandelbaum Verlagen, 2022), a book on Austrian "occupation children," had the wonderful idea that we organize a research workshop on the theme, "Children born of war and processes of state and nation building." The conversations that ensued with colleagues who attended the workshop, Karin Priem, Tereza Jiroutová Kynčlová, Philipp Rohrbach, and Dijana Simic, were intellectually stimulating and generative, providing a welcome perspective on parts of this book that I have tried to incorporate during the final editing stage. That Ajna Jusić, the president of the Association Forgotten Children of War, was my co-presenter on the topic of "Bosnian children born of war as political agents of change" at this event was especially meaningful for me, as I had not seen Ajna in person since our last conversation in Sarajevo in 2017.

Much of this research was supported by a grant from the Social Sciences and Humanities Research Council of Canada awarded in 2016 to a team project then entitled, "'Children of the Enemy': Narrative Constructions of Identity Following Wartime Rape and Transgenerational Trauma in Post-WWII Germany and Post-Conflict Bosnia." Agatha Schwartz, the principal xii Acknowledgments

investigator on this project, helped initiate some of the early contacts I made in Bosnia. The team also included Mythili Rajiva and Christabelle Sethna, and as a team, over the span of several years, we did a lot of good work together. I am very grateful to Ana Bogic, Ivana Amidzic, and Tea Rokolj for their initial work on transcriptions and translations. For all of them this was difficult work, as they were encountering the narratives of survivors for the first time and contending with the weight that they carry; thank you for taking care.

I owe heartfelt thanks to my colleagues at the Department of English Language and Literature and Saint Mary's University, especially Teresa Heffernan and Gugu Hlongwane, who took on additional administrative duties as Acting Chairs on my behalf and generously facilitated my sabbatical for research purposes in the fall of 2022, a precious six-month period that was instrumental in producing a draft of this work.

Neil Jordan is one of the kindest editors I have ever worked with, one who possesses a a special talent for inviting authorial reflection. Special thanks to Alice Salt, Gemma Rogers,Madii Cherry-Moreton, and Suba Ramya for their patience and generous assistance through the publication process.

At home, Steve Tucker's support of my work on this book has gone beyond what we could both imagine was called for. He held the fort for months and years on end, providing committed and patient daily care to our three children while I was traveling, discovering, mourning, crying, and celebrating with the amazing people I had been spending time with both here in Canada and in Bosnia. Among the most avid readers I have ever known in any language, and a serious student of Slavic history, intellectual traditions, and the Yugosphere, he has also been my first reader of drafts, tester of ideas, and a sparring after-dinner partner in conversation, polemics, and debate of all sorts. His unwavering affectionate support has had a grounding influence on my life and work, and I am grateful for it.

Introduction
Pathways to Bosnia

> Remembering is not a passionate or dispassionate retelling a reality that is no more, but a new birth of the past, when time goes in reverse. Above all it is creativity. As they narrate, people create, they "write" their life.
>
> *Svetlana Alexievich*, The Unwomanly Face of War

> Time renders most individual moments meaningless, or at least less important than they originally seemed, but it is only through the passage of time that life acquires its meaning. And that meaning itself is constantly in flux; we are always making it up and then revising as we go along, ordering and reordering our understanding of the past in real time.
>
> *Natalie Hodges*, Uncommon Measure

This book has several beginnings.

One of those is the year 2012, when I was pregnant with my youngest of three children. In late winter, Bryony House, a shelter and transition house for women and children leaving abuse and intimate partner violence in the Halifax Regional Municipality was looking for someone to deliver a public talk on women, children, and violence to mark events organized for the International Day of Women, on March 8. I interpreted this moment as an important confluence between my research and my personal experience, a moment in my life where, as Alexievich writes in her haunting oral history of the Russian women who fought in World War II, "time goes in reverse" as well as a "new birth of the past." I volunteered. Compelled as if by an invisible force, I began to seek and find ways to bring together my own transnational personal experience into the research process, to create a bridge between my past and my present and across different cultural identity thresholds. In the stages of advanced pregnancy—my daughter was born seven weeks later—I delivered a talk on sexual violence as a weapon of war during the war in Bosnia and the effect of that violence on women who experienced it, especially those women who conceived and gave birth to children because of rape.

DOI: 10.4324/9781003186168-1

2   Unforgetting and the Politics of Representation

In the late 1990s, I began reading first-person accounts of the war rape experiences of women survivors written in English and in Bosnian. The magnitude of the atrocities seemed incomprehensible to me and wounding in a way that was difficult to process. For a long time after, I read and wept. Their voices and their stories were all that I could hear. They consumed me with what I registered as an all-encompassing importance. I had not stopped thinking about them ever since. Their stories contained the meaning of the war itself, they resonated with multiple losses and harms: individual, as well as collective—of extended families, of communities, of nation. Through their stories and the memories of their harrowing war experiences they "wrote" their own lives, but they also strangely wrote my own—through reading their narratives I experienced a reordering of my own "understanding of the past in real time," as Hodges expresses this process through her scientifically inspired meditation on the relationship between one's own individual life and historical time.

I arrived in Canada in the fall of 1992 as a student of English linguistics and literature at the University of Belgrade, at a time when the war in Bosnia was intensifying. This was intended to be a short stay with my father and brother who were already in Toronto, my father since 1990, soon after my parents' divorce. When I left Yugoslavia, I did not know that the siege of Sarajevo had begun in April that same year; the Serbian media at the time, under Slobodan Milošević's authoritarian regime, still reported on the conflict in terms of small-scale operations carried out by the Yugoslav National Army as a form of national defense against secessionist elements. Belgrade, where I was born, was still the nominal capital of Yugoslavia, acting ostensibly on behalf of the country, but active political unrest and anti-government demonstrations, both spontaneous and well organized, had become a frequent occurrence by this point. I arrived in Canada with a Yugoslav passport, as a Yugoslav citizen.

My intention was to return to Belgrade to complete my studies before deciding what to do with my life afterwards. Spending a few months in an English-speaking country was going to be good, immersive language practice. However, two months after arriving in Toronto, I learned of the death of my mother who had remained in Serbia. While her death was not directly related to the war— she died of post-operative complications that could have, perhaps, been avoided had circumstances been different, the loss was unexpected, devastating, and largely incomprehensible to my 22-year-old self, who had only just left home a few months earlier. After traveling back to attend her funeral, I returned to Canada, and decided to remain. An existential maelstrom overtook my life. I was grieving an unexpected personal loss at the same time as I strove to overcome a culture shock and learn what it means to begin one's life in a new country, with new ways of being, seeing, and speaking. I struggled to understand a new environment, the demands of survival in a cultural and economic system very different from the one I grew up in. I also struggled to make sense of the loss of my country, as it was literally disintegrating in front of my eyes in Western news coverage. I witnessed it crumbling in violent ways mainly through Canadian and Anglo-American news, the reports of which I compulsively

Introduction   3

collected. By this time, my Yugoslav passport and citizenship had become historical documents. Being a citizen of a country that no longer exists made me feel in some strange way homeless and displaced, a state that would heighten each time I had to explain where I am from over the years. The question of identity started to preoccupy me, especially since I spent two and a half years without formal national identity and citizenship: my Yugoslav passport was no longer valid since the country it represented disintegrated after my arrival, while in Canada I existed on a temporary visa, awaiting permanent residency, without being able to legally work or continue my studies. It is as if I did not exist. I pondered the meaning of borders, their artificiality, their permeability.

On December 14, 1995, Slobodan Milošević, Alija Izetbegović, and Franjo Tudjman signed the Dayton Peace Accord, brokered through international help. This put an end to open warfare in Bosnia, the epicenter of the conflict for the previous four years. Earlier that same year, after two and a half years of being in legal limbo, I was granted permanent residency in Canada. I also gave birth to my first child and was allowed to pick up where I left off three years earlier with my studies. Grief was a constant companion, but there was no time to attend to it. From Canada, I witnessed the fall of Milošević's regime, the bombing of Belgrade by NATO forces, and the entrenchment of nationalist agendas in former Yugoslav republics, now newly established states. I realized that had I remained, I would have had to choose a national identity. Very little of it made sense. Such choices were incongruent with any discourse of home that permeated my childhood.

While I was born in Belgrade, I had grown up mainly in what is today the Republic of North Macedonia. My mother's family were a mix of, on the one hand, Bosnian Serbs via one of the Dalmatian Islands, likely Korčula, and on the other, Hungarian Croats who were settled by Maria Teresa—then 'sovereign of Austria, Hungary, Croatia, Bohemia, Transylvania, Mantua, Milan, Lodomeria and Galicia, the Austrian Netherlands, and Parma'—on the outer border of the Austro-Hungarian empire around the middle of the 18th century, to guard the southern border of the Austro-Hungarian empire from its Ottoman rival. My maternal great-great-grandmother spoke only Hungarian and struggled to raise her family in Sremski Karlovac in a Serb-speaking environment. Her husband was a soldier and seldom present. There are no stories about him, other than to recall that having failed as a small businessman, he ammased an increasing debt, and one day left his wife and daughters, leaving no trace of his subsequent whereabouts. Her daughter, my great-grandmother, remained there herself and raised her own family before moving back to Croatia after her daughters left home. My grandparents moved to the capital in the 1960s via Banja Luka and Sarajevo when my grandfather found work in his field, agricultural engineering. They spent much of their life in Belgrade, which is where my own parents met as university students. My maternal grandfather's family had settled and established itself in Banja Luka for at least two generations. His father's family were wealthy enough to send their only son to St. Petersburg, Russia, to the Theological Seminary. My grandfather subsequently learned Russian himself, among several other Slavic languages, and travelled to Moscow

4 Unforgetting and the Politics of Representation

and Kiev many times, bringing back with him tales of the people, the steppes, and the folklore, which he particularly admired.

My father's parents were Macedonian farmers from the northeastern Greek region of Drama. In 1944, on the back of a donkey, they fled Greece and headed north, ahead of the fascist Bulgarian armies. The newly formed Yugoslav Republic of Macedonia seemed to them a logical place to settle in, especially since the post-World War II Communist government was explicit about providing financial and other kind of support to all Macedonians who had to leave land and property behind in Greece during the war. Growing up, I addressed my mother in Serbo-Croatian and my father in Macedonian. In our extended households, differences in cultural and religious backgrounds were celebrated, or joked about, but certainly never emphasized as particularly important.

The violent conflation of nationality, culture, and religion in the political discourses that animated the war I experienced as foreign. Through my blend of cultural hybridity and the experience of migration, I embody transnational processes, movements, and encounters, a life shaped by thresholds, by crossings of geopolitical borders, by the sense of being both here, and there, except that "there" was itself in the process of redrawing of borders. I continued to ponder national identity, culture, and difference. I felt no particular allegiance to any one side in the conflict. However, I easily identified with victimized civilians, regardless of their nationality. Part of what I felt was akin to a survivor's guilt. Had I remained, had I happened to be living in Bosnia or Croatia, violence and torture could have easily marked my life as well. I was haunted by the violence and losses experienced by girls and women especially. Working to prepare the talk on March 8, 2012, therefore, felt like a strange, grim homecoming, an homage to those who lost their lives and those who survived, an unforgetting, an elegy to a country that is no more, a mourning of roots, the beginning of my own piecing together of my own life past and present, in the how, what, and why of the war.

Another beginning for the book is perhaps located in that very space of cultural hybridity and interactive cultural pluralism that marked my own identity growing up, bolstered through the Yugoslav multicultural ideology of *bratstvo i jedinstvo* (brotherhood and unity), becoming only multiplied and intensified upon landing in Canada. Just like the public framework of multiculturalism that has been institutionalized in Canada since 1982, the discourse of *bratstvo i jedinstvo* was institutionalized in Yugoslavia after World War II as public policy and a way to manage cultural, linguistic, and religious diversity. In the context of my family experience as well as the experience of many others who grew up in the Yugoslavia of the 1970s and 1980s, it provided a meaningful way to understand diversity, cultural and religious pluralism, and a way to relate to difference in positive manner for at least two generations of people who had grown up with it. In its general intention and institutional reach it was not unlike the Canadian discourse of multiculturalism: both have been represented as an official way to manage diversity. In Canada, this diversity initially did not go much further beyond the desire to settle British and French territorial claims in the region. Only later did the concept of multiculturalism begin to apply to a sense of Canadian national identity that officially includes immigrants. In Yugoslavia, *bratstvo i jedinstvo* from the beginning sought to diminish the importance of nationality asa defining feature of identity in favor of common belonging within a federation. Both frameworks have been criticized for failing to accomplish this goal.

The disintegration of Yugoslavia and the ensuing war invited vigorous public dismissal of the validity of the discourse and sometimes an outright rejection of it as artificial or synonymous with Yugoslav socialism. To date, there is very little scholarship both within the Yugosphere and Anglosphere[1] that analyses the complex historical and transhistorical dimensions of this discourse or its participation in global discourses of cultural diversity. Within the Anglosphere, most scholarship situates it in the context of socialist dictatorship pointing to it as an example of "the failure of the experiment," not only because of the ensuing war but also because of the socialist system within which it was institutionalized, a political system organized around concepts radically opposed to those on which capitalist, liberal democracies in the Anglosphere have been founded. Attempts to assess its significance more evenly have often been hastily labeled Yugonostalgia in the Anglosphere but also in some circles in the Yugosphere, where for a couple of decades after the war there was little discursive space to examine the socialist past more evenly and the diversity of people's relationships within it. Rather than being seen as a model of multiculturalism that was successfully implemented for over three decades, it is frequently still viewed as an artificial and oppressive ideological framework, very narrowly associated a socialist and Titoist past that the new nationalist parties sought to leave behind.[2] Based on my own memory and experience, however, and the experience of others who grew up with it, such accounts remain highly problematic, ideologically motivated, and woefully incomplete.

As an official framework for managing cultural diversity, the Canadian version of multiculturalism was starting to be criticized already in the early 2000s, only about two decades since it became enshrined as public policy. In Canada the multicultural framework is implicated in the politics of settlement, connected to Canada's status as a settler state founded upon colonial relations with Indigenous peoples, as well as a history of racial segregation, and colonial constructions of white superiority. The Canadian multicultural space has been constructed in the context of a state identity in which distinctions were made between white colonizers of primarily northern and western European descent—those who are 'in charge' and hold social, economic, cultural and other forms of power- and all others. Instead of integrating diverse racial, cultural, ethnic, and religious groups, critics have pointed to the fact that multiculturalism tends to reify and solidify differences, perpetuating forms of "Othering" of all minority groups and individuals, making social cohesion difficult, if not impossible.[3] While the

6 Unforgetting and the Politics of Representation

official Canadian framework generally does not tend to politicize cultural and religious differences, and valorizes the concept of political correctness to ensure tolerance and inclusiveness, this notion often devolves into a conversational veneer that hides deep-seated forms of discrimination and prejudice. Scholars have pointed out that certain forms of political correctness make it impossible to discuss, and possibly even to think about ideas that challenge the established order. It has also been pointed out that in the context of immigration it can function as "patriotic correctness" and foster structural forms of exclusion, and well as discourses of exclusion at the level of everyday interactions.[4]

My experience as a so-called first-generation Canadian—a category of identity that according to Statistics Canada includes Canadian citizens who were born outside Canada and have acquired citizenship through legal immigration channels—has been largely positive, especially during the first 12 years I spent in Toronto, which is where I completed both my bachelor's and graduate degrees. Toronto is a vibrant and vast metropolitan city, buzzing with the hum of different languages, and thriving on cultural hybridity. Its unabashed internationalism, at least in cultural and social terms, suited me well, as I felt to be an "other" among "others." When I was finally able to resume my studies, having waited in legal limbo for over two years to receive permanent residency, despite significant cultural and pedagogical differences, the university environments that I continued to inhabit represented a familiar and comfortable milieu, themselves a global microcosm comprising of people who deal in ideas and approach life with intellectual curiosity

In 2004, I moved to Halifax due to my appointment as professor at Saint Mary's University and a specialist in Renaissance non-dramatic literature in the Department of English Language and Literature. Since 2006, however, and after I became tenured, alongside teaching and researching the intellectual traditions of the European renaissance, I was able to devote time to my growing interest in the interdisciplinary scholarship of motherhood and the maternal, combined with my lingering orientation toward critical discourse and feminist theory. I became affiliated with the then-recently established *Journal of the Association for Research on Mothering* at one of my alma maters, York University, and took part in annual scholarly meetings. I discovered that the scope of topics and approaches coming together under scholarship on the "maternal" intersected meaningfully with my own personal and professional journeying through space—regions and countries—and time.

However, in Halifax, the only large urban center on the East Coast of Canada, a region comparatively less economically developed, more culturally homogenous, and isolated from Canada's large urban centers, my difference from the cultural majority was thrown into sharper relief, and at every corner in various subtle ways I was reminded that I do not fully belong, at least not in the same way as members of the cultural majority. Being a fully-fledged Canadian citizen, with all the civic rights and privileges of that designation, does not seem to significantly alter my status as "other." My next-door

Introduction 7

neighbor, a first-generation Canadian who emigrated to Canada with her husband and two children from Iraq several decades ago, told me recently that she is still habitually exposed to openly discriminatory and prejudicial remarks and behaviors from members of the Canadian cultural majority based on stereotypical and derogatory assumptions about Muslim women, as well as immigrants. Other friends, colleagues and acquaintances, also first generation Canadians, have told me the same thing about their experience with xenophobic and/or racial prejudice. This, even though the 1988 Canadian Multicultural Act states, among other clauses, that "multiculturalism is a fundamental characteristic of our Canadian identity,"[5] and equal rights under the law are guaranteed to all Canadian citizens.

The theoretical significance of this operative tension between official national policy and everyday practice indicates that there is no comfortable or singularly superior discursive or national space from which to assess and evaluate discourses of identity, nationhood, and negotiations over difference. Anti-immigrant sentiment in Canada, the US, the UK, and other countries of the EU in particular is fueled by nationalist forms of thought and popular conceptions of nationhood, that is, a dominant group's beliefs about the nation's symbolic boundaries and a sense of national (often bundled with racial/ethnic) superiority. Research suggests that immigrants and members of national minority groups are more likely to be viewed with suspicion and hostility by those dominant group members who subscribe to ethno-culturally exclusionary understandings of the national political community.[6] And such exclusionary ethno-cultural or ethno-nationalist understandings, as idealized forms of cultural and political community and nation, are clearly not limited to a particular part of the world.

These complex interfaces made visible through the lived experience of individuals and groups who are assigned and perceived as "different" on whatever basis reveal that peace, peacebuilding, and justice are in fact only some of the components of a larger, global ecology of social justice encompassing the interdependence of multiple elements within human systems, such as negative and positive peace; the psychology of peace; direct, structural, and cultural forms of violence; and inclusionary and exclusionary dynamics.[7] This awareness increasingly began to animate my interest in the private experiences of belonging, and the relationship among borders—actual and imagined—culture and identity, especially those experiences that stand in contrast to official, state-formulated, or nation-based ideologies of belonging. Such experiences and perspectives made visible the porousness of borders, their social constructed-ness as well as their irreducibility: a resistance to being made uniform, unanimous, impermeable, and seamless. It is their very porousness and permeability that most nation-states around the contemporary world, not only the countries of the former Yugoslavia, continue to perceive and reconstruct as a threat to belonging, a psychological and political justification for further fortification, defense, separation, exclusion, and a militarization of the mind.

8 Unforgetting and the Politics of Representation

The disintegration of Yugoslavia and the Bosnian war represent well-documented examples of the militarization of the mind, the reconstruction of psychological and actual borders as threats, and the political processes that co-opted and manufactured them as a justification for war.[8] Post-conflict Bosnia has also been studied extensively, particularly within the context of international relations, the relative successes and failures of peacekeeping missions, peace and conflict studies, the trials of the International Criminal Tribunal for the Former Yugoslavia (ICTY) and transitional justice, but, with notable exceptions, mainly in terms that take as axiomatic ethnicity as a dominant marker of identity: if not in a historical sense, then as a category institutionalized through the Dayton Agreement.[9] In connection with the use of rape as a weapon of war, feminist scholarship has studied conflict-related sexual violence and transitional justice processes through comparisons between the Bosnian example and other contemporary war-torn countries, such as Uganda, Colombia, Somalia, and the Democratic Republic of Congo. What continues to be under-documented, however, are the ways in which historically grounded individual and collective memories of war in Bosnia are constitutive of the psychology of peace and peacebuilding processes, but also the way in which they participate in and contribute to transnational discourses concerned with building sustainable ecologies of social and economic justice. More complex reassessments of various aspects of the Yugoslav socialist historical legacy would help highlight the future-oriented role of that legacy in building sustainable peace for Bosnia, and other countries in the region.

Moreover, the examples from contemporary Canada I am pointing to here illustrate that the absence of destructive conflict does not naturally translate into communities of peace either in the Canadian or in the Bosnian context. In both localities, within specific cultural and historical contexts, individuals and groups continue to experience structural forms of violence and exclusion (xenophobia, racism, sexism, poverty, etc.), as well as cultural forms of violence (intractable forms of structural violence perpetuated via social norms).[10] Continuing to reify the "post-conflict" dimension in discussions relating to contemporary Bosnia turns "post-conflict" into a normative lens, and obscures the extent to which equity, respect, and value of diversity, and the promotion of equal social, political, and economic rights are Bosnian as well as global issues. Centering the 'post conflict' lens in discussions of Bosnia therefore also channels a persistent if innovative form of Balkanism, conferring yet another type of intransigence to existing paternalist assumptions about "primordial patterns on violence" embedded within an otherwise deficient Balkan mentality.[11]

My own transnationally inflected awareness of irreducibility when it comes to the intersections among identity, culture, and nationhood has stood in contrast with reductionist representational and revisionist tendencies, here in the Canadian Anglosphere, as well as in the new, former Yugoslav countries. In the new official platforms of most political parties in Serbia and Croatia especially, the complex realities of the region prior, during, and in the aftermath of war

Introduction 9

were being ironed out into the homogenizing simplicity of official ultra-nationalism. A reigning form of politics for more than thirty five years, since recently it has started to be actively contested and critiqued by many groups and individuals in the two countries over the last decade. During the Yugoslav war and shortly after, I was experiencing a type of representational crisis, a cognitive dissonance every time I watched the news either here in the Anglosphere, or there in the Yugosphere. Having lived my entire life at the intersections of cultures, borders, languages, and political systems made me an outsider and an insider at once in all localities, sensitive to difference, hybridity, liminal spaces, discourse, and experience that resists assertions that there is anything single, pure, or straightforward about identity and belonging. My continued discomfort with Western narrativization of the Yugoslav region and recent events was validated by the publication of Maria Todorova's book, *Imagining the Balkans* in 1997.[12] The representational problem I was noticing was implicated with the role of media in reporting about armed conflict, especially through the extended tele-visual portrayals of war that became the norm in the 1990s, and that highlighted for me the relationship between language, representation, and power. It was clear that the process of meaning-making propagated through official media channels was "constitutive of the public sphere" and of public opinion, in that it not only exhibited reality but actively participated "in a strategy of containment, selectively producing and enforcing what will count as reality."[13]

The pervasiveness of the language of ethnicity in discussions relating to Bosnia have been a case in point. This language is comfortably familiar in the Anglosphere, since it is how the cultural majority conceptualizes immigrant identities. In fact, in everyday discourse ethnicity is often conflated with forms of embodied difference—what in Canada marks so-called "visible minorities"—namely representational identity category based on colonial constructions of color, in/visibility, and race. This is evident in the fact that it is only those who appear "different," who are marked as different, and who are either perceived or self-identify as people of color are imputed or expected to have an ethnicity. The white cultural majorty in Canada do not seem to conceptualize their own identity in terms of ethnicity.

The language of ethnicity is foreign and largely inaccurate to both how many peoples of the former Yugoslavia represent themselves and speak about the war, as well as to my own articulation of identity. Although since the break-up of Yugoslavia some authors in the Yugosphere and some media outlets have adopted the term "ethnicity" to analyze current events in the region, this is a new development and one that mirrors the hegemonic language of Western designations of identity. The term *nacionalnost* [nationality] as it is used by people in Bosnia and other former Yugoslav countries is both broader and more specific than "ethnicity." It focuses attention on both civic and cultural aspects of identification, which may or may not include religious denomination and has nothing to do with colorism or racialization. In the Bosnian,

Serbian, Croatian, and Macedonian languages, the term *nacionalnost* can describe one aspect of someone's identity, but often a distinction can be made between ethnicity (largely linked to a geographic location that may or may not coincide with state borders), nationality (largely linked to forms of civic belonging by birth or by rights of citizenship), and religion (which may or may not have anything to do with either of the previous two categories).[14] Getting this conceptualization right and using accurate language is particularly important in the context of discussions of Bosnia and Herzegovina, a country that has a long pluralist history and where the people themselves—despite official ethno-nationalist narratives cemented by the Dayton Accord—do not frequently rely on the language of ethnicity to address their differences. Snježana Kordić's point that in "Bosnia it continues to be difficult to assert what in fact does constitute the basis of difference among the three nationalities," is relevant in this context.[15]

The most easily traceable and most recent beginning of the book, however, is the decision to accept an invitation in 2014 to form a research team with colleagues from the University of Ottawa, Agatha Schwartz, Mythili Rajiva, and Christabelle Sethna, to work on a project that we at the time had articulated as "Children of the Enemy: Narrative Constructions of Identity Following Wartime Rape and Transgenerational Trauma in Post-WWII Germany and Post-Conflict Bosnia." Funding secured for this project through an Insight Development Grant of the Social Sciences and Humanities Research Council of Canada allowed me to spend a good part of the summer of 2017 in the Bosnian Federation entity, purposefully seeking to conduct a series of in-person interviews with women survivors of rape and Children Born of War.

To some extent, as Natalie Hodges reflects in her beautifully written meditation on her own life and the science of time in relation to the present, all my previous experiences had existed in my own perception as isolated from one another and hence also "meaningless" or, as she says, "less important than they originally seemed." They also seem to have lost the importance they may have held originally, precisely because of time's passage and constant flux, and the consequent reconstruction and reintegration of previous experience into each subsequent present. Finding myself in Bosnia in the summer of 2017, in the town where my mother grew up, at the confluence of my own pre-war memories of childhood in Yugoslavia and my then-present life as an emigree, and spending time in conversation with women and children survivors of war, provided the opportunity to revisit and reconstruct all of my previous experiences at this point in time and with a new purpose. As such, through the generative force of complex memorial reconstruction, many of those experiences were ordered and reordered, reordering my own "understanding of the past in real time," as Hodges says.

By 2014, I had already become increasingly preoccupied with the experiences of women survivors of war-related sexualized violence recorded in their testimonies, as well as the children born of such violence. In addition to the

Introduction   11

legal challenges of recognition both groups of people continued to face within Bosnia, they also faced representational challenges revolving around their social, legal, and discursive position as victims. The global media seized upon the experiences of women who survived rape during war and bombarded the public with sensationalist depictions of their suffering and victimization. The concept of woman victims gained currency in media and politics and succeeded in easily garnering public support for those who survived violence during war. The discourse relating to women as victims of war rape and other forms of sexualized and gendered torture was of key significance in the trials of the International Criminal Tribunal for Yugoslavia, where, alongside similar cases prosecuted at the International Criminal Court for Rwanda, the Special Court for Sierra Leone, and the Extraordinary Court Chambers for Cambodia, mass and systematic rape in war were not only acknowledged as a weapon of war but also definitively recognized as a crime against humanity with genocidal intentions.[16]

Within Bosnia itself these forms of international recognition in turn encouraged a social discourse of recognition that was instrumental for some women in achieving the legal status of "civilian victim of war" and associated rights. There is a politics to the recognition, however, one that reflects the peace politics introduced by the signing of the Dayton Accords in 1995. While the Accords ended the armed conflict, they also separated the formerly Yugoslav republic into two entities, the Federation of Bosnia and Herzegovina (the primarily Bosniak and Croat part of the country), and the Serb-dominated Republika Srpska, in addition to the small, neutral, and self-governing territory of the Brčko District belonging to both entities. The Federation is further subdivided into cantons dominated by a single nationality (either Bosniak or Croat). Even though the purported intention of the Dayton Accord was to "recreate multi-ethnic Bosnia through the right of return for refugees and internally displaced persons" (Guzina 2007, 223)—a right upheld in the Bosnian Constitutions—the political and social realities of daily life in Bosnia for the most part belie this intention and continue to be organized based on rigid ethno-national principles. As Guzina remarks, "the ambiguous constitutional and legal definitions of citizenship effectively preclude the re-emergence of overlapping, multiple national identities that were the norm in Bosnia before the war, when one could be, at the same time, a Serb/Croat/Bosniak, Bosnian and Yugoslav" (226). What this means in terms of identity and citizenship rights is that rather than being a country of "its citizens irrespective of their national identification," Bosnia is "primarily a country of its constituent nations," with the consequence that only those who belong to the "correct" ethnic majority within each local context are assured that their rights will be upheld (Guzina 227). What this meant for women survivors of war-related sexualized violence and the Children Born because of War is that their recognition as civilian victims of war and their ability to realize state funded benefits associated with this status, remained constrained by their nationality, or at least, by where they happened to find themselves after the war. Women survivors and Children Born of War in the Republika Srpska continue to face political and legal obstacles in obtaining official legal recognition.

Over the years Bosniak women from the Bosnian Federation entity have been the most willing to bring their stories to light. This is due to multiple factors. One is simply related to numbers: consistent estimates indicate that between 25,000 and 40,000 Bosniak women and girls were subjected to genocidal rape and enforced impregnation primarily, but not exclusively, by Serbian forces (Takševa 2023). The other reason is the continuous presence of international NGOs on the territory of the Federation entity both during and directly after the war, contributing to a more systematic form of record keeping and active documentation of cases of rape and other types of violence as well as a more prevalent discourse of rights. Many foreign-funded NGOs, such as Medica Zenica, for example -an organization that guartanteed physical safety and support of women who fled the violence—have been on the ground working with survivors and their families since 1993. In terms of data collection and related analyses, these reasons have contributed to the fact that the greatest number of studies, including my own work, focuses on Bosniak women survivors.

There is a small body of existing evidence that testifies to the experiences of war rape and sexual violence against Serbian and Croatian women, including enforced impregnation, as well as against women of other nationalities living at the time on the territory of the former Yugoslavia.[17] This situation is, therefore, a reflection of divergent political attitudes that the governments of the two large entities have taken toward the matter of rape during war and their openness to the wider international community. Historically, during and since the war, NGOs have had much harder time entering and operating on the territory of Republika Srpska because of its broadly conceived protectionist attitude. More recently, the government of Republika Srpska has moved to further formalize these political tendencies by introducing a draft law aimed at providing a distinct legal framework when it comes to non-governmental organization. The proposed law would restrict or entirely prevent the operation of NGOs that are receiving foreign funding and other forms of foreign assistance on its territory, reflecting the entity's mistrust of foreign influences. It envisages a special registry for such organizations, and additional administrative and financial reporting requirements, compared with local NGOs and those that can demonstrate that they are not receiving foreign support.

While the authorities in the Federation entity have been more willing and open to publicly acknowledging women who experienced sexual violence, especially when it serves the interests of an upcoming election to appeal to the women as voters, the government of the Republika Srpska has been overall more reticent about the issue, since public acknowledgment of the experiences of war rape and other forms of violence of the women living on their territories would

Introduction 13

inevitably draw them into public acknowledgment of Serb responsibility for much violence perpetrated against women of the neighboring entity. This acknowledgment has not been made to date, and continues to be connected to a more general ideology of political protectionism and denial of war crimes, reflecting Republika Srpska's refusal to engage in what its leadership perceives as foreign-led and/or foreign-funded processes of reconciliation and reparation.

The ideological wrangling over historical representation and responsibility in relation to the war has resulted in a situation where women in the Federation whose cases were documented and who had subsequently disclosed their experience of rape claimed and were granted the legal status of civilian victim of war, and have been entitled to a series of benefits and financial compensation. Conversely, women who live on the territory of Republika Srpska have been able to realize significantly fewer rights and benefits in terms of legal recognition. This has created large-scale inequities within Bosnia as a country when it comes to how it treats its victims of war, especially women, and the Children Born Because of War. The burden of proof rests within the victims, and many women have kept their silence for various reasons.

Within the Bosnian Federation the category of civil victim of war is legally defined as a person whose physiological and psychological health has significantly deteriorated due to direct threat of war and related violence, wounding, or other types of war-related torture. Family members of persons who are listed as missing or killed during war also fall under this category. The extent of what constitutes "significant" in this classification is legally defined as "at least 60% or significant deterioration of health," with women who have survived war rape and related torture defined as a "special category" of civilian victims of war under this legislative framework.[18] Establishing one's status as a civilian victim of war within Bosnia and before various commissions where one's victimhood needed to be ascertained as "true" and "significant" means the difference between having some form of social and financial support and having none.

At the same time, it has become clear to the women themselves that there is a politics to victimhood, and that it was actively shaped and perceived as a performative category: it seemed incumbent on the women who testified for the ICTY or domestic trials to perform their suffering in a credible way to be perceived—and recognized—as victims; their words and their experience were often not enough. There continued to be women who refuse to speak to anyone about their experiences, and whose silence has been explained with reference to the proverbial "wall of silence." The "wall of silence" is a compelling and resonant figure of speech, connoting women's interiorized feelings of guilt and shame stemming from traditionalist, religious-based, and patriarchal notions about female honor and chastity that were violated through rape. Yet, in some of the women's narratives and testimonies I recognized that the decision to remain silent is often very context-based and can in fact represent survivors' agentive resistance to the dominant logic of woman-as-victim. Their refusal to

14 Unforgetting and the Politics of Representation

name and speak of their experience can also be therefore an assertion of their dignity and strength as women and as survivors. The silence of many Serbian and Croatian women victims of war may also have to do with the fact that some of their own sons, husbands, and brothers are among those who have been named or accused of committing violent acts against women of other nationalities, some of whom have been indicted and tried. This is a reality and an experience for some women the details of which we know very little. Although I attempted, at the time I was unable to make contact with NGOs on the territory of Republika Srpska who were willing to share my call for research participation among the women survivors they were responsible for helping.

I became particularly interested in the stories of a small number of Bosniak women who decided to keep and raise children born because of war rape. My research relating to such women focuses on two main areas. The first centers on highlighting the positive potential of maternal ambivalence present within these relationships. Situating successfully managed maternal ambivalence within a more normative context typical of many close relationships, including mother/child relationships, results in the de-pathologizing of mothering practices of women who chose to raise children born of war. Through this approach, the Children themselves are destigmatized and discursively reinvested with dignity, since I examine their experience in the context of their own perspectives regarding their identity, well-being, and status within the community and broader society. The second approach is linked to the first, and it is rooted in challenging one-dimensional representations of women/mothers and children as victims. Instead, I focus on the often-overlooked forms of agency and embodied examples of their resilience when faced with great psycho-social challenges and struggles.[19]

This fieldwork changed my life in significant ways. My meetings with the women survivors, the children of war, and others whose lives were directly impacted by the war, started out as semi-structured interviews, but evolved into encounters and conversations that irrevocably marked my subsequent life, personally and professionally.

These encounters powerfully reordered for me the usual relationship between researcher and participant. What I was learning from my interlocutors went far beyond the information I was collecting for the purposes of a project on "children of the enemy" and implicated me in multiple ways. The journeys into their pasts and present ended up being journeys that unexpectedly illuminated aspects of my own past and the past of the country I was born in, the past that I had lived as well as the one that I would have lived had I not left the country. Through the conversations I had to confront my own mourning and reintegrate my personal grief—amalgamation of personal and collective loss—within a sense of time passing, its flux, but also its continuity. I realized that the sharing of stories and the resonance of the narratives within the annals of my biographical history represented a kind of unforgetting, an effortful process that is very different from the simple act of remembering.

Unforgetting is marked by a contradictory and powerful desire to remember, recall, and reconstruct events that are difficult, events that one may wish to forget, but cannot. Contestation over meaning is also part of unforgetting, as the meaning of the past is continually revisited and reconstructed through different social, political, and personal lenses in the present. As a memorial process, unforgetting is not linear or predictable, but rather cyclical and irregular, triggered by new events and pieces of new knowledge that add to one's existing memories, and reconstructed within the experience of the present. Unforgetting can unfold both as an individual and as a collective process. Mechanisms of transitional justice and reconciliation are in fact intended to foster and encourage unforgetting in the context of what is sometimes referred to as a culture of memory. They seek to identify and define what a culture of memory means for a society that is recovering from war, and for different groups within it, and what is important to remember and how. From the perspective of individual and collective psychology, unforgetting is, therefore, also intimately connected to recovery and healing.

And while my research team and I did write extensively based on the collected narratives, I was always aware of a "surplus of meaning," an abundance of signification residing in the stories I recorded, voices that needed to be yet more fully documented. Almost 30 years after the end of the war, the stories of the women and children capture a moment in time that is significant for understanding the complexity of individual lives, the power of self-representation, and occluded forms of resilience that co-exist with suffering and struggle. Articulated at the fault lines between the individual and the collective, the personal and the political, their stories also capture forms of recovery, well-being, and resilience that challenge a "linear rationality of the development of peace politics, embodied in the state and its position in modern regional relations and the global economy."[20] In this sense and from multiple perspectives, all chapters, therefore, engage the politics of representation, the struggle over the social and political meaning of images and depictions of gender and war, of women who survived violence, the Children of War, of Bosnian cultural and political identity, of the Yugoslav legacy, nationalism, ideology, and ideas about the Balkans. The politics of representation thus reveals the workings of social power structures locally but also internationally and globally, especially when it comes to the women who survived war violence and the Children Born Because of War, two groups whose experiences have often been the target of various forms of appropriation, while continually reinscribing their social marginalization.

The book is an attempt to write some of that complexity, to inscribe as far as possible within a limited scope some parts of a gendered history and politics of self/representation where many voices speak at once, where, as Elsa Barkley Brown says, voices are heard "in multiple rhythms being played simultaneously."[21] It hopes to show through the narratives that peace and recovery are located within everyday processes, processes that embody transformational

16 Unforgetting and the Politics of Representation

struggles through which new Socialities (ways of being together) and identities are generated over time. As such, the book contributes to feminist peacebuilding by recognizing the "fuzziness of intersections between different local and international actors, agendas, and structures."[22] In being attuned to the "diversity of the personal," the local in its hybridity, and the irreducible, multilayered, and multidirectional nature of recovery, the book contributes to transnational feminist scholarship on contemporary Bosnian society, war-related sexual violence, and its historical aftermath, as well as the peacebuilding project itself located at the intersections of the local, the personal, the international, and the global.

My own cross-border, transnational positionality regarding the material is an integral aspect of such hybridity, embodying the slippages and in-betweenness of the local and the international, insider and outsider, researcher and participant in ways that are constitutive of this project. Such understanding further seeks to assert that the lines between a state of war and a state of peace and recovery are often not definitive and easily demarcated but can be observed in the everyday actions and utterances of individual people, self-identified collectives, and in the lived experience of those for whom war, violence, and peace co-exist at the crossroads of past memory and present reality. It is my conviction that the possibility of sustainable peace emerges from within these irreducible spaces of meaning, actualized through everyday habits and communicative patterns.

Chapter Outline

The book is divided into three parts. Each part contains rich archival material based on my conversations with individuals who have survived the war in various ways, and those who have been born because of the war. Over five chapters, Part I brings together conversations and published material whose purpose overall is to deconstruct and problematize the fetishization of ethnicity as the main determinant of identity, culture, and politics that still creeps into many scholarly and media accounts of contemporary Bosnian society. While ethnicity has been encoded into the constitution through the Dayton Agreement, and thus represents the official politics of the country, each of the chapters shows in different ways people's resistance to this discourse through specific counter-narratives representing a complex worldview based on the concept of *suživost* (living peacefully together). The chapters build a conception of peacebuilding in connection with a multi-directional understanding of individual and collective memory that contributes to recovery, as it is also future-oriented.

In Chapter 1, Why Stories Matter, I highlight the central role of storytelling and narrative in constructing peace understood relationally, through the continuities and interdependence between larger, social peacebuilding frameworks and initiatives, and people's private experiences of peace and well-being. I examine the relationship of individual stories about war, suffering, and survival to

Introduction 17

process of memory and recovery, arguing in turn that memory, recovery, and peacebuilding are functions of embodiment that are narratively conveyed, in public discourse as well as private storytelling and life narratives.

Chapter 2, Ecologies of Peace, develops the concept of peace ecologies as emerging from the multifaceted nature of traumatic experience and acts of narration as forms of agency and authority over painful aspects of the past as well as constructive orientation toward the future. Here I posit that traumatic experience encompasses the social and physical ecologies or "ecosystems" that constitute people's habitats, interlinked in survivor accounts of sexualized violence as something affecting not only the person it was perpetrated against but their families, communities, and all those who may have witnessed the violence, thus acquiring a social or discursive dimension. Such understanding entails that we begin to think of peacebuilding in terms of individual, community-based, and state-level capacities to develop ecologies of peace, and recognize the diverse ways in which diverse human lives are defined through interactions between individuals and their environment. Such a perspective also challenges totalizing accounts of victimization and reveals agency in various spaces and across different levels of identity, not only measured in terms of large, state, or group-based intervention.

Chapter 3, Bosnia Beyond Balkanism, further engages with embodied and irreducible categories of experience, individual stories, and perspectives to show the diverse and often critical ways in which Bosnian citizens interact with official Bosnian politics, and that inherently deconstruct Balkanist forms of thought and representation. This diversity and critical engagement fly in the face of homogenizing accounts of Bosnia's internal politics, civil society, and the peace process, both within Bosnia and in commentary generated about Bosnia by scholars, politicians, and media representatives from the outside.

Chapter 4, Sarajevo the Beautiful, features the words of Vahdeta, a small business owner in Sarajevo's old town market, as well as published materials commemorating the siege of Sarajevo through the words of people who survived it. Their collective historical experience and the way in which they re/construct the siege as a memorial form stems not only from memories of the recent war in isolation but also the recent war as remembered in the context of the city's other history and the complexity of people's social and cultural experiences that both pre-dated and were contemporaneous with the war. My reading of these narratives suggests that memorial forms, such as the one of the sieges of Sarajevo, contain references that link memories of the past to the present moment but also to the future as they tend to take a longer, historical view based on different aspects of a shared past.

In Chapter 5, Growing Up Under Siege, two young women narrate their experiences of war through a contemporary perspective of Bosnian society. Their memories of childhood during the war are embedded in their current perceptions of living within the Yugosphere and of culture, the bankruptcy of ethno-nationalist discourses, as well as an active critique of the current

18　Unforgetting and the Politics of Representation

political regime. As such, their memorial reconstruction of the past in the present resonates with the political power of presence, occupying the space of irrepressible individual utterance and actions that "encroach incrementally to capture the trenches" from the power base of patriarchal, as well as official ethno-nationalist structure, while "erecting springboards to move on."[23]

The two chapters in Part II, Unforgetting the Children Born Because of War and What Does It Mean to Be a Child Born Because of War?, deal with the experiences of a particular group: Children Born as a Result of War Rape in Bosnia. In the first chapter, I trace the proverbial silence or "forgetting" surrounding the group within Bosnia, to reveal that it has not been a total silence, but a decades-long process leading toward "unforgetting" them, punctuated and propelled by multiple events and the activist work of many individuals, including some of the children themselves. I especially highlight the important peacebuilding work of Ajna Jusić done on behalf of the Sarajevo-based Association of Forgotten Children of War whose advocacy within Bosnia and globally has resulted in formal recognition of this group within some Bosnian legal jurisdictions. In the second chapter of Part II, I bring forward long sections from the conversations I had with three Children Born of War in 2017. I have organized the narratives by grouping their words thematically, to highlight the significance of their perspectives on particular issues, the similarities as well as the differences among them. In my search for an adequate and ethical way to handle their stories and present them to readers, I have been inspired by Svetlana Alexievich's documentary novel *The Unwomanly Face of War* and her collection *Last Witnesses: Unchildlike Stories*, both presenting recollections of survivors of World War II in a life-affirming way, privileging the strength and unique cadences of each survivor voice. Through the Children's narratives emerges a complex picture of war, national identity, private experiences of belonging, barriers to peace and well-being, recognition, and inclusion, but also personal courage, resilience, and determination to redefine the meaning of peace in Bosnia.

Over the span of three chapters, Part III deals with multiple forms of agency demonstrated by women who survived the war in different ways: as survivors of war-related sexualized violence, as women who lost children and other members of their close family during war, and as women who fought in the war. In The Space of Dialogue, I provide some contextual and demographic details about the women who shared their stories with me and emphasize the relevance of their truth narratives in redefining the scope of peace, justice, and recovery. In The Vulnerable and the Brave, I bring forward the women's firstperson narratives. I arrange their narratives using the same approach as I do with the children's stories, grouping them thematically to emphasize the courage and diversity of their perspectives. Their perspectives actively contest reductionist representation of women survivors of sexualized violence during war, and challenge one-dimensional discussions of victimhood. Justice in a judiciary sense, as punishment or correction for those who have perpetrated criminal acts, is of key importance to some of the women, but not to all. Each

Introduction   19

conversation represented both a confirmation and a re-inscription of each woman's authorial, storytelling agency and her own healing path. Each woman ascribed explicit value to the act of narration that is of benefit to themselves. None of them—even the one who has been bed-ridden for 19 years—were fully at ease with the self-concept of a victim. Although all women articulated past and present challenges, all of them exhibited resilience and agency. In the last chapter of Part III, I focus on Esma D., a woman who fought for the Bosnian army during the war, by providing her own narrative account of what it meant to be a woman fighter, and the way in which this type of involvement in armed conflict affected her.

Placing the narratives of women who survived sexualized violence during war and various other forms of torture, including enforced impregnation and/ or witnessing the torture and murder of loves ones, alongside the narrative of a woman who survived violence but in a way that she was responsible for afflicting it, highlights the range of female agency during war and the complexity of violence, traumatic experience, and recovery, as well as the multiple ways in which women work on their own healing, and rearticulate the goals of justice and peace. In all of the narratives, memories of the past are retold refracted in the present, and thus also looking toward a possible or desired future. As such, women's private memories and sometimes active engagement with the community and other survivors connect to, draw upon, and in turn reshape collective forms of memorialization and thus participate in peacebuilding.

In the concluding chapter, I reflect on the narratives through the perspective of home, an idea that was violently reordered by the war for each of the speakers. I examine the concept in connection with real and perceived borders, as well as being one that is often defined through the porousness of such borders. I connect the acts of narration and telling to forms of peacebuilding at the personal level, in the context of "being well in the world," as well as the collective level, in the context of "being well with others." Here I make the point that conceiving of home in the context of personal, collective, and national belonging has relevance beyond Bosnia and the other countries in the Yugosphere, as it necessitates recognition of the pervasiveness of nationalist forms of thinking and their embeddedness in many everyday social actions and modern institutions.

Notes

1 Tim Judah was first to use the concept of Yugosphere in "Yugoslavia Is Dead, Long Live the Yugosphere," in *LSEE Papers on Southeastern Europe*, 2009, accessible at: https://www.lse.ac.uk/LSEE-Research-on-South-Eastern-Europe/Assets/ Documents/Publications/Paper-Series-on-SEE/Yugosphere.pdf Judah also discusses the concept of the Anglosphere, and *la Francophonie* as similar in meaning. In his account, the Anglosphere comprises Britain, Ireland, the US, Canada, Australia, and New Zealand. I will continue to use both Yugosphere and Anglosphere throughout, since I agree that within each respective sphere, despite many differences, people also have many things in common.

20 Unforgetting and the Politics of Representation

2 An exception is Nena Močnik's recent work, where she puts forward the position that multicultural discourses globally have much to learn from the way in which the Yugoslav discourse of Brotherhood and Unity strove to provide a common civic identity that supersedes differences. See Močnik, "Brotherhood and Unity Goes Multiculturalism: Legacy as a Leading Path toward Implementations of New European Multiculturalism," in ed. Ognjenović, Gorana, and Jasna Jozelic, *Titoism, Self-Determination, Nationalism, Cultural Memory: Volume Two, Tito's Yugoslavia, Stories Untold* (New York: Palgrave Macmillan US, 2016), 215–251. Systematic analyses of Jugosolvenstvo (Yugoslavism), Yugonostalgia and Titonostalgia have also begun to shed greater light on the complexity of the discourse of *bratstvo i jedinstvo*. See Mitja Velikonja's *Titonostalgia: A Study of Nostalgia for Josip Broz* (Ljubljana: Mirovni inštitut, 2008), and the work done by Larisa Kurtovic, such as for example, "Yugonostalgia on Wheels: Commemorating Marshall Tito Across Post-War Borders: Two Ethnographic Tales from Post-War Bosnia and Herzegovina." University of California Berkley, *Newsletter of the Institute of Slavic, East European and Eurasian Studies*, 28.1 (2011), 2–22.

3 See Tatjana Takseva, "What it Takes to Feel Canadian: Multiculturalism and the Logic of Home," *Canadian Ethnic Studies* 56.1 (2024): 55–81, DOI: 10.1353/ces.2024.a921080, and Joseph Garcea, et al. "Introduction: Multiculturalism Discourses in Canada." *Canadian Ethnic Studies*, 40.1 (2008), 1–10. doi:10.1353/ces.0.0069; and Joseph Garcea, "Postulations on the Fragmentary Effects of Multiculturalism in Canada." *Canadian Ethnic Studies*, 40.1 (2008), 141–160. doi:10.1353/ces.0.0059.

4 Waleed Aly and Robert Mark Simpson, "Political Correctness Gone Viral." In ed. Carl Fox and Joe Saunders, *Media Ethics, Free Speech, and the Requirements of Democracy* (New York: Routledge, 2018) (chapter 7).

5 See Laurence Brosseau and Michael Dewing, *Parliament of Canada: Canadian Multiculturalism*, accessible at, https://lop.parl.ca/sites/PublicWebsite/default/en_CA/ResearchPublications/200920E. Also see, Beryle Mae Jones, "Multiculturalism and Citizenship: The status of 'Visible Minorities' in Canada." *Canadian Ethnic Studies Journal* 32.1 spring (2000), 111, accessible at: link.gale.com/apps/doc/A82883501/AONE?u=hali76546&sid=bookmark-AONE&xid=4ae007c1. Accessed 29 Nov. 2022.

6 Yuval Feinstein and Bart Bonikowski, "Nationalist Narratives and Anti Immigrant Attitudes: Exceptionalism and Collective Victimhood in Contemporary Israel," *Journal of Ethnic and Migration Studies* 47.3 (2021), 741–761, 742. DOI: 10.1080/1369183X.2019.1620596; Bonikowski, "Ethno-Nationalist Populism and the Mobilization of Collective Resentment." *The British Journal of Sociology* 68 (2016), 181–213; Bonikowski and Paul DiMaggio, "Varieties of American Popular Nationalism," *American Sociological Review* 81 (2016), 949–980; Noah Lewin-Epstein and Asaf Levanon, "National Identity and Xenophobia in an Ethnically Divided Society," *International Journal on Multicultural Societies* 7 (2005), 90–118; Anatol Lieven, *America Right or Wrong: An Anatomy of American Nationalism* (New York: Oxford University Press, 2004); Victoria M. Esses, "Prejudice and Discrimination Toward Immigrants," *Annual Review Of Psychology* 72 (2021), 503–31. Paul May, "French Cultural Wars: Public Discourses on Multiculturalism in France (19952013)," *Journal of Ethnic and Migration Studies* 42 (2016): 1334–1352.

7 Linda M. Woolf, "Social Justice and Peace," in ed. Maria Gloria C. Njoku, Leonard A. Jason, and R. Burke Johnson, The *Psychology of Peace Promotion: Global Perspectives on Personal Peace, Children and Adolescents, and Social Justice* (Cham: Springer International Publishing AG, 2019), 219–235.

Introduction 21

8 There have been numerous studies detailing the reasons for war and debating the presence and/or the manufacturing of differences in the Yugosphere over the last thirty years. See for example, Robert J. Donia, Robert, John V. A. Fine and John Van Antwerp Fine, *Bosnia and Hercegovina: a Tradition Betrayed* (New York: Columbia University Press, 1994); Swanee Hunt, *This Was Not Our War: Bosnian Women Reclaiming the Peace* (Durham: Duke University Press, 2004); Sabrina P. Ramet, *Thinking About Yugoslavia: Scholarly Debates About the Yugoslav Breakup and the Wars in Bosnia and Kosovo* (Cambridge: Cambridge University Press, 2005); Dubravka Zarkov, *The Body of War. Media, Ethnicity and Gender in the Break-up of Yugoslavia* (Durham and London: Duke University Press, 2007); Torsten Kolind. *Post-War Identification: Everyday Muslim Counterdiscourse in Bosnia Herzegovina* (Aarhus: Aarhus University Press, 2008).

9 In addition to the studies listed in the above note, also see, Timothy Donais, *The Political Economy of Peacebuilding in Post-Dayton Bosnia*. 1st ed. (London: Routledge, 2005) which examines Bosnia's ongoing economic crisis by exploring the interactions of an inappropriate international model of economic reform with the country's particular post-conflict and post-socialist political economy. See also V.P. Gagnon, *The Myth of Ethnic War: Serbia and Croatia in the 1990s* (Ithaca: Cornell University Press, 2013), and Olivera Simić, Zala Volčič and Catherine R. Philpot (eds.). *Peace Psychology in the Balkans: Dealing with a Violent Past while Building Peace*, (New York: Springer 2014). Both approach the Balkans as a microcosm of peacebuilding, in terms of both the traumatic past that must be addressed and prospects for future nonviolence, and the range of peace objectives in the region, from promoting the absence of conflict to advocating for justice, equality, and positive relations between groups, the peacebuilding potential of the schools, the arts and media, national symbols, and other cultural institutions ten years after the war.

10 For a still useful definition of structural and cultural violence see Johan Galtung, *Peace by Peaceful Means: Peace and Conflict, Development and Civilization* (PRIO, the International Peace Research Institute, Oslo, and London, UK: Sage, 1996).

11 Danijel Dzino, "Imagining Bosnia: Review of C. Carmichael's *Concise History of Bosnia,"* *Croatian Studies Review* 11 (2015), 141–159, 144.

12 Maria Todorova, *Imagining the Balkans* (New York: Oxford University Press, 2009), 59. Todorova begins from the question, "How could a geographical appellation [Balkans] be transformed into one of the most powerful pejorative designations in history, international relations, political science, and nowadays, general intellectual discourse?" (7). In the book she answers this question conclusively by demonstrating that the Balkans have been historically constructed as a repository of negative characteristics against which the a positive and self congratulatory image of the 'European' and the 'West' has been reinforced.

13 Judith Butler, *Frames of War: When Is Life Grievable?* (London: Verso, 2009), xii–xiii.

14 The concept of 'ethnicity' as it is used in Anglo-American pluralist social contexts has connections to both racial and/or territorial belonging, but less to religious denomination. In North American society, the term 'ethnicity' has racializing connotations while being very vaguely connected to territory. In fact, when it is used, it denotes minority status both in terms of race and origin. In Canada, we never hear of Canadian Catholics, or Quebec French Canadians as ethnic groups, for example. The identities of so-called White Canadians of British, Irish, or Scottish ancestry are also never conceptualized in terms of 'ethnic identity' even though they do fulfil the criteria of most definitions of that term. Discursively, the term seems to be used to represent an identity that is based on minority- group-belonging established

22 Unforgetting and the Politics of Representation

through either through racial categories or territories that are not Canada. On some of the challenges and limitations associated with the term ethnicity, see Maykel Varkuyten, *The Social Psychology of Ethnic Identity* (London: Taylor and Francis Group, 2004); Martin Doornbos, "Linking the Future to the past: Ethnicity and Pluralism," *Review of African Political Economy* 52 (1991), 53–65, and Hiroyuki Hino, *Ethnic Diversity and Economic Instability in Africa: Interdisciplinary Perspectives* (Cambridge University Press, 2012).

15 In the original: "U Bosni ni do danas nije shvaćeno sto zapravo cini osnovnu razliku izmedju triju nacija."Kordić, *Jezik I Nacionalizam* , Durieux 2010, 322. Translation is mine.

16 See Gaggioli, Gloria. "Sexual Violence in Armed Conflicts: A Violation of International Humanitarian Law and Human Rights Law." *International Review of the Red Cross* 96.894 (2014), 503–538. doi: 10.1017/S1816383115000211; Fraciah Muringi Njoroge, *Evolution of Rape as a War Crime and a Crime Against Humanity* (July 25, 2016). Available at SSRN: https://ssrn.com/abstract=2813970 or http://doi.org/10.2139/ssrn.2813970; and Patricia Viseur Sellers, *The Prosecution of Sexual Violence in conflict: The Importance of Human Rights as Means of Interpretation*, OHCHR, UN Nations and the Rule of Law, 2008, accessible at: https://www.un.org/ruleoflaw/blog/document/the-prosecution-of-sexual-violence-in-conflict-the-importance-of-human-rights-as-means-of-interpretation/.

17 See Vesna Nikolić-Ristanović, "Living Without Democracy and Peace: Violence Against Women in the Former Yugoslavia," *Violence Against Women* 5.1 (Jan 1999), 63–80. doi: 10.1177/10778019922181158; and Vesna Nikolić-Ristanović, ed., *Women, Violence, and War: Wartime Victimization of Refugees in the Balkans* (Budapest: Central European University Press, 2000); Amra Delić (2015), the video documents "Duhovi Prošlosti' Ghosts of the Past" (2014, Radio Free Europe, TV Liberty episode 953, https://youtu.be/oDvEKbV_paM?si=NKtJSoeZGnZuejVB) and "Sjećaš li se mene u ropstvu/Do you remember me enslaved" (2017, Radio Television Serbia).

18 See *Vodič za civilne žrtve rata: kako ostvariti pravo na zaštitu kao civilna žrtva rata u Federaciji BiH* (Medjunarodna komisija za nestale osobe [ICMP], [*Guide for Civilian Victims of War in the Federation of Bosnia and Herzegovina*- my translation], published by the Institut za nestale osobe/lica Bosne i Hercegovine [INO/INL], Centar za Slobodan pristup informacijama [CSpi]: Sarajevo, 2007.

19 Tamara P. Trošt and Danilo Mandić, ed. *Changing Youth Values in Southeast Europe: Beyond Ethnicity* (Routledge 2018). In my contribution to this collection, "Negotiating Identities in Post-Conflict Bosnia and Herzegovina: Self, Ethnicity and Nationhood in Adolescents Born of Wartime Rape," 19–38, I discuss the limitations of current discourses of nationalism and ethnicity in the social sciences and look at how adolescents born of war in Bosnia, with their unique positionality in dominant ethno-nationalist official politics challenge ethnicity as the most important identity marker. This book builds on some of the ideas presented in that chapter and extends them to considering how other individuals, such as women survivors of war actively 'negotiate' self-identity in relation to official politics.

20 Oliver P. Richmond, Sandra Pogodda and Jasmin Ramović, ed. *The Palgrave Handbook of Disciplinary and Regional Approaches to Peace* (London: Palgrave Macmillan, 2016), 3, accessible at: https://doi.org/10.1007/978-1-137-40761-0.

21 "What Happened Here," *Feminist Studies* 18.2 (1992): 295–308. See also Susanna Campbell et al., ed. *Liberal Peace? The Problems and Practices of Peacebuilding* (Cambridge: Cambridge University Press, 2011); Oliver Richmond, *A Post-Liberal Peace* (London: Routledge, 2011); Roger Mac Ginty, *Routledge Handbook of Peacebuilding* (London: Routledge, 2013).

Introduction   23

22 Laura McLeod, "A Feminist Approach to Hybridity: Understanding Local and International Interactions in Producing Post-Conflict Gender Security," *Journal of Intervention and State Building* 9.1 (2015): 48–69, 51. A small body of recent scholarship is beginning to articulate the connections between peace and conflict studies and feminist theory and approach, such as, for example, Elizabeth Porter, "Feminist Building Peace and Reconciliation: Beyond Post-Conflict," *Peacebuilding* 4.2 (2016):210–225; and Donna Pankhurst, "The 'Sex War' and Other Wars: Toward a Feminist Approach to Peace Building," *Development in Practice* 13.2 (2003): 154–177. While not explicitly feminist, *Hybridity on the Ground in Peacebuilding and Development*, ed. Joanne Wallis, Lia Kent, Miranda Forsyth, Sinclair Dinnen and Srinjoy Bose (Canberra: ANU Press, 2018), offers a useful conceptualization of hybridity in peace and conflict studies that recognizes the profound differences that exist between sociopolitical models on which international peacebuilding endeavors are carries out and the lived reality of local populations. In a similar vein, Maria-Adrianna Deiana's *Gender, and Citizenship: Promise of Peace in Post-Dayton Bosnia-Herzegovina* (London: Palgrave, Macmillan 2018), represents a rethinking of peace and conflict based on empirical research and stories of women survivors of war in the context of feminist international relations.

The concept of hybridity in peace studies seems to be replacing (or is sometimes being used alongside) earlier conceptions of the two levels at which peacebuilding can take place: at the official, state level, involving international actors and organizations, and 'from below', involving the interpersonal, and various types of civil society actors. For a lucid discussion of how 'peace from below' may operate in Bosnia and Herzegovina see, Julianne Funk, 'Invisible' Believers for Peace: Religion and Peacebuilding in Postwar Bosnia-Herzegovina," PhD Thesis (Katholieke Universiteit Leuven, 2012). The metaphor of 'ecology' in relation to how peacebuilding takes place seems to me most accurate and encompassing, although historically, the connection between the concepts has been made primarily, and rather narrowly, through environmental studies. The concept emerged from the debate on 'environmental security' and 'environmental peacemaking'. A shortcoming of this approach is "the lack of a common worldview and the absence of a shared philosophical space in relating ecology with peace"as outlined by Christos Kyrou, "Peace Ecology: An Emerging Paradigm in Peace Studies," *International Journal of Peace Studies* 12.1 (2007): 73–92. Kyrou provides a framework for a broader conceptualization of peace ecology, away from one directional 'functionalism' and environmental determinism that often downplays the significance of social, cultural and political factors in peace building. He proposes a more encompassing definition ofpeace ecology as:

a theoretical framework, broad and integrative enough to allow a full understanding, functionally as well as philosophically, of the inherent capacities of the environment to inform and sustain peace…[one that] creates conceptual space for looking at the peacebuilding potential of environmental practices and projects regardless of whether they are driven by problem solving or by a worldview; whether they focus on some task at hand or on human consciousness..

(73, 75)

The direct impact of this reframing on feminist peace and conflict studies is difficult to gauge. More recent research has revisited the need for a more encompassing definition of peace ecology but has done it in relation specifically to political ecology or political geo-ecology. Political ecology studies emerged in the late 1980s primarily through perspectives that combine Marxist political economy and cultural ecology, to demonstrate the importance of uneven power relations and politics within environmental degradation processes and struggles over resources. See for example, P. Robbins, *Political ecology: A Critical Introduction*. 2nd ed. Oxford: Wiley. 2012, Úrsula Oswald Spring, Hans Günter Brauch and Keith G. Tidball (eds.), *Expanding Peace Ecology: Peace, Security, Sustainability, Equity and Gender. Perspectives of IPRA's Ecology and Peace Commission*, Springer Cham, 2014, and. Philippe Le Billon and Rosaleen Duffy, "Conflict Ecologies: Connecting Political Ecology and Peace and Conflict Studies," *Journal of Political Ecology*, 25.1(2018): 239-260.

The way in which I use the term encompasses this understanding but nsists on a definition of ecologyas the relationship of living things to their environment and to each other, emphasizing that interpersonal relationships include multiple and complex dimensions that are connected to physical environments but also go beyond it to refer to multiple individual identities understood intersectionally, with gender, culture, education level and nationality playing key intersectional roles.As a framework, peace ecology must also draw upon developments in social ecological models that owe some of their models to Urie Bronfenbrenner's ecological framework for human development. For Bronfenbrenner's work see "Toward an Experimental Ecology of Human Development", *American Psychologist*, 32 (1977): 513-531; *The Ecology of Human Development: Experiments by Nature and Design*, Harvard University Press, 1979; "Ecology of the Family as a Context for Human Development: Research Perspectives," *Developmental Psychology*, 22.6 (1986): 723-742, and "Interacting Systems in Human Development: Research paradigms: Present and Future," in N. Bolger, A. Caspi, G. Downey, & M. Moorehouse (Eds.), *Persons in Context: Developmental Processes* (pp. 25–49), Cambridge University Press, 1988. A feminist framework for peace ecology has yet to be developed. I hope that this book lays some groundwork for the development of this research and theoretical model. Monika Palmberger, in *How Generations Remember: Conflicting Histories and Shared Memories in Post-War Bosnia and Herzegovina* (Palgrave: Macmillan, 2016) and the collection, *The New Bosnian Mosaic: Identities, Memories and Moral Claims in a Post-War Society*, ed. Xavier Bougarel, Elissa Helms and Ger Duijzings (Aldershot: Ashgate, 2007), provide accounts of post-war Bosnian society that are based on the model of peacebuilding 'from below'. The first work contextualizes how people remember in post-war Mostar, demonstrating that they do not suddenly overwrite their previous memories with new public history, while the second demonstrates the extent to which the war affected the proverbial Bosnian mosaic and focuses on other categories such as urbanity and rurality, gender, generation, class, and occupation in addition to ethno-nationalist categories.

23 Asef Bayat, *Life as Politics: How Ordinary People Change the Middle East* (Stanford University Press, 2010), 98.

References

Guzina, Dejan. "Dilemmas of Nation-Building and Citizenship in Dayton Bosnia." *National Identities*, 9.3 (2007): 217–234. https://doi.org/10.1080/14608940701406195

Takševa, Tatjana. "Challenging Conceptions: Children Born of Wartime Rape in Bosnia and Herzegovina," in *Challenging Conceptions: Children Born of Wartime Rape and Sexual Exploitation*. Eds. Kimberley Theidon, Dyan Mazurana and Dipali Anumol, Oxford University Press, 2023, DOI: 10.1093/oso/980197648315.003.0012.

Part I

The universe is made of stories, not atoms.

Muriel Rukeyser, The Speed of Darkness

Chapter 1

Why Stories Matter

The centrality of storytelling and the importance of words and narrative within my own family sensitized me to look for and appreciate the meaning of stories within other cultural and discursive frameworks. Very early on, I learned that language and the words we use have the capacity to transform our experience, and that "it is through story ... that we can distinguish what is true" (Lopez 1999). This is another way of saying that "the universe is made of stories, not atoms" as Muriel Rukeyser's line states in the preceding epigraph. This means that in its imaginative, narrative, and creative quality, language is especially useful in asserting a human truth, in "being a poem that rests on material evidence," especially in a context of great complexity.[1]

The stories of my maternal grandfather were told to me in different languages; he was a linguist at heart who actively spoke seven languages and who taught me that language is the measure of true wealth and value: the more languages one knows, the more people one can understand and communicate with. His people must have come from the coast, one of the islands off southern Dalmatia, he said. And there was always an expansiveness to his outlook on life, a migratory restlessness, and a curiosity about what lies beyond the visible line of the horizon. The stories he told were sometimes interspersed with songs which he sang in their original language. Singing them did not always represent an expression of happiness and joy. Experiences of imprisonment, dispossession, privation, and displacement were also part of this narrative. What he conveyed to me through story and songs was an intensely relational narrative world where relatives both living and deceased played an active part and where the present appeared to be only one variety of what happened before and what is likely to happen in the future.

My maternal grandmother's stories were drawn from Western mythology and art. Having grown up with a very strict, Hungarian-speaking mother and grandmother, and raised in the Srem District on the Danube on Habsburg values of earnestness, industry, and forbearance, she did not sing, nor did she smile a great deal. But she appreciated the didacticism that permeated myths, the stern lessons they taught about human folly. When I was a child, she had

DOI: 10.4324/9781003186168-3

28 Unforgetting and the Politics of Representation

decided to take art history in university as a mature student, as a subject she had always been interested in but never had the opportunity to study formally. This meant that she often contextualized my own childish actions with reference to various mythological figures, saints, and paintings, as well as departed ancestors who, in her view, made their genetic presence manifest in some of my own emerging character traits and behaviors.

My paternal grandparents told stories of World War II and hardship from the perspective of farmers who remembered in vivid detail what it meant to grow tobacco and tend a vineyard in their childhood village in Northern Greece, and to flee during the night and across borders ahead of advancing hostile armies. Their understanding of their own national identity was shaped by the experience of growing up as Slavic speakers in Greek Macedonia, a regional minority that inhabited the Aegean parts of Greece. Their memories were interspersed with stories of the widespread Hellenization in Greece following the end of World War I, where personal and topographic Macedonian names were forcibly changed to Greek versions, and they were forbidden to speak their maternal language at school and in public. Under the regime of Ioannis Metaxas, a Greek prime minister between 1936 and 1941, the situation for Slavic speakers became intolerable, causing many to emigrate. A law was passed banning local Macedonian dialects. Many people who broke the rule were deported to the islands of Thasos and Cephalonia. Others were arrested, fined, beaten, and forced to drink castor oil, or even deported to the border regions in Yugoslavia following a staunch government policy of chastising minorities.[2] My grandparents chose to leave, and fled their village at night, after receiving news that one of their young, politically outspoken relatives had disappeared.

Some of their stories, therefore, involved narratives about family members who were no longer among the living but whose remembered words and deeds were forever imprinted on their, and through their stories, also my mind. Their children—my father, aunts, and uncle—told stories from the perspective of being raised by parents whose lives were marked by the trauma of having lived through World War II, and who themselves recalled through vivid detail what it meant to grow up in a post-war climate. Many of the stories that shaped my childhood, and that would over time become integrated into primary aspects of my personal and social identity, were in fact family memories, past events reconstructed through the prism of a present where official lines of history comingle and sometimes stand at odds with the unique details of individual experience. The stories of my extended family, therefore, functioned as a memorial narrative community, one within which I could locate myself along the continuum between past and present while looking toward the future. I grasped very early on the connections between narrative and memory, and the importance of story to one's sense of identity, orientation to others and the world.

The importance of stories amid great losses and burdens of the past at the individual, community, and national levels was impressed upon me powerfully as well over the course of the first decade I spent in Canada. While I was coming to terms with a personal loss, loss of life in the recent war, loss of country, and with what it means to be a first-generation Canadian, I was listening to stories of Indigenous survivors of trauma in the Residential School system and their children, and stories about the missing and murdered Indigenous women and girls that were slowly coming to light for the first time on the mainstream Canadian media. My first-generation Canadian identity was being formed as the Residential Schools Settlement Agreement was being implemented, the largest class-action settlement in Canadian history, and the establishment of the Truth and Reconciliation Commission of Canada "to facilitate reconciliation among former students, their families, their communities and all Canadians."[3] It is estimated that at least 150,000 Indigenous children were removed and separated from their families and communities to attend Residential Schools following the establishment and dominance of the colonial government. While most of the 139 Indian Residential Schools ceased to operate by the mid-1970s, the last federally run school closed in the late 1990s, after I had arrived in Canada. Over the following two decades, it became apparent that first-person and community narratives shaped by lived experience of unspeakable loss and suffering as well as acts of resistance, agency, and resilience, represent the building blocks of recovery and peace, rooted in seeking to understand and heal the intergenerational legacy of pain that Indigenous peoples carry because of genocidal colonial policies. Indigenous stories, like healing and peace, are also a form of unforgetting; they do not always unfold according to a linear logic, and a clear conflict-crisis-resolution format, but are said to exist in a spiral way, "within the time and space as they happen, and in each subsequent telling."[4] I recognized the grief of many losses in what I was hearing, and this made me listen better, more closely, more deeply.

What was also becoming apparent is that the emerging truth and reconciliation framework in Canada is part of a global wave of historical transformations that have taken place following the end of the Cold War, the fall of the Berlin Wall, and the dissolution of the Soviet Union, alongside a steady and a powerful current of postcolonial discourses and voices demanding accountability from governments in postcolonial settler societies. These global changes have clear and broad implications for how we study memory and cross-border, transnational representation of past and present events. Diverse memories and identities that existed on either side of the Iron Curtain and across the Global North and Global South have since continued to come into better view of one another. The collapse of binary structures between "Eastern" and "Western" memory cultures has been unfolding in the context of growing globalized flows of capital, goods, and services, but also of people. These flows triggered waves of migration, contributing to the increasingly multi-memory cultural nature of most modern societies.

Over the late 1990s and the first decade of the 21st century, truth and reconciliation frameworks were being formulated in response to these changes in

30 Unforgetting and the Politics of Representation

many different nation-states, representing societies' cultural memory work that instigated negotiations of memories, histories, and identities in a largely pluralist context and in the effort to build sustainable peace.[5] Life-writing, testimonies, and other forms of first-person narratives emerged powerfully onto local and global cultural, literary, and political scenes, providing a situated, truth-based approach to grasping the individual implications of compelling and often polyphonic memories, histories, and experiences.

Given the continuities between individual and collective remembrance, however, storytelling has political and historical implications as well. Storytelling is a path toward peace, justice, and "getting at meaning" in more than one way.[6] In the case of sexual violence in war, Bosnian and Rwandan survivor stories and testimonies that started to emerge over the course of 1993 and 1994 helped codify rape legally and for the first time as a recognizable and independent crime within the statutes of the International Criminal Tribunals for the Former Yugoslavia (ICTY) and for Rwanda (ICTR). These became the historic foundation upon which crimes of rape and sexual violence are punished. Survivor first-person narratives brought the world's attention to the systematic nature of the violence, and the use of rape as a weapon of war, propelling closer investigation and the setting up of criminal courts of justice. The presence of Bosnian women's stories in the global public eye encouraged German women who were raped by the liberating Allied forces at the end of World War II to start narrating their own memories and experiences about this largely occluded history.[7] This, in turn, has prompted other investigations of specific gendered and conflict-related, "taboo" history in other regions, such as in Austria, where much interesting work is currently being done on so-called "occupation children" and the children of Black GIs in Austria.[8]

Since the war in Bosnia, "transitional justice" mechanisms were established within the constitutional framework of the Dayton Accord as Bosnia's equivalent to negotiating post-conflict truth and to accomplishing peace and reconciliation. Following a wave of testimonies and published narratives about the lived experience of war, attention has shifted to the relative successes and failures of the local criminal justice system. Although the formal mechanisms of transitional justice resulted in 540 verdicts between 2005 and 2022 spread between the ICTY and the judicial courts in various former Yugoslav states, the legal perspective is of continuing relevance, as many perpetrators remain at large, and sometimes still inhabit the same communities as those whom they have harmed.[9] But coming to terms with the past and achieving peace and reconciliation are multilayered, multidirectional, and linear processes that unfold simultaneously and over long periods of time across many arenas: personal, familial, community-based, legal, and national, as well as across the intersectional layers of lived experience, such as gender, class, nationality, and religion. Their implications and their relative successes or failures can only be assessed with some measure of accuracy on a longer timeline, sometimes spanning several generations.

Studies by legal scholars, sociologists, political scientists, and scholars in international relations, development, and peace and conflict studies continue to shed important light on the tension among macro forces that animate peace projects, nationalism, and transitional justice. However, personal narratives are an effective way to get at the intangible qualities that mark individual lives in context, and issues that have to do with emotion, socialization, and identity in ways that are not captured in other forms of study. Attention to such narratives helps identify, without giving in to simplification, the means of reversing internalized oppressions, and the broad range of agency that people assert in the context of their everyday lives. As such, those narratives also help identify the functioning of nonviolent interactions, mutual recognitions, and the everyday means to reconciliation itself.[10] Focusing attention on individual people, the stories of individual women survivors and some of the Children Born Because of War almost 30 years after the war, as I do in this book, shows not only the diverse ways in which members of these two groups who were directly affected by war violence have been engaged in memory work, but also how those stories and perspectives told from their particular social positions, actively participate in the weaving of communicative and cultural memory within the larger context of justice and peacebuilding.

Communicative memory in particular depends on stories and narrativization. It is defined as "an interactive practice located within the tension between individuals' and groups' recall of the past," but "bound to the existence of living bearers of memory and to the communicators of experience and encompasses three to four generations."[11] Scholars of memory distinguish between communicative memory and cultural memory. Cultural memory has been defined as more stable in that it usually represents a "collective concept for all knowledge that directs behavior and experience in the interactive framework of a society, and one that obtains meaning through generations in repeated societal practice and initiation."[12] Communicative memory is usually located in proximity with the everyday, and with individual speakers in interactive, interpersonal contexts. Communicative memory resides in the stories that people tell, stories that sometimes confirm and reinscribe aspects of cultural memory, but also stories that contest, subvert, and redefine established cultural memory. There is no real distinction between communicative and cultural memory, however, except in theory. The forms and methods of both are intermixed in the actual memory practice of individuals and social groups.[13] It is "through stories that people draw connections between human experiences and the complexity of deliberation, inviting us to consider the dilemmas and difficulties of choice in spaces of extremity."[14] Individual stories, therefore, shed light on the process of memory, recovery, and peacebuilding in a distinct manner that is constitutive of larger justice processes and reconciliation mechanisms. In this sense, both memory and peacebuilding must also be understood as embodied, and as residing in the personal, the individual, the communal, and the everyday, as functions of embodiment.

Storytelling is also an important aspect of traumatic experience that carries within it the potential for healing and peace at the individual level. Due to the nature of trauma—a shocking event or a series of events that take place entirely outside of the scope of ordinary physical, physiological, and/or neurological and cognitive experience—survivors often feel that they cannot succeed in making other people understand or even believe the complexity of their experience.[15] At the same time, survivors of trauma often feel compelled to keep retelling the story of the traumatic event since each act of retelling brings with it another opportunity to recreate and reconstruct another aspect of the complex experience. Each reconstruction, in turn, increases the survivor's mastery as the storyteller of one's own history, a historian of one's own life, one who acquires a greater amount of control over a seemingly overwhelming amount of incoherent details through a process of molding them and shaping them into a story, the storytelling process of having to order them and reorder them with some sense of a beginning, middle, and an end. In this sense, storytelling always brings benefits for the storyteller as well, especially in the context of first-person storying by survivors of violent events. Each reordering brings a new perspective on the past from the position of each present act of telling.

Each of these memorial reconstructions, in turn, also contain a political dimension, through what Asef Bayat terms "the power of presence," distinguishing between the politics of the powerful, which is patriarchal and authoritative, and the politics of "ordinary persons" who are subject to such politics. Arguably, survivors of war-related violence are on an important level not "ordinary persons" to the extent that their experiences are shaped by events that are precise opposite of ordinary, i.e., events and experiences that are inherently extraordinary. However, to the extent that their power within larger social and political structures is limited and constrained in varying degrees, they speak to ruling power from the perspective of those who are subject to official politics. As such, they generate a specific "power of presence" which acts as a critical political tool, an agentive space for defying, resisting, negotiating, making oneself heard, seen, and asserting the power of the collective "from below."[16]

In terms of methods and ethics of representation, feminist epistemology, which foregrounds individual ways of knowing, experiencing, and narrating, provides a usable set of concepts and representation strategies to engage with the perspectives of individual survivors. The emphasis on embodiment and intersectionality in feminist epistemology challenges dominant sites of knowledge and meaning-production and replaces them with the recognition of alternative ways of knowing that validate individual experience and voice.[17] Within this epistemological context, the individual and the self are understood not as private, distinct structures that exist in isolation from social context, but as entities formed and enacted within a complex network of inter-relational, communal, and social spaces. The self in feminist epistemology is experientially grounded and understood to be "continually both in the process of being shaped by social practices, and at the same time, the means by which we are able to express our resistance to socio-cultural and bodily norms."[18] As an act of personal agency, narrative is the main vehicle through which such embodied knowledge is revealed and validated. Research has shown that narratives of experience are not only reports of the experience but are also fully elaborated interpretations—or what may be called cases, examples, or exemplars—of experience.[19]

Grounding discussions relating to survivors of war and Children Born Because of War within a feminist epistemological framework thus has the potential to reveal not only oppression and suffering within each individual story, but also overlooked forms of agency and parallel individual histories of resistance to normative, revisionist, and other oppressive discourses and social practice. Personal narratives in particular showcase these feminist commitments because they reveal the continuities between oppression and resistance. Their value lies precisely in rearticulated definitions of subjectivity, "as constructed and socially produced rather than biologically determined."[20] Contextualizing the lives of individual survivors thus assumes that each of them "nonetheless exists as a thinking, feeling subject and social agent, capable of resistance and innovations produced out of the clash between contradictory subject positions and practices."[21] In the book I highlight such embodied means of knowing to show how through their commonalities but also differences from one another survivor narratives challenge stereotypical conceptions about their own victimhood. This approach question a what Lydia Sklevicky has referred to as the "customary relation between the general and the particular in the hierarchy of relevance usually asserted in the writing of official history."[22] As such it renders women survivors visible beyond their victimization by reframing how we understand the realm of political agency in relation to women's experience in war.

Finally, the stories of people who have survived war, and especially those who have survived different forms of war-related violence, have archival value in that they document individual experiences as well as memorialization of that experience at a particular historical moment. While the experiences of women who survived war rape during the war have been documented more extensively, the narratives of Children Born of War Rape, and the stories of women fighters have received significantly less attention. Such forms of documentation augment our knowledge of post-war recovery as they intersect with gender and provide a basis for further study of those phenomena in relation to Bosnia and the Balkans, but also as they may apply to different global settings. Moreover, what I hope is self-evident is that each one of their stories speaks about experience, past events, the present, healing, and trauma, from a distinct position, reminding us that although they are all survivors of the same war, each narrator is positioned differently in relation to each aspect of the war as well as peacebuilding.

Notes

1 Barry Lopez, *About This Life: Journeys at the Threshold of Memory* (Vintage, 1999), and Muriel Rukeyser, "The Education of a Poet" (1976), in ed. Janet Sternberg, *The Writer on her Work*, Revised ed. (W.W. Norton, 2000), 226.

2 Neil Simpson. *Macedonia Its Disputed History* (Victoria: Aristoc Press, 1994), 101, 102 & 191; *The Rising Sun In the Balkans* (The Republic of Macedonia; Sydney: International Affairs Agency; Pollitecon Publications, 1995), 33. Andrew Rossos. *Macedonia and the Macedonians: A History* (Stanford, California: Hoover Press, 2008), 145.

3 Truth and Reconciliation Commission of Canada was established in 2008, following the Indian Residential Schools Settlement Agreement, whose implementation began in 2007, 9 years after the Liberal Government of Canada issues the "Statement of Reconciliation" in 1998. For more on the timelines and the TRC see, https://www.rcaanccirnac.gc.ca/eng/1450124405592/1529106060525.

4 Suzanne Methot writes about the central status of stories in Indigenous knowledge systems in Legacy, *Trauma and Indigenous Healing* (ECW Press, 2019).

5 For different models of cultural memory and its relation to the field of memory studies as well as media and literary production, see Astrid Erll, *Memory in Culture*, trans. Sara B. Young (Original German language edition published by J.B.Metzlersche Verlagsbuchhandlung und Carl Ernst Poeschel Velrag GmbH Stuttgart, 2005; English translation published by Palgrave Macmillan, 2007). Also see, Astrid Erll, Ansgar Nünning, and Sara B. Young. *A Companion to Cultural Memory Studies an International and Interdisciplinary Handbook* (Berlin: Walter de Gruyter, 2008). On the transnational implications of these global developments in connection to memory, see Chiara DeCesari, and Ann Rigney, ed., *Transnational Memory: Circulation, Articulation, Scales* (Berlin/Boston: De Gruyter, 2014).

6 The relationship between storytelling and peace has only recently received scholarly attention. See for example, Maria Gloria C. Njoku and Jessica Senehi, "Peace Stories: A Model for Creating and Sustaining Peace," in ed. Maria Gloria C. Njoku, Leonard A Jason, and R. Burke Johnson, *The Psychology of Peace Promotion: Global Perspectives on Personal Peace, Children and Adolescents, and Social Justice* (Springer Cham International Publishing AG, 2019), 237–250.

7 Agatha Schwartz and I looked more closely at these connections in "Between Trauma and Resilience: A Transnational Reading of Women's Life Writing about Wartime Rape in Germany and Bosnia and Herzegovina," *Aspasia: The International Yearbook of Central, Eastern, and Southeastern European Women's and Gender History* 14.2020, 124-143. doi: 10.3167/asp.2020.140109.

8 See, for example, Flavia Guerrini, *Vom feind ein kind: Nachkommen allierter Soldaten erzählen* (Mandelbaum Verlag, 2022). Philipp Rohrbach, a historian with the Vienna Wiesenthal Institute for Holocaust Studies (VWI)since 2010, and a PhD Candidate at the Institute for Contemporary History at the University of Vienna, has curated and collaborated on exhibitions and projects relating to memory, "taboo history" and the category of children born because of war: "recollecting" (MAK/Austrian Museum for AppliedArts/Contemporary Art, 2008), "Kampf um die Stadt" (Wien Museum 2009), "Black Austria. The Children of African-American GIs" (The Austrian Museum of Folk Life and Folk Art, 2016); "Forgotten Children" and "Lost in Administration. Afro-Austrian GI Children –A Research Project" (University of Salzburg, 2013–2014, 2015–2017); since 2013 he has been co-head with Mag. Adina Seegerof of the project "The Austrian Heritage" (Verein GEDENKDIENST/VWI).

Why Stories Matter 35

9 For more details, see the publications of the Balkans Transitional Justice Program, accessible at: BIRN, https://balkaninsight.com/balkan-transitional-justice-home/publications/.
10 See Njoku and Senehi, 241.
11 Harald Weltzer, "Communicative Memory" in ed. Astrid Erll, and Ansgar Nünning, *Cultural Memory Studies: An International and Interdisciplinary Handbook* (De Gruyter, 2008), 285.
12 Weltzer, 285.
13 Weltzer, 285.
14 Erin Baines, *Buried in the Heart: Women, Complex Victimhood and the War in Northern Uganda* (New Rork: Cambridge University Press, 9).
15 See, for example, Primo Levy's The *Drowned and the Saved*, in ed. Ann Goldstein, *The Complete Works of Primo Levy, Volume III* (New York: Liveright Publishing Corporations, 2015); and Susan Brison's *Aftermath: Violence and the Remaking of a Self* (Princeton University Press, 2003).
16 Asef Bayat, *Life as Politics: How Ordinary People Change the Middle East* (Stanford University Press, 2010), 98.
17 Sharlene Naggy Hesse-Biber, ed. *Handbook of Feminist Research: Theory and Praxis*, 2nd Edition (Sage, 2012).
18 Karen Barbour, "Embodied Ways of Knowing: Revisiting Feminist Epistemology." In ed. Louise Mansfield, Jayne Caudwell, Belinda Wheaton & Beccy Watson, *The Palgrave Handbook of Feminism and Sport, Leisure and Physical Education* (Palgrave Macmillan, 2018), 209–226, 220.
19 D. J. Clandinin and J. Rosiek. "Mapping a Landscape of Narrative Inquiry: Borderland Spaces and Tensions." In ed. D. J. Clandinin, *Handbook of Narrative Inquiry: Mapping a Methodology* (Sage Publications, 2007), 35–76.
20 Barbour, 212.
21 Chris Weedon, *Feminist Practice and Poststructuralist Theory* (Oxford: Basil Blackwell, 1987), 124.
22 Lydia Sklevicky, *Konji, žene, ratovi* (Zagreb: Ženska infoteka, 1996), 14.

Reference

Lopez, Barry. *About This Life: Journeys on the Threshold of Memory*, Vintage Books, 1999.

Chapter 2

Ecologies of Peace

The multifaceted nature of traumatic experience was apparent in my conversations with survivors. Their narratives show the consequences of trauma on their sense of self, resulting from the nature of rape and sexual violence as the physical, psychological, and moral violation of a person. At the same time, also visible within the narratives are the relational, communal, and social aspects of traumatic experience that structure how survivors understand their experience, as well as how they describe the process of healing.[1] Their stories show the interdependence of individual and collective psychic and social mechanisms that play a part in how trauma is experienced, manifested and, in some cases, overcome. They also show that each individual at different points in time and in different settings can experience and represent themselves in terms of either or both victimhood and suffering, as well as in terms of resilience, as a survivor. Traumatic experience is to some extent dialectic and even kaleidoscopic: it results from unspeakable suffering that continuously demands to be heard and recognized. At the same time, traumatic experience frequently resists being defined through suffering only. People resist being defined through a single experience of victimization and seek to assert agency over different aspects of their lives in multiple ways, thereby also asserting their right to see themselves and be seen as complex human beings, outside of the singular prism of victimhood. Identifying oneself as either a victim or a survivor or alternating between the two forms of identification is, therefore, neither static nor permanent. Such identification can and does exists on a spectrum. This spectrum encompasses what has been understood as a continuum of violence[2] as well as instances marked by agency, forms of healing, and peace building.

The concept of a continuum of violence against women was developed by Liz Kelly in 1988 to help shift how instances of violence against women are categorized. Rather than categorizing violence against women and girls as episodic and deviant incidents (defined in law as crimes) of extreme cruelty and harm, the concept helps us to recognize the normative and functional elements of such violence, existing in the everyday, ongoing context in the lives and experiences of women and girls all over the world.[3] Isolated attention on manifestations of severe, horrifying, and excessive physical and sexual violence

DOI: 10.4324/9781003186168-4

against women, leads investigators to seek explanations for such violence in individual pathology and abnormality (of perpetrator and/or victim), or in the context of war, in the aberrant behavior of specific groups of perpetrators. This approach distances the acts and their motivations from the structures and norms of "acceptability," "decency," and "civilized society" at the individual level, but also at the level of the politics of representation, suggesting that the men of some nations, races, or ethnicities are more prone to committing such violence than men who are white, Western, or "civilized."

The law tends to recognize as crimes, albeit only under specific circumstances, only aberrant forms of violence against women. Rape of women during war now constitutes one of these contexts, in no small measure thanks to Bosnian and Rwandan women who testified in the criminal courts about their experiences. These testimonies, in connection with other forms of testimony relating to war crimes, enabled international criminal tribunals to establish the systematic, intentional nature of mass rapes in situations of armed conflict, leading for the first time to the legal codification of rape as a weapon of war rather than a "natural" by-product of war as it was generally considered until 2008. This has been an immensely significant development.

However, this ruling, as significant as it has been, exists simply at one extreme end of a broad spectrum of socially sanctioned male aggression, coercive behavior, notions of entitlement, and deep-rooted patriarchal norms. So, for example, "stranger" rape exists on a continuum of normalized behavior, including misogynist jokes, sexual harassment, intimate intrusions, and coerced sex with dates or partners. These are all included in the everyday experiences of women and girls, for which there is widespread tolerance, not only in Bosnia and the Balkans, but in other societies, inlcuding those in the so-called Global North. For example, a study cited by a 2022 report of the Scottish Women's Aid Society Tolerance found that up to one in two young men and one in three young women in Scotland believe that forced sex is justifiable in certain circumstances.[4] Scholars have been pointing out that most global societies normalize deeply misogynistic, male-dominated cultures and behaviors, where certain levels of men's mistreatment of women are so prevalent that they remain barely visible or noticed.[5]

It has been very important for research, policy, and practice to categorize and investigate diverse settings of gender-based violence: domestic abuse, rape, sexual assault, and sexual harassment, forced marriage, child abuse, culturally sanctioned harmful practices, sexual exploitation, economic and structural discrimination, internet porn, stalking, and abuse of women and girls in immigration and refugee contexts. But all of these instances, as different as they, also possess some things in common. In terms of function, they are instrumental forms of coercion and intimidation; their impact manifests either as constraint or outright abuse or both at the same time. In terms of consequences, they function to control and limit the status, movement, integrity, opportunities, and rights of many women and girls. These shared circumstances rooted in different types of patriarchal logic reinforce stereotypical ideas about victim blaming and perpetuate socially sanctioned mistrust of women who survived violence,

38 Unforgetting and the Politics of Representation

Although violence against women in war takes place in the context of conflict which represents a disruption of all ordinary life patterns, the forms of thought that make this violence possible in the first place exist in peace time as well. The normative patriarchal frameworks within which gender based violence against women occurs are evident in the challenge that many victims encounter when trying to assert the legal validity of evidence, especially in cases where the only evidence is the woman's testimony. In this sense, the reluctance of some women survivors to disclose or report their experiences of violence must be understood not only in the context of traditional feminine values of honor, chastity, and shamefast sexual purity that was perceived to be violated through rape, but also in connection with the fact that the women are well aware of the misogyny underlying the social propensity toward victim blaming. Furthermore, there are many cases where women continue to reside in the same community and meet daily the perpetrator of violence himself and/or close members of his immediate and extended family and friends. These are all important factors in assessing the reasons for some women's silence. These factors also help us assess the extent of women's politically motivated agency involved in choosing to speak out and make their stories public.

Just as violence against women exists on a continuum, women survivor's agency, just like agency for most people, is not asserted in an absolute sense and from a perspective of absolute power and autonomy. Agency exists in dialectic interplay with instances of victimization, is mediated through time, is context-specific and further determined by many factors, not least the contingencies of daily living that often demand a singular label (victim or survivor). The event of narration itself, and how people use words to locate themselves and others in language constitutes "agentive discourse." It is "within the space of agentive discourse through which we ascribe rights, and claim them for ourselves, as well as place duties on others."[6] Not everyone involved in interactive exchange has equal access to rights and duties to perform particular kinds of meaningful actions at a given time. This intersectional sensitivity becomes a great obligation in the context of a research relationship, but in itself does not remove narrative agency from any research participants. However, agency is never exercised in an absolute sense, nor does it exist outside of specific contexts. All agents are embodied, and as such we are in different degrees encumbered, enmeshed in our own individual and social contexts, historically and legally embedded. Agency, therefore, resides within the very level of subjectivity, intention, participation, and decision making, and the ways in which those become articulated through language and discourse and based on an individual social position.

For survivors of traumatic experiences, more so than for any other individual, the act of telling is neither easy nor straightforward. Hence, the unforgetting. The women who spoke with me related that they needed to prepare themselves for the conversation, even though they chose to engage in it, and saw the benefits. Despite this, however, they all displayed clear agentive consciousness around the process and meaning of narrativization, what they can expect from it, why they are choosing it, and how to manage the aftereffects.

Ecologies of Peace   39

For all of them—even for those who have not spoken about their war experiences to anyone for more than ten years, or in the case of one woman, never up to that point—this agentive awareness created an "epistemic distance" between the immediacy of relived traumatic events and their perception of them, a way to step out of the "temporal flux" of painful sensations.

Each instance of storying past and present experiences involves a series of decisions speakers make as they actively construct and reconstruct within their stories their past in their present and future selves. Deciding in a relational and interactive context what to say and how reflects a sense of authorship and, therefore, also authority, personal responsibility, and autonomy. Through telling, speakers create a sense of meaning that is shaped by and shapes in turn a variety of cultural meanings, symbolic as well as embodied. Narrative constructions of meaning are, therefore, expressions of agency and subjectivity through which survivors of war actively shape and reshape themselves as agentive historical and political subjects through individual life histories. Recollections themselves often assume "the form of a story or are at least constituents of a story, which can be narrated and has usually been repeatedly told."[7]

The relationship between trauma, memory, agency, and recovery is multifaceted and complex, predicated on the myriad ways we develop to live with the pain of the past. Recent interdisciplinary writing on trauma has highlighted that "the way we remember the past and imagine the future affects the way we live in the present," and that trauma, memory, and imagination are united in our understanding and way of being in the world.[8] Although there is a range of so-called "typical responses" recorded across a wide spectrum of traumatic experiences, trauma and its effects on each individual cannot be fully grasped in a purely cognitive manner.[9] To the extent that trauma is a loss of connection, as Peter Levine has described it, loss of connection to a coherent and historically continuous sense of self but also the self's social and natural environment, the healing of trauma must involve a web of relational elements that help restore the lost connection, and reestablish social and interactional connectivity.[10]

The loss of interconnectivity at the individual level, the challenge of "finding one's way home," is further compounded when trauma is the consequence of war, an event that causes disruption in the macro-social sphere as well as in micro-social settings, where the objective forms that have defined home and belonging have been violently reordered in a literal sense for all those whose lives were disrupted by war. Finding one's way home, therefore, or restoring the lost sense of cohesion at the personal and collective level both literally and figuratively requires the generation of multiple polyphonic narratives that call for public recognition and awareness, and, at the personal level, that allow each person to re-story and re-narrativize traumatic events at different times and in different settings, with different words even, to facilitate the regrowing of a cohesive and agentive sense of self.

Traumatic experience thus encompasses the social and physical ecologies or "ecosystems" that constitute people's habitats. This is a term I borrow and

40 Unforgetting and the Politics of Representation

adapt from the life sciences to refer to a range of habitat factors that comprise the complex physical environment of daily living. The individual and collective remain interlinked and interdependent in survivor accounts since sexualized violence affects not only the person it was perpetrated against but their families, communities, and all those who may have witnessed it. For many who experienced sexual violence during the war, this was only one type of loss they remember or unforget, daily. For some, witnessing the torture and murder of loved ones represents an experience harder to live with than the harm that was inflicted onto their own bodies and spirit.

The survivors' personal experiences, and the extent to which they feel at peace or not at peace are also refracted through the nature of the support or lack thereof that they have been able to access and receive. Such factors have as much to do with health and legal systems within which survivors are led to or discouraged from seeking help, as with the individual survivors' personal resources and physical access. Since traumatic experience is multifaceted, it demands a multifaceted approach that resists binary constructions relating to self/other, public/private, individual/collective. As such, traumatic experience both exists as relational and is recalled relationally since it has taken place and is remembered in specific interpersonal and social contexts.

A relational understanding of trauma in turn means that recovery, or "being at peace" at the individual level must also be articulated in a relational sense, through the study of processes that enable—or prevent—individuals and communities to be at peace or fail to develop peaceful ecosystems of cohabitation. Such understanding entails that we begin to think of peacebuilding in terms of the interdependence among individual, community-based, state level, and international, geopolitically situated capacities to develop ecologies of peace. Understanding peacebuilding in terms of ecologies of peace means that we recognize the diverse ways in which diverse human lives are defined through specific social positionality, and specific interactions with complex environments. Such a perspective enables that we begin to locate political agency in various social and cultural spaces and across different levels of identity, not only measured in terms of large, state- or group-based interventions.

Researching motherhood and the maternal, I have been particularly struck by the narratives of women who have given birth and/or raised children born because of war rape. The central event of the war experience for them focused on the fact of motherhood and their negotiation of motherhood as a social role, yet very little had been written about it from this perspective. Much of the discourse on pregnancies resulting from war rape—a reality that has affected great numbers of women across the globe in areas of conflict—is focused on detailing the social stigma affecting mothers and children, and the legal, socioeconomic, and cultural marginalization experienced by both. The mothers' strong feelings of rejection and sometimes hatred toward the children who throughout both of their lives continue to trigger traumatic memories from the mother's past is also discussed in some literature. These issues are without doubt a significant aspect of this type of mothering.

However, in the context of the Bosniak women that I spoke with, maternal subjectivity, agency, care, and love toward the children were particularly prominent. The maternal role, dependent on an active, rational, and emotional commitment to the long-term, daily care of children, is separable from the biological act of giving birth. This is evidenced not only in the examples of women who have raised their own biological children born of war rape, but also in the examples of those women and men who have adopted children born because of war and have provided them with committed parental love and care. In so far as one of the main goals of maternal care is to prepare the children for social acceptability, when it comes to the life stories of two of such mothers who raised their biological children born of rape, they have shown exceptional forms of agency and personal courage in contending not only with their own trauma and recovery but also with systemic barriers and cultural prejudices their children have had to contend with. Both mothers have succeeded in navigating with great dignity and with deep commitment to their children's well-being the complexity of their own maternal feelings and the hostile environments affecting their own lives and the lives of their children. So my analyses have situated their accounts within the context of feminist maternal theory and philosophy, examining the women's mothering practices as embedded within their specific social, cultural, and psychological settings.[11] Rather than continuing to reconstruct them and their stories exclusively through the lens of "children of the enemy," victimhood, and contested identity boundaries drawn in terms of ethnicity, I highlight the ways in which their narratives show resilience, distinct types of personal responsibility and agency through which they re/shape their ways of being in the world and contribute to social and political narratives of recovery and peace.

Building awareness around the experiences of children born of war and women who have experienced sexualized war-related violence continues to be of key importance in many different spheres, within Bosnia, but also globally. Conceptually, the category of victim appears both irreducible and easily manipulated and co-opted through its embeddedness in multiple contexts. As such it poses representational challenges. Media and scholarship often participate in a problematic logic according to which women's experiences and identities are continuously framed and reframed with an emphasis on their victimization.

Many of the women I spoke with remarked very pointedly that the government remembers the civilian victims of war only before or during elections. It is not uncommon that the war experiences of women survivors are disbelieved and discredited by others in their communities, or that they are shamed and blamed for being responsible for what happened to them. Despite this, they expressed fatigue and frustration with the narratives of their victimization

42 Unforgetting and the Politics of Representation

being instrumentalized for purposes that have nothing to do with their own well-being, continuously repeated over the media when it appears to be politically convenient. All of them are keenly aware of the instrumental utility of the conceptual category "victim" in civic, medical, and legal frameworks. Achieving the formal status of "civilian victim of war" [*civilna žrtva rata*] is a pre-condition to realizing indispensable post-war benefits, such as a disability pension and medical insurance, or post-secondary tuition relief for themselves and their children. Being formally accorded the status "civil victim of war" also represents a form of official acknowledgment of the harm that was done to them during the war, and the ensuing suffering. For the children born because of war, being accorded this status means decreasing forms of systemic stigmatization and fuller civic integration. At the same time, however, the public dimension of this recognition is something that some women continue to avoid.

Women also expressed frustration with the number of different types of documenters, journalists, students, and researchers, who come to ask them for their stories, treating their stories as an endless repository of suffering and pain to be tapped into when it comes to the topic of women, children, and war. The women expressed moral fatigue with being asked the same questions repeatedly. They spoke about being protective of their stories and selective in terms of when they want to share them and with whom, based on previous negative experiences. Some of them remarked that there has been enough talk about the war—that everyone needs to look forward, into the future. At the same time, many of them still believe that it is exceptionally important for their stories to be told, recorded, and remembered.

On the one hand, not calling upon their experiences of victimization runs the risk of those experiences being unrecognized, trivialized, diminished, or forgotten. On the other hand, the utilization of their stories to illustrate the gendered nature of war rape without situating them in the specific social, cultural, and political setting within which this violence took place, runs the risk of misrepresenting crucial aspects of their experience, and occluding crucial aspects of agency, autonomy, and resistance that may be embedded in episodes of unspeakable violence. Many women, while seeking respect for the experiences they have survived, feel trapped by the singularity and reductionism of the concept of victim. The complexity of the discursive social space they have occupied since the war and have learned to navigate with varying degrees of success, the space that they are all negotiating through acts of personal courage, pride, and determination, draws attention powerfully to the need to revisit and reconstruct the way victims/survivors of war are discussed and represented.

The validation of the survivor's experience in a way that neither reduces nor overstates the relative importance of either victimhood or survival in people's self-concept is at the heart of survivor-centric perspectives.[12] The benefit of this perspective is that it is spacious and allows for people to identify and assert various kinds of agency at various times in the context of telling or not telling their experience. In a theoretical, philosophical as well as practical sense, survivor-centricity starts from the premise that all policy, analysis, and support of those who have survived sexualized and gender-based violence must remain rooted in the perspective of the survivor. While there has been much discussion of the term in scholarship and policy, and while practitioners in many fields strive to apply it in practice, "survivor-centered approaches are yet to be fully translated into meaningful practice by [nation] states, especially in relation to health and justice systems."[13] The issue lies in their systemic implementation across all sectors of government, as well as a large-scale discursive shift in how we understand sexualized and gender-based violence in conditions of conflict. Such a perspective in turn depends upon a redefinition of the very logic of the nation-state and its global investment in security and militarization.[14]

A continued emphasis on survivor-centricity in public discourse over the last decade has, nonetheless, been pivotal in highlighting for first response teams, providers of medical and psychological support services, as well as for researchers, the inadequacies and patriarchal bias in existing policies and approaches to rape and sexualized violence across various systems and institutional contexts. The concept and the philosophy behind it also highlight the ways in which survivors themselves can be systemically empowered as documenters of their own experience. The recent work of Ute Baur-Timmerbrink, Sabine Lee, Heide Glaesmer, and Barbara Stelzl-Marx, as well as Amra Delić, the *Association Forgotten Children of War* in Sarajevo ("Zaboravljena Djeca Rata") led by Ajna Jusić, and *The Museum of War Childhood* in Sarajevo founded by Jasminko Halilović, among others, have each in a different way foregrounded the legal, cultural, and personal consequences of conflict upon the lives of survivors, men and women alike, and the importance of understanding multi-level forms of conflict and the impact of long-term war-related violence within the context of agentive, survivor-led, and survivor-centric reframing of those experiences.[15]

This book builds on such work. It challenges totalizing accounts of victimization that grow out of war, especially when it comes to the assumption that women survivors are in "constant need of rescue and rehabilitation."[16] Stressing the importance of self-representation to engage with the stories of survivors of war violence, I hope to highlight the conceptual and experiential thresholds of victim/survivor categories and the continuities between them, as well as how many individuals adopt silence in an agentive manner to resist one-dimensional social representations of themselves. Rather than assuming a straightforward connection between silence and victimization, the silences of survivors must be understood within the larger context of human agency, which is never absolute, but always contingent and socially embedded across multiple intersections of identity.[17] The emphasis on narrativization of experience and memories foregrounds the transformative power of survivor language as a path to social transformation and peace. In all of this, I strive to follow the lead provided by survivors themselves.

Notes

1 I have recently explored, with Mythili Rajiva, some of the consequences of this binary understanding of traumatic experience in relation to survivor narratives and proposed an alternative approach in the context of feminist trauma studies. See Mythili Rajiva and Tatjana Takševa, "Thinking Against Trauma Binaries: The Interdependence of Personal and Collective Trauma in the Narratives of Bosnian Women Rape Survivors." *Feminist Theory* 22.3 (2021), 405–427. doi: 10.1177/1464700120978863.

2 The concept of the continuum of violence was introduced by Cynthia Cockburn to denote a line of continuity between phases of peace and conflict. See Cockburn, "A Continuum of Violence: A Gender Perspective on War and Peace." In ed. Wenona Giles and Jennifer Hyndman, *Sites of Violence: Gender and Conflict Zones* (Berkeley, CA: University of California Press, 2004), 24–44.

3 Kelly Liz, *Surviving Sexual Violence* (Cambridge, UK; Oxford, UK: Polity Press, 1988).

4 Scottish Women's Aid Society, "Equally Safe in Practice Framework: Continuum of Violence-Making the Connections," Knowledge, Skills, Change 2022, accessible at: https://womensaid.scot/wp-content/uploads/2022/12/ESiP-Continuum-of-Violence.pdf.

5 Jackson Katz, *The Macho Paradox: Why Some Men Hurt Women and How All Men Can Help* (Naperville, IL: Sourcebooks, 2006).

6 Rom Harré, "Positioning Theory: Moral Dimensions of Social-Cultural Psychology. In ed. J. Valsiner, *The Oxford Handbook of Culture and Psychology* (New York: Oxford University, 2012), 191–206, 193.

7 Jurgen Straub, "Psychology, Narrative and Cultural Memory: Past and Present," in ed. Astrid Erll and Ansgar Nünning, *Cultural Memory Studies: An International and Interdisciplinary Handbook* (Berlin, New York: Dee Gruyter, 2008), 215–228, 216.

8 Stephen K. Levine, *Trauma, Tragedy, Therapy: The Arts and Human Suffering* (Jessica Kingsley Publishers, 2009), 16–17.

9 See for example, Stefanie Marie Margarete Dinkelbach, "Finding the Way Home: An Interdisciplinary Perspective on Trauma and Trauma Resolution Practices," in ed. Elspeth McInnes and Anka Mason., *Where to From Here? Examining Conflict Related and Relational Interaction Trauma* (Brill, 2019), 191–212.

10 Peter Levine, *Trauma and Memory: Brain and Body in a Search for the Living Past: A Practical Guide for Understanding and Working with Traumatic Memory* (North Atlantic Books, 2015).

11 Takševa, "Raising Children Born of Wartime Rape in Post-Conflict Bosnia: Maternal Philosophy Perspective," in ed. Tatjana Takševa and Arlene Sgoutas, *Mothers Under Fire: Mothering in Conflict Zones* (Demeter Press, 2015); Takševa, "Mother Love, Maternal Ambivalence, and the Possibility of Empowered Mothering," *Hypatia: Journal of Feminist Philosophy* 32.1 (2016). doi: 10.1111/hypa.12310; Takševa, "Raising Children Born of War in Bosnia: Reframing Perspectives on Mother Love through a Mother-Daughter Case Study," In ed. Carole Zufferey and Fiona Buchanan, *Intersections of Mothering: Feminist Accounts* (Routledge, 2020), 141–155, and Takševa, "'Where Would You Send the Pain?': Agency and Resilience in Three Children Born of War in Bosnia and Herzegovina," in ed. Kimberly Theidon, Dyan Mazurana, and Dipali Anumol, *Challenging Conceptions: Children Born of Wartime Rape and Sexual Exploitation* (Oxford University Press, 2023).

12 The concept of survivor centricity goes back to Resolution 2467 of the UN Security Council, the most recent addition to the Women, Peace, and Security (WPS) agenda, where the Council embraced the idea of a "survivor-centred approach" to

preventing and responding to conflict-related sexual violence. Most recently, the concept has emerged powerfully in a variety of global contexts, in part due to the recognition of sexual violence during war as a crime against humanity that publicized its significance through the awarding of the Nobel Peace Prize in 2018 to Nadia Murad Basee Taha, Iraqi Yazidi human rights activist and Denis Mukwege, an African gynaecologist for the efforts of both people to end sexual violence as a weapon of war. Murad subsequently founded Nadia's Initiative, an organization dedicated to helping women and children victimized by genocides, mass atrocities, and human trafficking to heal and rebuild their lives and communities. Nadia's Initiative was one of the organizations that initiated The Murad Code project, as a consultative initiative involving partners from across the globe, including survivors and other individuals, civil-society organisations, governments, inter-governmental and other international organisations, and funders. The idea of a global code of conduct for the gathering and use of information about systematic and conflict-related sexual violence originated with the Institute for International Criminal Investigations (IICI) (www.iici.global). The founding partners of the project are IICI, Nadia's Initiative (www.nadiasinitiative.org) and the Preventing Sexual Violence in Conflict Initiative of the UK government (PSVI). The Code defines survivor-centric approaches in gathering testimonies and documenting them, and promotes them for adoption by any organization and agency providing support to victims and survivors of violence.

13 A statement made by Hilary Douglas of the British Red Cross in an International Committee of the Red Cross publication, *Sexual Violence in Conflict: Putting the Individual First*, Geneva, November 2020, accessible at: https://www.icrc.org/en/document/putting-individual-first.

14 A nation state can be defined as a self-declared and independent geopolitical entity that asserts control within boundaries of land and water and is populated by a citizenship. There is emerging literature calling for reconceptualizing what we mean when we say that we are committed to survivor-centric approaches, and that sheds light on the interdependence of the individual and the collective aspects of violence, trauma, and recovery. See for example, Janine Natalya Clark, "Beyond a 'Survivor-Centred Approach' to Conflict-Related Sexual Violence?," *International Affairs* 97.4 (2021), 1067–1084. doi: 10.1093/ia/iiabo55.

Among studies that have highlighted the connections between sexual violence against women in particular and national, political and cultural discourses are Susan Brownmiller's now classic study of, *Against Our Will: Men, Women, and Rape* (Simon and Schuster, 1975)/Fawcett Columbine 1993; Nira Yuval-Davis' *Gender and Nation* (Thousand Oaks: Sage, 1997), shaped understanding about the interdependence of national projects, including war and women's symbolic –and actual-- roles within those projects. Mrinalini Sinha's more recent work extend these ideas within a postcolonial perspective in *Gender and Nation*, Publication of the American Historical Association, 2006. Alexandra Stiglmayer's collection, *Mass Rape: The War Against Women in Bosnia and Herzegovina* (University of Nebraska Press, 1994), remains an important collection on the war in Bosnia as it was unfolding. Christina Lamb's *Our Bodies, Their Battlefields: War Through the Lives of Women* (New York: Scribner, 2020), adds to this body of knowledge, and it includes several chapters based on her interviews with Bosnian women who survived sexualized violence during the war.

15 R. Charli Carpenter, *Born of War: Protecting Children of Sexual Violence Survivors in Conflict Zones* (Bloomfield, CT: Kumarian Press, 2007), and *Forgetting Children Born of War Setting the Human Rights Agenda in Bosnia and Beyond* (New York: Columbia University Press, 2010); Sabine Lee, *Children Born of War in the Twentieth Century* (Manchester, England: Manchester University Press, 2017); Camile Oliveira and Erin Baines, 'Children "Born of War": A Role for Fathers?,'

46   Unforgetting and the Politics of Representation

International Affairs 96: 2 (2020), 439–455. Additionally, there are multiple international and national scholarly projects on Children Born of War with presence on the Internet, which provide some insight into the scope of research on this topic. Ute Baur-Timmerbrink's book, *Wir Besatzungskinder: Töchter und Söhne alliierter Soldaten erzählen*, ("We, the children of the occupation: narratives by the daughters and sons of soldiers of the allied forces" – my translation), was published in German in 2015. The following year it was translated by S. Fischer Fondacija into Bosnian as *Mi Djeca Okupacije: Pripovijesti Kćerki I Siniva Saveznićkih Vojnika*, and published by Traduki, Sarajevo (2016). It has not been translated into English to date. This is an important book as it deals with the long-term consequences of being a child of war. Additionally, due to the decades-long distance from the events themselves, the book provides a unique perspective on transgenerational memory and trauma, as well as agency and resilience over an extended period.

My own work on the topic has foregrounded a maternal theory context include the edited collection, Tatjana Takševa and Arlene Sgoutas, ed. *Mothering Under Fire: Mothers and Mothering in Conflict Zones* (Toronto: Demeter Press, 2015); "Challenging Conceptions: Children Born of Wartime Rape in Bosnia and Herzegovina," in ed. Kimberley Theidon and Dyan Mazurana, *Challenging Conceptions: Children Born of Wartime Rape and Sexual Exploitation* (Oxford University Press, forthcoming); "Raising Children Born of War in Bosnia: Reframing Perspectives on Mother Love Through a Mother-Daughter Case Study," in ed. Carole Zuffrey and Fiona Buchanan *Intersections of Mothering: Feminist Accounts. Interdisciplinary Research in Motherhood Series* (Routledge, 2020), 141–155; "Negotiating Identities in Post-Conflict Bosnia and Herzegovina: Self, Ethnicity and Nationhood in Adolescents Born of Wartime Rape," in Ed. Tamara P. Trošt and Danilo Mandić, *Changing Youth Values in Southeast Europe: Beyond Ethnicity* (Routledge, 2017). 19-38; "Building a Culture of Peace and Collective Memory in Post-Conflict Bosnia and Herzegovina: Sarajevo's Museum of War Childhood," *Studies in Ethnicity and Nationalism* 18.1 (2018). doi: 10.1111/sena.12265; "Response to Whether the Definition of the Term 'children Born of War' and Vulnerabilities of Children From Recent Conflict and Post-conflict Settings Should Be Broadened," *Acta Medica Academica. Academy of Sciences and Arts of Bosnia and Herzegovina* 46.2 (2017), 177–179. doi: 10.5644/ama2006-124.206; "Hybridity, Ethnicity and Nationhood: Legacies of Interethnic War, Wartime Rape and the Potential for Bridging the Ethnic Divide in Post-conflict Bosnia and Herzegovina," Tatjana Takševa and Agatha Schwartz, *National Identities*. April, 2017. doi: 10.1080/14608944.2017.1298580; "Mother Love, Maternal Ambivalence, and the Possibility of Empowered Mothering." *Hypatia: Journal of Feminist Philosophy* 32.1 (2016). doi: 10.1111/hypa.12310.

I am grateful to Amra Delić for sharing her master's thesis with me: *Kvalitet života i dugoročne psihičke posljedice u žena sa iskustvom ratnog silovanja* (Magistarski rad, Univerzitet u Tuzli, Medicinski fakultet, 2015) [The quality of life and long-lasting psychological consequences in women survivors of rape in Bosnia and Herzegovina]. Delić's engaged research has been instrumental in helping the founding of the Sarajevo-based Association Forgotten Children of War, fostering its membership and supporting the leadership in their efforts to remove multiple types of stigma against the population of children born because of war in Bosnia, but also globally.

The activist work of Ajna Jusić, the president of the Association Forgotten Children of war, and a child of the Bosnian war herself, has been, since 2017, has contributed immensely to raising awareness around the issues surrounding this population. Jusić has advocated very vocally across many media platforms and in many languages for the rights of children of war in Bosnian society and beyond. It has been a true pleasure and a privilege getting to know her. More about the Association and its activities can be seen here: https://zdr.ba/.

16 Simić, Olivera. "Challenging Bosnian Women's Identity as Rape Victims, as Unending Victims: The 'Other' Sex in Times of War," *Journal of International Women's Studies* 13.4 (2012), 129–142, 133. Since the end of the war, the work of Zilka Spahić Šiljak, in English and Bosnian, the work of Olivera Simić, Dubravka Žarkov, Jasmina Husanović, and Vesna Nikolić-Ristanović has helped shape a more complex understanding of the war and its aftermath, as well as of women in war as survivors but also active agents in particular gendered ways. Recent publications issued by local agencies such as My Voice Echoes…by Masha Durkalić, published by CURE Foundation in 2015, and "We Are Still Alive," a research projects published by Medica Zenica in 2014, based on women's survivor narratives of those who have been supported by Medica's services since the war, are also significant in this regard. They contribute to a more complex understanding of the impact of the war and its aftermath on communities and on the individual lives of women survivors through a lens that encourages us to see resilience and agency as co-existing with struggle and suffering, and as 'twin' or hybrid factors in survivors' everyday peacebuilding efforts.

17 There has been some recent feminist work that is beginning to theorize silence, showing that it is not always incompatible with agency. See for example, George, Nicole, and Lia Kent. "Sexual Violence and Hybrid Peacebuilding: How Does Silence 'Speak'?" *Third World Thematics: A TWQ Journal* 2.4 (2017), 518–537 and Björkdahl Annika and Johanna Mannegren Selimovic, "'Gendering Agency in Transitional Justice'." *Security Dialogue* 46.2 (2015), 165–182.

Chapter 3

Bosnia Beyond Balkanism

The relationship between narrativization and agentive discourse is relevant to reconceptualizing victim/survivor identities in relation to trauma, memory, and recovery, but also in relation to how the peace process is represented in an international context. Personal narratives highlight the "diversity of the personal" in relation to trauma and memory, the local in its hybridity, and the multilayered and multidirectional nature of both identity and recovery. By offering embodied and contextually situated insights into irreducible categories of experience, individual stories and perspectives highlight the diverse and often critical ways in which Bosnian citizens within the Federation interact with official Bosnian politics. This diversity and critical engagement fly in the face of homogenizing accounts of Bosnia's internal politics, civil society, and the peace process, both within Bosnia and in commentary generated about Bosnia by scholars, politicians, and media representatives from the outside.

Official Bosnian politics continues to operate along the lines of the ethnic divides that have been institutionalized by the Dayton Peace Agreement. Signed on November 21, 1995, the agreement was intended as a temporary solution to end direct armed conflict. It separated the former Yugoslav republic into three areas: two entities (the Federation of Bosnia-Herzegovina, with majority Bosniak and Croat population, and the Republika Srpska, where the majority is Serb) and the small neutral, self-governing territory of the Brčko District belonging to both entities. The current political structure and the cultural and civic systems emanating from it have only solidified the divide, perpetuating a logic of national belonging that is entirely identified by "ethnicity" or nationality. Political elites have seized on the benefits of this divisive logic and continue to "ethnify" differences, generating and working to maintain a climate defined by a continued threat of violence, thereby exploiting people's worst fear of another war, and propagating a version of nationalism based on "ethnic" quotas, protectionist policies, and "us" vs "them" exclusionism. This political strategy diverts attention from social and economic issues that affect all Bosnian citizens equally and from the possibility of building a civic basis for national identity founded on pluralist values.

DOI: 10.4324/9781003186168-5

The ethnicization of the population that was produced by the war[1] and cemented through the cumbersome constitutional framework of the Dayton Accords remains the dominant backdrop to discussions of post-conflict recovery, despite a recent turn in the academic study of Bosnia and Herzegovina that seeks to challenge one-dimensional representations of the contemporary political landscape in the Yugosphere. This turn coincides with growing critiques of the epistemic efficacy of Western social science, growing internal "contradictions within the liberal democratic, capitalist peace model" itself, and increasing awareness that "liberal peace interventions are not the work of omnipotent and omniscient powers" from the West.[2] It is not only becoming clear that the Global North cannot transform other societies into quiescent and orderly states in their own image, but also that this image itself is crumbling as a viable model for populations within the Global North, especially in so-called Western democracies and much of the Anglosphere.[3] Much of this work is developing a resonant critique of neoliberalism as a dominant political and social ideology that has taken hold via the unregulated force of the capitalist market economy and that was promoted internally as well as through foreign policy as being able to solve all social issues, including inequalities, all the while upholding the cherished ideals of democracy. It has become more than apparent, especially since the global pandemic, that in the Global North, for the most part, this neoliberal project is failing: authoritarian and nationalist politics is on the rise, wealth disparities are on a sharp incline, the unregulated housing market has created staggering numbers of homeless populations, the prices of consumables, especially food, is reaching absurd levels due to food industry corporate monopolies, the basic working wage is insufficient to support a single individual let alone children or other family members, and basic social support systems, such as access to daycare, health, and education, are either greatly diminished, privatized, or altogether non-existent.

When it comes to Bosnia and other post-socialist spaces habitually constructed as "Europe's periphery," or "semi-periphery," this turn is marked by studies that transcend the static, taken-for-granted assumptions about the primacy of ethnic categories and Western representations of the peace process in the region. Recent collections like *Welcome to the Desert of Post-Socialism: Radical Politics After Yugoslavia*, edited by Srećko Horvat and Igor Štiks (2015), *Changing Youth Values in Southeast Europe: Beyond Ethnicity*, edited by Tamara Trošt and Danilo Mandić (2018), and the recent work by Siniša Malešević challenge one-dimensional representations of the contemporary political and social landscape in the countries of the former Yugoslavia and the surrounding region. Outlining a multifaceted political and cultural situation in post-socialist countries, such studies chart the flourishing of diverse forms of political and anti-regime protests, as well as mobilizations for the commons (the defense of public and common goods against unregulated, aggressive privatization), student and workers movement (such as the ones in

50 Unforgetting and the Politics of Representation

Slovenia, Croatia, Serbia, Bosnia and Herzegovina, and Montenegro), and intellectual challenges to dominant media discourses.

This book contributes to such work in showing that the peace process cannot be understood fully only in relation to laws, courts, quotas, and other agents of social and political control. How people think about these processes beyond what is articulated at the level of official politics is equally important. What is particularly evident from the stories of my interlocutors who all reside within the entity of the Bosnian Federation is the tension between the official, normative level of politics and governance associated with political elites and lawmakers, and the operative level, visible at the level of their everyday perspectives and practices. By normative national ideology I mean the official ideological and discursive frameworks propagated and reinforced through mainstream media, educational and legal structures, and embedded into economic and political systems. By the operative level of national ideology I mean the multiple ways in which the normative level is being implemented, applied, contested, subverted, reinterpreted, and brought to life or rejected through the everyday social practices of people within the nation.[4] In my articulation of the normative level of ideology in particular, I depart from current sociological explanations whereby the normative is held to be represented in "ideal-typical terms" and most often "deduced from authoritative texts and scriptures, such as religious 'holy books'...philosophers, prophets, scientists, or documents with powerful legal, ethical or semi-sacred status...the constitutions of sovereign states," etc.[5] A significant body of feminist scholarship, especially scholarship written from a postcolonial perspective or originating from the so-called Global South has extensively analyzed the ways in which various types of normativity, political, racial, and gendered—types that often emanate from the universalist claims of patriarchal, colonial ideologies—are in fact asserted and reinscribed as hegemonic through school curricula, mainstream and official media channels (news programs, political and commercial adverts, film, social media, and other forms of cultural content), the speeches of political leaders, social work policies, welfare policies, child protection agencies, etc.[6] Social institutions are therefore complicit in maintaining and reinforcing normativity. Consistent with my intersectional feminist orientation and the value feminist epistemology accords to experience and specific positionality as sources of knowledge, I therefore treat the particular perspectives of individual people as constitutive of the complexity with which ideology functions at the operational level within the Bosnian Federation.

The tension between the normative and the operative level of ideology becomes pronounced in the narratives of women survivors of war violence and the Children Born Because of War, two groups of people in Bosnian society who have endured great harm during and after the war and have since faced lack of social and legal support and lack of social recognition. Their understanding of justice and recovery, and their critique of official state-level nationalist politics shows their active contribution to an alternative vision of the nation and national well-being. It also shows an alternative conceptualization of the nation, and forms of individual and collective belonging. Their vision aligns categories of belonging more with a set of common civic, secular values than with identity based in imagined forms of ethnic purity backed by a common religion. These counter-narratives of the nation and nationality are also visible in the case of the children born because of war, whose relationship to the majority in their communities (predominantly Bosniak populations) and to official ethno-nationalist politics is contested through their very origins.

However, the critical stance is not limited to only these two groups within the Federation. On the contrary; ordinary citizens' active critique of official nationalist politics represents the most widespread and unifying civic discourse in the Federation in ways that are unmatched, for example, either in Serbia or Croatia, or for that matter, in the Canadian mainstream media sphere where I reside. Such critiques of official politics are also evident in the narrative of Esma D., the woman fighter in Part III, Chapter 10 of this book, and the stories of the two young women who grew up under siege, Merima Omeragić and Selma Beširević in Part I, Chapter 5. Multiple media news outlets and channels in Sarajevo, including several daily news, such as *Avaz*, *Oslobodjenje*, *Danas*, and *Dnevni List*, critically engage with the political establishment, and focused on outcomes, challenge the very bases of official ethno-nationalist politics. The incommensurability of interests between members of the political, governing class and ordinary citizens is affirmed, analyzed, and debated across many media platforms, within many institutional settings, as well as in everyday social interactions. Through these perspectives it becomes evident that ethnicity, or *nacionalnost* as a category of identity that has been assigned extraordinary prominence in the country's constitutional framework and international discourses, may have ambivalent or context-specific relevance for most ordinary people in the Federation, not least those who have suffered irreparable harms during and because of the war.

Failing to consider such tensions and their distinct manifestations in the perspectives of individual people runs the risk of reinscribing harmful Balkanist stereotypes about the region and its people, and occluding the diversity of perspectives, forms of civic engagement, and vigorous critiques of the existing political regime. Remaining focused on state-centered mechanisms for retributive justice (systems based on deterrence, retribution, social defense, and rehabilitation in a narrow sense) or the realm of international relations, obscures the complex forms of civic discourse embodied in how people in the region remember the past and envision the future in relation to peace, justice, and nation-building.

Remembering the past, moreover, does not stop at the recent war. It has as much to do with memories of the socialist past, as well as memories of World War II, which were central in establishing the distinct national character of the former Yugoslavia. The term "post-socialist," while convenient in denoting former socialist societies and polities after the formal collapse of socialist

52 Unforgetting and the Politics of Representation

regimes, just like the term "post-conflict," can be problematic and misleading, as both erroneously imply a hard break with the past. Just as the absence of war does not imply peace and well-being—in Bosnia and elsewhere social and political discourses of security remain militarized—the formal termination of the socialist system with the break-up of Yugoslavia does not mean that people's subjectivities have changed overnight or disappeared, even after a bloody war. The expectation that they should change, along with the assumption that most people should find the transition to a capitalist neoliberal economic and political system inevitable, "natural," or even unambiguously desirable, or that the current manifestation of political subjectivities in the region is an indication of some form of political immaturity, are all problematic examples of reductionism at best, and Balkanism at worst.

For all of us who were born in Yugoslavia, the war changed the way we think about our identities, our former and current neighbors, how we articulate citizenship, religious denomination, and our nationality. But no assumptions should be made about any of it, especially as more of us begin to publicly remember Yugoslavia in many diverse ways and from various intersections of identity. Remembering one's life in the Yugoslav state does not automatically equate to Yugonostalgia, any more so than anyone's memories connected to their place of birth and related social, economic, and cultural contexts can be assumed automatically to be rooted in nostalgia.[7] Memory is not a faculty for storing the past, but rather a flexible process of construction and reconstruction across various dimensions of past and present lived experience. In that sense, remembering is always constructive and functional, both at the individual and at the collective level.

More work remains yet to be done on the relationships between the present moment in Bosnia and Herzegovina and other post-Yugoslav states on the one hand, and socialist forms of subjectivity, on the other. Recent work in political science notes that "subjectivity can be considered the primary concern of socialism,"[8] recognizing that the life and development of the socialist state depended more upon a strong philosophical and social vision than upon either politics or economics.[9] It is hardly surprising that leading cultural, politicial and economic features of a given social and national sustem result in the creation of a preferred or even a 'habitual' self. Much intersting work has been done on the neoliberal self, as the preferred form of life and subjectivity in the economic, political and cultural circumstancesof present day developed and developing capitalism.[10] Each ideology and regime results in structuring the subjectivities of those who live within them in a variety of ways. Subjectivity, in turn, is not a static quality. According to feminist epistemological traditions, each thinking, feeling subject, and social agent "is capable of resistance and innovation produced out of the clash between contradictory subject positions and practices." Subjectivity thus understood is, therefore, always contingent, "incomplete, heterogenous, and constantly shifting," which renders each subject, too, "an unstable, fragmented, and fluid notion, rather than a single and unified identity constant over time."[11]

Memories, just like lived experience and subjectivity, are contextual and embodied, interlinking individual with the collective, and are continually reconstructed in the present time. In that sense, the current moment in Bosnia and other former Yugoslav countries is one that charts a unique path to nation-hood, a path that is consistent with not only the aftereffects of the recent war and the socialist past, but the longer history of the Balkan region and its multilayered cultural specificity.

While this is not a book that deals explicitly with the politics of the Yugosphere, the complex and diverse political realities as seen and experienced by individuals within the Yugosphere do inform the context for much of what the people in this book say about themselves, how they remember the war, how they integrate those memories into their present, and how they look toward the future. This political backdrop very clearly informs the perspectives of the group Children Born Because of War, who, although a group defined by difficult stories of biological origin resulting in social prejudice, nonetheless, belong to the country's youth, those whose values are intricately linked to Bosnia's social, cultural, and political future. When their identities are considered in accordance with how they see themselves, it becomes apparent that their specific positionality within contemporary Bosnian youth culture—across and beyond constructions of identity based on an imagined form of pure ethnic belonging—has positive implications for the construction of possible new models of national identity that are emerging alongside, from within or counter to the official ethno-nationalist ones that nurture ethnic divisions. Their perspectives serve as a reminder that "ethnic intolerance was not a precursor to the war but its consequence,"[12] which in turn also represents the future possibility of overcoming it. Their lives unfold in the post-war period, and in this sense, they belong to the post-war generation, shaped by the failure of neoliberal reforms to translate into a better standard of living and greater emphasis on human rights. The identity of the children born of war, alongside their expressed discontent and social demands, is agentive and symbolic tool for reconfiguring new, more enabling forms of civic identity.[13] Through the leadership of the Association *Zaboravljena Djeca Rata*/Forgotten Children Born of War, they have emerged into a visible, active political presence in the Federation, as well as internationally, something that I discuss in greater detail in Part II, Chapter 6. In fact, the Association has recently started to organize their political advocacy around the premise that children born because of war form a specific national heritage for Bosnia, a legacy that must not be erased or occluded, and that as such they must receive legal recognition.[14]

My own positionality regarding the topic, I hope, also contributes to a more complex understanding of identity and the polyvalent signification of the socialist past and nationality. Because I come from the same general locality as my research participants, I share aspects of their cultural and linguistic background, both of which shaped the way we interacted when we first met and, likely, how the conversations unfolded. I, like many of my interlocutors, grew up in socialist Yugoslavia. This meant that we also had a shared collective past and a shared frame of reference for some cultural and political realities, dates, names, etc. In many of the conversations this was an easy and shared frame of reference, and something that the women possibly even emphasized, based on their understanding of my identity. Most of my interlocutors were women, and thus we also share a gender identification, as well as the knowledge of what it meant to be a woman in socialist Yugoslavia in a general sense. It was often implied that some aspects of what they were narrating would be readily understandable to me from this perspective. We also share the same language/s, which eliminated the need for an interpreter to mediate or translate the intended meaning. This in turn ensured an uninterrupted flow of conversation, one that more easily departed from the traditional question-answer qualitative model, adding a more spontaneous, natural dimension to the communication.

At the same time, the cross-nationality aspects of my Yugoslav identity position me in a very specific way regarding the women who have been subjected to sexualized violence primarily because of their nationality. While the children born because of war and I do share aspects of a cross-national identity, the women I spoke with were targeted for rape based on nationality understood as a defining category of identity, in this case either Bosniak or Croat. For some of them, in fact, their nationality became more important as a marker of personal identity in part because of the experience of being targeted for it. Clearly, my looking back on the Yugoslav past of my childhood and youth after having lived in Canada for 30 years, at a distance, and without the living pressure to declare a single nationality, is very different from the perspective of lived, historical continuity between Yugoslavia's dissolution, the reality of the ensuing war, and the daily aftermath of war in a newly articulated political entity.

Yet, because of the shared language and shared frame of historical and cultural reference, it became clear from the first encounter that I was being asked to take an active part in the conversation. My interlocutors were not content to simply answer my well-thought-out questions. As soon as I addressed them in the Bosnian language, they wanted to know more about me, who I was, and where I come from. The fact that we could converse in the Bosnian language contributed to how they may have chosen to shape, tell, and retell their stories, and engage with the questions I had posed. In some cases, we shared a meal, a lunch, or a dinner, and much of the conversation unfolded while smoking and drinking coffee. And it is not unlikely to assume that the complexity of my insider/outsider positionality, vis-a-vis each of theirs,may have shaped what they chose to say or not say to me, in more than one way.

This was no conventional research context. It was inevitable that I became part of the narrative that emerged during those encounters. In some cases, both I and my interlocutors cried during our conversation. They cried recalling with me the horrors through which they had lived, many traumatic memories still being triggered through the narrative occasion. I, because of being profoundly moved and awed by their suffering and courage, perturbed by the blind, misogynistic inhumanity of ethno-nationalist male violence against women, of what it meant then that the perpetrator was a Serb, or a Croat and what this fact may mean now to the women themselves, and to the people who now live in Serbia, or Croatia. I felt implicated by association in the identities of the perpetrators, as well as the identity of the victims simultaneously.

My shifting outsider-insider status creates both potential and limitations generated in the relational space of identity and difference. My reading of Bosnia and the personal narratives of the people I spoke with, alongside my own positionality, destabilizes comfortable singular frames through which their experiences are interpreted, and through which Bosnia is discussed. The polyphony of voices that remember and converse about the past contests, in fact, any singular frame on memory, recovery, violence, and trauma, within Bosnia and the Yugosphere as well. Instead, this reading hopes to situates their storie and the perspective on Bosnia emerging from them at the intersections of embodiment variously manifested on the continuum of self-other, individual-collective, inside-outside, identity-difference, victimization-agency, trauma-resilience.

Notes

1 See Dubravka Žarkov's *The Body of War: Media, Ethnicity and Gender in the Break-Up of Yugoslavia* (Duke University Press, 2007).

2 See Oliver P. Richmond and Jason Franks, *Liberal Peace Transitions: Between State Building and Peacebuilding* (Edinburgh University Press, 2009); Roger MacGinty, "Hybrid Peace: The Interaction Between Top-Down and Bottom-Up Peace," *Security Dialogue* 41.6(2010), 391–412; and Roger Mac Ginty and Oliver Richmond, "The Fallacy of Constructing Hybrid Political Orders: A Reappraisal of the Hybrid Turn in Peacebuilding," *International Peacekeeping* 23.2(2026), 219–239. doi: 10.1080?13533312.2015.1099440.

3 For recent critiques that seek to reach broader audiences see for example, George Monbiot, *How Did We Get into This Mess?* (London: Verso, 2017); Ben Rhodes, *After the Fall: The Rise of Authoritarianism in the World We've Made* (Random House, 2022), and Paul Verhaeghe, *What About Me?: The Struggle for Identity in a Market-Based Society* (Scribe Publications, 2014). Rhodes' book, although documenting and castigating the rise of authoritarianism in the US, nonetheless, manages to convey its points from a position of typical Western arrogance, assuming a sort of divine pre-eminence for America as a country that is supremely and single-handedly responsible for all good and bad things that happen in the entire world, starting from the perspective that as a nation, the US "held within its hands the capacity to destroy, shape, and enlighten all human life on earth." This position it itself a self-serving example of a neoliberal subjectivity that is formed on the concept of competition with others and shaped through the need to assert a hierarchical and domineering attitude over all things, animate and inanimate.

4 For the conceptualization of the two levels of ideology, the normative and the operative, I am drawing upon Siniša Malešević's work, particularly his, "Nationalism and the Power or Ideology," In ed. Gerard Delanty and Krishan Kumar, *The Sage Handbook of Nations and Nationalism* (Sage Publications, 2006). I agree with the position that "the relationship between the normative and the operative realms, that is, between the two levels of ideology, is always a question of empirical evidence" (310), which is why I extend his approach to show the complexity of relationships that can exist between the two levels when our empirical sample is very specific, that is, when we look at how particular groups of survivors engage with the normative level within the Bosnian federation. I am reluctant to apply the terms of my analysis to the entirety of Bosnia and Herzegovina since the relationship between the two

56 Unforgetting and the Politics of Representation

levels of ideology appear to operate in a different way among different groups in Republika Srpska, perhaps a way that is more consistent with Malešević's analysis of that relationship in post-socialist Serbia and Croatia.

5 Malešević', "Nationalism and the Power or Ideology," 309.

6 Out of a very large field of studies based on such analyses, I can refer to only a few to indicate their scope: Nira Yuval-Davis', *Gender and Nation* (Sage Publications, 1997) and *The Politics of Belonging: Intersectional Contestations* (Sage Publications, 2011); Philippa Levine, *Gender and Empire* (Oxford University Press, 2004); Maile Arvin, Eve Tuck and Angie Morrill, "Decolonizing Feminism: Challenging Connections Between Settler Colonialism and Heteropatriarchy," *Feminist Formations* 4.1 (2013), 8–34; Mrinalini Sinha, "Gender and Nation," *Feminist Theory Reader: Local and Global Perspectives*, 5th ed. *(Routledge, 2021), 155–168; Amrita Basu and Tanika Samkar, ed., *Women, Gender and Religious Nationalism* (Cambridge University Press, 2022).

7 Svetlana Boym's *The Future of Nostalgia* (Basic Books, 2001) remains among the most sensitive and detailed accounts of the different uses and functions of nostalgia in relation to memory and history. In her book nostalgia is defined through different tropes all of which are, however, informed by the notion of nostalgia as "longing for the past." Even in this capacity of longing for an unrecoverable past within post-communist memory, Boym identifies the constructive qualities of nostalgia, referring to it as a "double-edged sword," in that "it seems to be an emotional antidote to politics, and thus remains the best political tool" (58). My own position has been that there are political elements to personal memories, even when they are of the distinctly nostalgic variety in that recalling and reconstructing aspects of the past in the present often takes place in response to some form of lacking perceived in the present, and as such constitutes a critique of the present. If not always a fully formed political act, a critique of the present is at least always a necessary precursor to political action.

8 Dominic Martin, "Postsocialism," Sep. 14, 2021, Website. Cambridge Encyclopedia of Anthropology, 2022., n.p.

9 See for example, Boris Groys, *The Communist Postscript* (London: Verso, 2009), which discusses communist politics in the Soviet Union. Some of his insights, however, have relevance for how the development and functioning of the Yugoslav socialist state was conceptualized, at least in in the first decade after the second world war.

10 Jim McGuigan's "The Neoliberal Self," *Culture Unbound* 6 (2014): 223–240, and Stephen Vassallo's *Neoliberal Selfhood*, Cambridge University Press, 2020.

11 Chris Weedon, *Feminist Practice and Poststructuralist Theory* (Oxford: Basil Blackwell, 1987), 125; Karen Barbour, "Embodied Ways of Knowing: Revisiting Feminist Epistemology," in ed. Louise Mansfield, Jayne Caudwell, Belinda Wheaton and Beccy Watson, *The Palgrave Handbook of Feminism and Sport, Leisure and Physical Education.* (Palgrave Macmillan UK, 2018.), 209–226, 212.

12 Barbara Matejcic, "Cruel Wars Cast Shadow Over Mixed Marriages," *Balkan Insight*, October 30, 2009. Accessible at: https://balkaninsight.com/2009/10/30/cruel-wars-cast-shadow-over-mixed-marriages/. Dubravka Žarkov, *The Body of War* (Duke University Press, 2007).

13 I have written more about this process in "Negotiating Identities in Post-Conflict Bosnia and Herzegovina: Self, Ethnicity and Nationhood in Adolescents Born of Wartime Rape," in ed. Tamara PO. Trošt and Danilo Mandić, *Changing Youth Values in Southeast Europe: Beyond Ethnicity* (Routledge, 2018), 19–38. On their perspectives on Yugoslavism and Yugonostalgia as a distinct form of cultural "memory" and a form of critique of the present, I have written in "Post-war

Yugoslavism and Yugonostalgia as Expression of Multi-Ethnic Solidarity and Tolerance in Bosnia and Herzegovina," *New Diversities* 21.1 (2019), 87–101. Most recently, I wrote about the personal narratives of three young adults born of war, foregrounding the ways in which they challenge conceptions of themselves as victims, and as so-called children of the enemy: "Where Do You Send the Pain? Agency and Resilience in Three Children Born of War in Bosnia and Herzegovina," in ed. Kimberly Theidon, Kimberly and Dyan Mazurana *Challenging Conceptions: Children Born of Wartime Rape and Sexual Exploitation* (Oxford University Press, 2023).

14 Ajna Jusić, the President of the Association, shared this piece of information during the recent research workshop we both attended, "Children born of war and processes of state and nation building," May 22, 2024, Universität Innsbruck, Austria.

Chapter 4

Sarajevo the Beautiful

Vahdeta B. is a small business owner in her forties, slim, and agile. Her antique and souvenir shop is located on a busy corner of Baščaršija, the old market in the center of the city. I approach to take a closer look at various objects representing Tito's image or his distinctly familiar signature. Although Vahdeta's is not the only shop in the busy market that sells such objects, I am intrigued by their prominence in her display. When I introduce myself, ask her about the souvenirs bearing Tito's image, and tell her about the project I am working on, Vahdeta offers to make coffee for us, and invites me to sit with her in front of her shop.[1]

People here love Tito, and I was growing up during Tito's time—this is why you see this merchandise. It was clear to one that if there is no brotherhood and unity and no strong leadership, what took place here would happen. And it did. In Tito's time I was not wealthy, but I was free. My parents were not preoccupied with acquiring wealth. They devoted their time to our well-being and contentment instead. I raised my children in the same way. I taught them that in this world, there are good and bad people, regardless of where they come from. My son learned this lesson when he was three and a half years old. This is when the war started, when he was three years old. This is also when my son learned about Tito, and what he stood for. I didn't idealize Tito for him, but simply it was important for him to know who he was, and what he stood for.

My husband was wounded on the head during the war. This caused his entire right side to remain paralyzed. He has also been unable to speak since. My husband was 33 when the war began, and this is also the year he was wounded. We were without food, water, and electricity, with a young child. My brothers were distributed to serve at the defense lines. It was very difficult for children during the war. They did go to school, in the basements of the city. People did not give up. We were also going outside even though grenades were falling. One cannot remain indoors forever. Parents were perturbed, upset. I had to fetch water for us, but I couldn't leave my son at home alone. In the middle of summer, we used to burn toys and books to create a fire, so that we can bake bread. We kept clean; not just us, everyone around here. I do remember though that my son came home one evening in 2000 and said that Senja had told him that there would be another war.

DOI: 10.4324/9781003186168-6

If there is war, I said, I will sit in the middle of the street right now and wait for the first grenade to hit me so that I don't have to endure what we endured then. This was my worst moment psychologically. At the time, I had a young child, I used to have a husband who was strong and capable...

With all of that there were refugees coming. My son is playing outside, and one day he comes inside to say, mama, Lola hit me. He said to me that Srdjan[2] is a četnik, and I said to him, Srdjan is not a četnik, that his father and mother are here with us, that we are neighbors. If he were a četnik he would have run away to the mountains to shot at us from there. This is when Lola hit me. My son was barely 4 years old when this happened. I explained to him that there are četniks, and ustaše, and that there are also Serbs and Croats as well as Muslim extremists. And he understood me although he was four years old. He understood that Srdjan's dad was a member of a civil defense and our neighbor, that he is not a četnik. He understood this, but the other child did not. Children were not to blame though. The grown-ups around him clearly did not explain this to him. And so, children grow. Without thinking. Our people often do not use their heads.

On the other hand, people in Sarajevo are wonderful. Do you remember the 2001 film "No Man's Land"?[3] Do you remember the last scene, where the character played by Branko Djurić remains lying down, covering an unexploded mine with his body—because he knows that if he moves the mine will explode? The response of the international community in the film was that they have freed Bosna,[4] while he is left in an impossible situation, where he is facing a certain death. So was Bosna left to lie as if on a mine and cannot move. In whichever direction Bosna moves, it's impossible, it will explode. There is no agreement that is possible among the three sides. The Dayton Accord was necessary. And Alija[5] signed the Accord to stop the armed conflict but in itself the Accord is not functional. It doesn't work since it is built in a way that the three sides can never agree on anything. They agree about silly, stupid things, but not about things that matter to Bosna as a country. Still, people have kept their soul, their spirit, although they have now accumulated debts and loans but have no salaries. In Tito's day, even a manual laborer could live well and feed his family. Now, people must save up to 200 marks to sign up their children to school.

There is a small number of Serbs and Croats left here. Run from here, they will destroy you, is what they are being told. The same way that in Serbia and Croatia Bošnjaci and whoever is not the majority is told to leave. But let me tell you something. Recently a man passed away, a Serb, who lived here all his life, who was here during the war, who never took up arms. He was well respected. He received a proper burial. He had a family of his own here.

During the war my colleague Gaga was imprisoned by the četniks. We at work did all we could to have him released. Serbs came for him—I can't say Serbs, they were četniks, since we can't put the two in the same bag as it were, they came for him, to mobilize them to fight on their side. When he refused, they killed him in front of his wife and child. There were all sorts of things that took place. There was raping and pillaging on all sides. Slowly it's all coming to light. But many do not understand that the first to suffer in war are the worker, the farmer, the civilian. When my son was little, he would sometimes say, I will be a defender, too. I said to him, I will take the gun and give you a good beating with it, you will not be defender, you will not be shooting, because in this war it is not clear who is shooting at whom.

There was a Bošnjak man from here who was imprisoned and taken to a concentration camp. And there was a soldier in this četnik army who took him behind the building and released him, let him go. He said to him, when I see that you are far away, I will fire three bullets and I will tell them that I killed you. This is why I can never lump all people into the same bag. What I see even now is that people get along well together. I have two very good friends, Senka and Zana. Zana I have asked many times during the war, what are you, Serbian or Croatian. She wouldn't tell me; I still don't know. I remembered that I had asked her this only after the war, and even then we joked about it, I need to know so that I know who I am dealing with, we laughed. This is not really important to me. And it wasn't just me. Sarajevo is like that, it's very special. But then, Yugoslavia was like that as well. And yet, here we are at elections again…and we will each vote for our own, because if the "they" come to power, who knows what will happen.

How do we change this sort of thinking? Many people don't leave their homes, they sit at home and listen to what is served to them on the news, in the media, by politicians, so they are easy to manipulate. The programming that we see here from Serbia is truly terrible—the tone of it is problematic, threatening, and sometimes, the words are as well. It is irritating. But I am sure that this is all planned, to show only certain kinds of programs to us here, to keep us fearful. As soon as nationalism is stirred, there is revolt. I feel like calling in sometimes to give them my opinion. They sit there, the three of them, representatives from each constituent people, and they are supposed to provide answers to people's questions. People do call, young people especially ask very pointed questions, but the host tells them they don't have to answer if they don't know the answers, or they feel uncomfortable.

But young people are asking uncomfortable questions, the right questions, and they demand answers. Have you heard about Jajce? The students of one school in Jajce took to peaceful demonstrations because they wanted to study under the same roof and to study the same curriculum. They were protesting the "two schools under one roof" policy.[6] I take pride in their demands, and in their perspective. My own daughter never speaks about her friends in terms of their nationality.

War was mentioned recently in the news. And my neighbor feels so afraid. This is how it all works. They tell you, hush, whatever it is, it's ok as long as there is no war. This is a tactic to keep people afraid, and to keep the status quo. As long as there is no war, people will endure anything. And in this atmosphere, who will stand up and demand solutions from politicians, who will hold them accountable? If we all decided to close our shops, and stop everything for ten days or more, demanding real solutions to the problems we are all facing, then they would have to consider us. I think that a state is a like a family, like mother and father who look out for the best interest of all of their children, and the interest of the family. But we don't have this kind of thinking. People are good, but we have lost our faith in the possibility of change for the better, we have lost trust in politicians and the system. What we live with now is a form of rotten capitalism.[7] Some people have yachts and others don't have enough to eat, but they can't say anything about the boats since it will seem like jealousy or envy. It is not envy. It is people feeling heartbroken because they can't provide the most basic sustenance to their children.

One Predrag calls my husband for Ramadan to say Bajram Šerif Mubarek Olsun [may this noble holiday be blessed]. My husband calls him on Orthodox Easter to say Hristos Voskrese [Christ has risen]. My son has friends who are Serbs and Croats, and we respect each other's customs and traditions. I think people got frightened directly before the war, became afraid for their own lives. I refuse to follow the news or watch TV. No help from it. I don't recall that there has been an incident here in Sarajevo based on someone's religious denomination. Nothing is black and white.

Only during the last census[8] did I realize that being Bosnian is classified as "other" and that we are all still supposed to declare according to our nationality, Serbian, Croatian, Bošnjaci. Why aren't we all Bosnian? What does it mean that Bosnian is classified as "other"? I don't understand. I understand people very well, but I don't understand this. We need to abolish politics, to abolish any programming on the media that does not address our reality. Instead, they only fire people up. I think that all of us would feel and act as Bosnian.

I will give you two examples. In 1994 my husband and I wanted to leave Sarajevo via the tunnel for Italy. We made it over Igman, and into Croatia. So here we are in Croatia, my husband with his Bošnjak disability ID, where it says that he was a member of the Bosnian Muslim army. People helped us, with whatever we needed, got us on the bus. No one asked us any questions or was unkind. My brother also has a disability designation on his license plate. And the Serbs [in Republika Srpska] lower his premiums on the basis of his disability, even though it is clear from his paperwork that he is a Bošnjak and that he fought for the Bosnian army during the war. What I mean to say that there is a lot of propaganda about how bad things are. We have to start using our own heads A lot of time has gone by since the war, and we are at a standstill…There were things you couldn't say when Tito was in power, but living was good. Now we supposedly live in a democracy where there is freedom of expression—well, we are certainly free to curse.

This is my second visit to Sarajevo, but my connection with the city and Bosnia run deep. Last time I was there was in 1987, as part of a school trip across Yugoslavia at the end of high school. I went to high school in North Macedonia, where it was customary that in the final year all graduating students take a week-long trip across the country together, and visit historically significant sites. The city holds a meaningful place in my family genealogy as

62 Unforgetting and the Politics of Representation

the place where my mother grew up. Although she was born in Banja Luka in 1946, she moved to Sarajevo very soon after that, so that her mother, my grandmother, could take up the post of primary school teacher. My grandparents' and my mother's anti-nationalist political orientation and their humanist vision of tolerance, cultural interdependence, and pluralism was in large measure shaped by the experience of living in this city. When I met Vahdeta, I was staying in Vratnik, the Muslim *mahala* (city quarter) where I could see the Sebilj, the Ottoman-style wooden fountain in the center of Baščaršija Square built by Mehmed Pasha Kukavica in 1753. The food and smells felt familiar, like the smells of home, as was the lilt of people's intonation. Also familiar was the way in which Vahdeta narrates her story. She communicates meaning by emphasizing the inter-relational embeddedness of specific people in specific situations. Individual relationships shape the way in which she remembers the past as well as how she sees the present.

In a representational sense, Sarajevo's most distinguishing trait has been its cultural fluidity, its diversity and religious tolerance, and its reputation as the only city in Europe where a mosque, a Catholic church, an Orthodox Church, and a Synagogue stand within 100 meters of each other, still standing.[9] The people of Sarajevo have a distinct, proud, and loving relationship to the city, and in some ways being from Sarajevo is a form of belonging that tends to override any other designation of identity, despite official politics. When Vahdeta refers to the people "here" who are wonderful, she means the people of Sarajevo, people she lived with before the war, through the siege, and those she has continued to live with since the war. The relationship between Sarajevans and Sarajevo is one that transcends the recent war, or at least, one that integrates the experience of the last war into a much longer historical memory. The following description of Sarajevo comes from Dževad Karahasan's *Dnevnik Selidbe*. The book was first published in Zagreb, in Serbo-Croatian-Bosnian in 1993 during the siege, and translated into English by Slobodan Drakulić as *Sarajevo, Exodus of a City* the following year. The war which Karahasan witnessed prompted his reflection on the city as "a dramatically constructed cultural system," whose most pronounced trait is "an exciting interplay of dialogue and opposition between the open and the closed, the external and the internal." He writes:

> Approximately a hundred year after its founding [c. 1440], the city had gathered within itself people from all the monotheistic religions and the cultures derived from them, with myriad languages and ways of life. Sarajevo became a microcosm, a center of the world that contained the whole world within itself, as mystics would say…. Everything that is possible in the world existed in Sarajevo—distilled, reduced to its nucleus…. Sarajevo is like a fortune-teller's crystal ball that contains all events, all that any human being can experience, all the phenomena of the world. Like Borges' Aleph, showing in itself all that ever was, that ever will be, and even all that could be, Sarajevo holds within itself all that constitutes the world to the west of India…. when

it was founded, the city was settled by people from three monotheistic religions—Islam, Catholicism and Eastern orthodoxy—and the languages spoken in it were Turkish, Arabic, Persian, Bosnian, Croatian, Serbian, Magyar, German, and Italian. And then, some fifty years after Sarajevo was founded, the Spanish rulers Ferdinand and Isabella banished the Jews of Spain, some of whom took refuge in Sarajevo. They brought to the city its fourth monotheistic religion and a new culture—constituted around that religion and around centuries of wondering—and they brought new languages, too. Sarajevo became a new Babylon, and a new Jerusalem—a city of new linguistic mingling and a city in which temples of all faiths of the Book can be seen in one glance.[10]

Karahasan mourns the destruction caused by the recent war; yet, his sadness is punctuated by a distinctive blend of lightness, fortitude, and forbearance that comes from the capacity to situate one's current grief into a longer and broader perspective. This is a perspective that I hear in Vahdeta's voice, as well as the voices of all others I spoke with, including in my casual interactions with restaurant staff, shopkeepers, and taxi drivers.

Vahdeta's recollection of the war centers on the siege, a three-year-long event that for Sarajevans marks the experience of the recent war. On May 4, 1992, the Yugoslav People's Army aided by Bosnian Serb militias surrounded and blockaded the city of about 500,000 inhabitants. Sarajevo's geography, nestled in the Miljacka River valley and surrounded by mountains, made possible a near total blockade. The destruction of the post office towers prevented a connection with the outside world.

The outside world included the neighboring Serbia, and the copper mining town in eastern Serbia where I was living with my mother at the time the siege began. After my parents' divorce in 1990, my mother had taken a post as the head of obstetrics and gynecology in the local hospital, while my father emigrated to Canada, motivated to turn a completely new leaf personally, as well as to leave behind the increasingly bleak economic situation in North Macedonia. We did not know what was taking place in Sarajevo. Six months after the siege began, as I was leaving for Toronto to join my father in Canada, Serbian media was still reporting on fighting between "the Yugoslav People's Army and its enemies" on the territory of the republic of Bosnia and Herzegovina—the Bosnian government's recent declaration of independence seemed to classify it as an enemy—but the details of the siege or its impact on the civilian population were not been released.

However, my mother's decision to send my then 16-year-old brother to Canada to join my father in the following year, 1991, had by that point already acquired political urgency, as Slovenia, Croatia, and Macedonia had all declared independence in quick succession during that year. It was becoming clear that to remain in Serbia with the onset of armed conflict in both Croatia and Bosnia likely meant that he would be drafted and sent to one of the front

64   Unforgetting and the Politics of Representation

lines. Had my brother not left Serbia then, he could have been one of the soldiers sent to shell Sarajevo during the siege.

I would find out what happened much later. FAMA, established in 1990 as
the first Bosnian independent media company with the aim of documenting
the transition from communism to the impending war, and then the war itself,
indicates that approximately 4,000 shells were fired at the city every single day.
FAMA also documents that snipers and other artillery were so positioned
around the city that there was not a 50-meter length of any street that was
beyond their reach.[11] Electricity and gas supply in the city were cut off, and
water supply was reduced to one small water source within the city, and another
one just on the outskirts, at Hrasnica. Citizens of Sarajevo were subject to
constant shelling and sniper fire. The food supply was disappearing. The first
UN humanitarian airlift supply to the citizens of Sarajevo began in July 1992.
According to what was available via airlift, every citizen was entitled to humanitarian aid consisting of 1,250 grams of beans, 300 grams of sugar, 300 grams
of oil, and 1 kg of flour. The Sarajevo tunnel that Vahdeta references in her
story through which she and her family used to escape to Croatia was constructed between March and June of the second year of the siege, 1993. The
tunnel now has commemorative value, and it features in the war memories of
everyone who lived in Sarajevo at the time. At the time, it provided a way out
of the city, not without risks, and allowed a way in for food, war supplies, and
humanitarian aid.

The siege ended on March 19, 1996, when the aggressor forces left Grbavica,
the last part of the city to be returned to the government of Bosnia and
Herzegovina under the Dayton Peace Agreement. It lasted 1,395 days, which
counts as the longest siege in modern warfare history. The death toll was severe:
over 11,000 people lost their lives, of whom close to 1600 were children. Some
50,0000 people were wounded, and many of them, like Vahdeta's husband,
were disabled for life.[12]

What is compelling now, more than 30 or so years after the war, is how the
siege is remembered and reconstructed in individual stories like Vahdeta's, as
well as in the broader cultural sphere of the Bosnian Federation entity. Given
that memory "is not a faculty for storing the representations of the past, but
rather, a process or activity of using the past to meet current needs for action,"
the way people construct memories is both personally and socially situated,
and an active space for asserting distinct forms of individual and collective
agency. Human remembering is, therefore, deeply relational, enmeshed in
social relationships, a fact that has implications for how we understand distinct
forms of peacebuilding and recovery embedded in everyday interactions.

The siege has by now acquired the status of memorial form. Memorial
forms represent a language that is used to articulate historical experiences.
They can also be a medium for experiences to be translated into, focusing on
transfers, imitation, copying, and the process of translation.[13] As a memorial
form, the siege is reconstructed in the cultural sphere as an affirmative act of

survival revealing the vibrant, darkly humorous, and resilient way in which the city and its people see their connection with the past. Memorial forms are enabling, and they evolve over time. As such they are both temporally distinct as well as deeply contextual, although individuals and groups may avail themselves of such existing forms, borrowing them and "translating" them within the context of their own individual remembrance. The nature and functioning of memorial forms in individual and collective discourse focus our attention to the intersections between individual and collective remembrance. Such intersections have the potential to redefine how we think of war-related trauma in cases where survivors utilize them in their narratives and use them to shape recollections of traumatic experiences. A memorial form depends "not only on the relationship between past and present, but on the accumulation of previous such relationships and their ongoing construction and reconstruction." The memorial form of Sarajevo under siege is thus constructively connected to people's existing orientation toward the city and its meaning. This perspective is grounded in a longer history and knowledge, one that preceded the war, and to which the war simply added another memorial dimension.

All the Sarajevans I spoke with can recall in an instant the number of days the siege lasted, some of them jokingly, remarking about how some facts, for better or worse, remain indelible in the mind. Memories of life under siege, which defined the recent war for citizens of Sarajevo, have been woven into the fabric of people's daily memories and integrated seamlessly into current cultural references and colloquial idiom. The siege has thus become a model of shared remembrance communicated in the specific language used to articulate collective historical experience, connecting it to the present in meaningful ways.[14]

Their collective historical experience, therefore, and the way in which they re/construct the memorial form stems not only from memories of the recent war in isolation, but also the recent war as remembered in the context of the city's other history and the complexity of people's social and cultural experiences that both pre-dated and were contemporaneous with the war. As a memorial form, the siege of Sarajevo also contains references that link these remembrances to the present moment and to the future, as they tend to take a longer, historical view based on different aspects of a shared past.

Vahdeta's story uses the siege as a memory form that complicates simplistic, victim-focused accounts of life under siege, and deconstructs the idea of ethnicity as the single most important marker of identity for Bosnian people. Her perspective is consistent with the perspectives of the other people whose stories I bring forward in the following chapters. None of them suggests that ethno-national labels are irrelevant: those labels have certainly been made more prominent by the war and through their subsequent exploitation in official post-Dayton Bosnian politics. But they do suggest that their relevance is neither all-encompassing, nor capable of overriding a sense of community built on daily social interaction. Vahdeta's recollection relating to the neighbor

66 Unforgetting and the Politics of Representation

whose ethnicity she wasn't sure of and with whom she joked about its alleged importance points to the historical and psychological distance that she and others like her have placed between the language of ethno-nationalist and ethno-religious labels in the political sphere, and their everyday lives and interactions. This is also shown in how quickly she moves from recalling why her son was hit by the child of their wartime neighbors to the reference of a film aimed to capture her dissatisfaction with the current Bosnian political scene.

Vahdeta makes an easy conversational distinction between members of different perpetrator armies. Each one is associated with a different nationality but is not fully identified by it. Serb and Croat Bosnian friends and neighbors who are all members of the same Sarajevan community are distinct from Serb, Croat, and Bosniak members of paramilitary, political groups such as četnici, ustaše, and Muslim extremists. Serbians and Croatians, as now citizens of different countries, are distinct even further. Her firsthand awareness of cases where even members of a specific perpetrator army—četnik's, in her example—did not all uniformly exercise inhumanity over Bošnjak prisoners points to the very specific way in which she recalls instances of violence and humanity.

Understanding the dynamic and evolving nature of memorial forms makes it impossible to study war-related trauma in connection with memorialization and peacebuilding as static, immutable experiences. Because memory is an activity shaped by imaginative construction and reconstruction, each reconstruction is iterative, in that it is built on the speaker's or the collective's attitude toward an entire active mass of organized past reactions and experience.[15] The attitude is reflected in the language of each reconstruction, which is also the language of self-representation, that is, a set of semantic constructions that capture how speaker or collective sees themselves in relation to the past, and in turn, seeks to be seen by others in the present.

Sarajevo's embrace of this difficult recent history manifests in several affirmative ways throughout Vahdeta's story, but also in other cultural narratives that shed light on the importance of self-representation, and the ecology of peacebuilding in contemporary Bosnian society. I will point to several such examples.

When I visited the Art Gallery of Bosnia and Herzegovina, I picked up two volumes containing selections of Milomir Kovačević 'Strašni's' candid photographs documenting life under siege. The volumes were published in 2010 and 2016, respectively. They feature photos that were part of the March 1998 exhibit in the Museum of Contemporary History in Paris, "From Unification to Dissolution of Yugoslav Territory: A Century of History." 'Strašni' used photography to convey powerful forms of social and political critique going back to 1990 and has a reputation as an engaged artist and humanist, a chronicler of cultural events. The exhibit of his war photography called "Sarajevo, Strašni Grad," playing on the meaning of the artist's nickname, *the terrible* [Sarajevo, the Terrible City], had just closed a week before I arrived in Bosnia.

Sarajevo the Beautiful   67

In the preface, the artist styles his intention around the desire to create a memorial form of the siege, to connect the past to the future: "to use my own form of expression, photography, to bring back memories of these not-so-distant events and to motivate all to think about the future." The brief biography that accompanies the 2010 volume clearly identifies this connection as affirmative, contrasting it to how the war was being represented from the outside. Stašni's war photography, the introduction highlights,

[D]iffers dramatically from those taken by his foreign colleagues. While they strived to photograph death in the most bizarre ways, he showed life and resistance to the difficult times. Despite the chaos, his photographs attempted to create harmony and visual purity. In fact, his own work was a particular form of resistance to the destruction of the city.

The titles of both volumes self-consciously pun on the meaning of the photographer's nickname, 'Strašni,' *the terrible*. The first is titled *$trašnizbori1990. Milomir Kovačević* ["Terrible elections1990"], providing additional symbolic commentary on the greed for power and wealth that stood behind the democratic elections with the dollar sign that doubles as an "S." The second, entitled, *Djeca u Ratu, Sarajevo 92–95: Godine Strašnog Djetinjstva* [Children in War, Sarajevo 92–95: The Years of Terrible Childhood], blend the photographer's name with the experience of the children whose experiences of war he captures on camera.

The editorial comment relating to the photographed children guides the viewer to accurately interpret what the photographer saw through the cameral lens: "faced with a reality beyond their understanding, and despite the difficult conditions in which they lived, Sarajevo children have always continued to play and have fun…The children crossed the war with a smiling face, defying those for whom innocence is worth nothing. Even sick in their beds, wounded in the head and legs, they kept their mischievous smile which is the mark of Sarajevans."[16]

In a 2017 interview with Radio Slobodna Evropa that promoted the exhibit, asked about how he remembers Sarajevo and its people during the siege when he took the photos, Strašni replied:

People showed a lot of solidarity. We helped each other in any way we could. We shared all that we had. On the streets there was great solidarity. In passing we conveyed news and information about where to go to get water, where not to go because of snipers. Even though there was no electricity and television, we always knew what was going on.

Having spent the last 22 years of his life in France, in some of his comments Strašni also draws explicit attention to the problematic representation of post-war Sarajevo, Bosnia, and the Yugosphere in French media:

68 Unforgetting and the Politics of Representation

Whenever we are mentioned on the media, it is in a negative context, not just Bosnia and Herzegovina, but the entire former Yugoslav space. It usually has to do with destruction, minefields, how many people were killed, immigration. After a while, one gets tired of hearing it. I think to myself, there are other things to remember, not only that. These are all facts about Sarajevo. Sarajevo has been standing here for centuries: there was life here before the war, and there is one after the war. I wanted to tell a different story about Sarajevo.[17]

Like Vahdeta in her story of life in Sarajevo before and during the war, like Karahasan in his descriptions of Sarajevo, Strašni too draws upon Sarajevo's long historical past to contextualize complex forms of memorialization and representation of people and the war. He offers art as an intervention in inadequate, one-dimensional representation, deconstructing through his assertion of a different kind of remembrance, resulting from a different way of seeing the past.

The explicit construction of art and creativity as a form of political commentary and resistance, and an affirmative act of post-war, post-socialist memorialization, is a recurring theme in other cultural narratives in the Yugosphere. Strašni himself was among 50 other artists from Bosnia, Serbia, Croatia, and Slovenia whose work was featured in Rijeka and Goli Otok in Croatia in 2020 and 2021, as part of the project, "Artistic Interventions in Public Space: Environment of Remembrance—Art as a Resistance to Repression." The project was organized by the Goli Otok Ante Zemljar Association from Zagreb, in partnership with the art organization Art De Facto (Zagreb). The project was created as a reaction to the artists' visits to the concentration camp in Goli Otok from 2016 to 2019. Goli Otok, a high security prison mainly for Yugoslav political prisoners ran from 1949 until 1989, together with the nearby Sveti Grgur Island, which held a similar camp for female prisoners. Prisoners included known and alleged Stalinists, but also members of the Communist Party of Yugoslavia or even non-party citizens accused of exhibiting sympathy or leanings toward the Soviet Union, as well as anti-communists and nationalists from all former Yugoslav nationalities. The project was intended to redefine how we see places where crimes have occurred, emphasizing that they are also "places of remembrance, learning and memory." The project was exhibited alongside the permanent exhibit on *Galeb*, the Yugoslav Navy training ship and Tito's official yacht. The *Galeb* exhibitdeals with the history of the ship and Tito as a man "who made a small country, which included Croatia, an important and recognized factor in the global arena and who was also a leading figure in the Non-Aligned Movement of which Yugoslavia was a part."[18]

Another example of active and affirmative forms of remembrance of the siege as a memorial form are the "FAMA Projects" founded by a Sarajevo team, Suada Kapić and Miran Norderland and launched in 2012. FAMA houses what is considered the world's largest independent Collection of multi-media projects pertaining to the Siege of Sarajevo and related events in reference to the Fall of Yugoslavia (1991–1999).[19] The founders or FAMA define the purpose of the collection as aid to collective memory building as well as a body of evidence and a set of materials for use in research and education.[20] The language used to define the siege does not deny the suffering and hardship, but instead emphasizes resourcefulness, strength, and resilience, as well as a particular form of dark humor. An example is the reference to the historical value of the collection in tackling what the authors call the "Phenomenon of Survival," comprising of "lessons learned" and an absurdly comical comparison of "obstacles and opportunities."

The print publication comprising selections from FAMA's materials is entitled *The Art of Survival: Extreme Urban Conditions and Human Resilience Based on Evidence from the Siege of Sarajevo 1992–1996*. It was published in 2016. Authored and edited by one of the FAMA founders, Suada Kapić, the volume utilizes de-identified and boldly illustrated individual survivor statements about life under siege. Echoing the early modern dramatic tradition in Europe where plays that were publicly performed often provided a short title as well as a long, descriptive one, the collection's long title is "The Art of Survival which the city of Sarajevo mastered during the four-year siege could offer answers to many challenges facing our civilization at the outset of the 21st century—how to survive disasters caused by nature or by humans and how to overcome fear from threats and terror induced by an *invisible enemy*." In the editorial preface, the author explains the rationale for the book in terms of a perceived global need to establish a "resilience module for the sake of terrified individuals and unprepared societies alike." In the same spirit, Kapić writes:

> Extreme urban conditions produced a parallel civilization in which creativity was a basic necessity. The process of adaptation left no space for stagnation and helplessness. Work was the law of mental and physical survival. Working toward resilience kept people's minds occupied—work eliminated thoughts that could destroy their motivation…During the siege, the continuation of *normal* [emphasis on the original] life in the city, the continuation of creativity, was as important as bread or medicine for all citizens of Sarajevo. In this book we are not presenting here a theory, but real-life evidence of an open mind potential to win in the face of the unknown, the new, the uncertain, and the unthinkable.[21]

The normalcy referred to in the text does not negate or deny the terror and suffering experienced by the people of Sarajevo during the siege. On the contrary, by emphasizing the term, the author indicates that these were "extreme" circumstances far from anything that can be counted as "normal." What the term means to show is a mental attitude, a kind of fortitude espoused by people precisely in response to the extremity of the circumstances in which they found themselves. In Kapić's text, the word "normalcy" comes to stand as an

70   Unforgetting and the Politics of Representation

equivalent to creativity, a kind of resourcefulness which the book emphasizes as the key to resilience.

The suffering and hardship are implied in survivor statements within the book, but always only as the backdrop to their resilient striving to live as fully as possible within the "new, the uncertain and the unthinkable":

At the time we couldn't prevent the destruction of the city, but there was some kind of resistance—we maintained at least the city's spiritual pulse. If we had left this city's spirit die, then the city would have been truly dead. (55)

My friends and I would party for no reason, just to relax. We used truck batteries to listen to music. (54)

I would invent recipes. One of them was for bean pie: boil the beans well, add some onions and pepper if you've got any; mash all of that well and spread it over filo pastry sheets, before baking it. It's a real speciality. (54)

When going to college to take my exams, all dolled up (as much as possible), I would walk along the rear of whatever was there to protect us from sniper fire, although it was more for mental than actual protection. I could never be sure if I'd come back alive. At times I would take my shoes off and run across intersections. (58)

We created a professional ballet performance of Ravel's Bolero. As important as it was for us dancers to come to rehearsals every day and challenge our physical and mental endurance, it was also important for the audience to come and see the performance. It was a kind of assurance that after all, we did live in a world where it was possible to achieve things that even in normal life were not easy to achieve, namely, a ballet performance. (15).

I was preparing for journalism exams. (16).

Despite the shelling, exhibitors brought their dogs; some poodles even had bows, like in the best of times. People were amazed when I told them to feed their dogs yeast as a supplement. They thought the yeast would make the dogs swell. A dog is not bread; the yeast cannot make it swell. (58)

You could tell that those dresses brought out of mothballs were beautiful, and those young girls looked beautiful in them. The fashion show was actually cheerful; although shells were falling all around, the atmosphere was nice. There were torches instead of electric lights or reflectors. (59)

I was making jewellery even though nobody had ordered it. But it was something to do. I worked very hard. I carefully followed patterns, crafting every piece with care—to make them beautiful. (57)

I went to several weddings. Each time we had great fun. (58)

I trained in athletics. (9)

Every morning, I had to run across intersections. On Sundays, when I was hosting the morning program, my greeting of the day would be: 'Good morning, people, listeners old and young. I'm still alive. If you are, too, let's start.' (12)

Constructing life under siege as an art of survival and choosing not to portray it through a primary emphasis on victimization and suffering, survivor statements actively shape how they see and understand the war and their relationship to it. Vahdeta, too, refers to aspects of this "normalcy" during the siege in the example of her son continuing to go to school as well as to play outside with the neighborhood children. In both narratives, remembering the experience of war and hardship represents "a temporal process, involving continuous construction and reconstruction, which puts into focus issues of change, history, conflict."[22] Through very distinctive self-representational power, memory thus builds an orientation toward the past in the present.

These forms of remembering are also acts of recovery, as they highlight the functional and creative characteristics of memory, primarily in how they alter the relationship between individual people and the environment and open avenues for action and agency.[23] First-person memorialization lays down a potential path toward the future and sets the authoritative terms of how one and one's past should be seen and recognized by others. Given that these discursive strategies are connected to deliberate acts of self-representation, their theoretical significance cannot be overstated. From a linguistic standpoint, the English noun "survivor" does not have a noun equivalent in Bosnian, but only a gerund form, as it is derived from the verb "to survive": *preživjeo*, (masculine singular), *preživjela* (feminine singular), *preživjeli* (plural), the form in which it is most often used. While in English constructions it appears natural to speak of a person with reference to the nouns "victim" or "survivor," in Bosnian, the only nominal equivalent is *žrtva* (victim). The term, however, is seldom used as a self-referential label in conversation, unless it is in the context of a formal conversation or to emphasize one's legal status. In most Bosnian linguistic constructions—as well as the linguistic constructions of most former Yugoslav languages—the emphasis falls on the circumstances and events that contribute to tragedy and hardship, as something that people or individuals actively respond to.[24] So, the only effective way to describe one's relationship to the past experience of war in Bosnian is by using the active verb "to survive": *Preživjela sam rat* ["I survived the war"] rather than with the noun equivalent in English, "I am a survivor of war." This linguistic feature has implications for discussions relating to peacebuilding and how the members of each community interpret past events.

Vahdeta's narrativization of Tito and socialist Yugoslavia for her young son, used to teach him about pluralist values, participates in this affirmative connection with the past, much like the permanent exhibit on *Galeb*, the Yugoslav Navy training ship and Tito's official yacht stationed in Rijeka, Croatia, alongside the Goli Otok exhibit. Similar forms of affirmative narrativization of Tito and life in socialist Yugoslavia emerged in all my other conversations. Vahdeta's memories of Tito are associated with her individual happy childhood, as well as her subsequent, post-war reassessment of the foundational political values of socialist Yugoslavia embodied in the well-known slogan, *bratstvo i jedinstvo* ["brotherhood and unity"].

The phrase, *bratstvo i jedinstvo*, coined during the Yugoslav People's Liberation War (1941–45), became the slogan of the League of Communists of

72 Unforgetting and the Politics of Representation

Yugoslavia. After World War II, the slogan was used as a guiding principle of pluralism in all formal speeches, government-issued documents, and announcements. Tito himself would also very frequently state on many public occasions, "Protect brotherhood and unity like the pupil of your eye" (*čuvajte bratstvo i jedinstvo kao zjenicu oka svoga*). Yugoslav national iconography represented the meaning of this phrase in different ways, and it permeated public life. Its official meaning was integrated into the solemn oath of responsibility recited by pupils entering grade one:

Danas, kada postajem pionir	[Today, when I become a pioneer]
Dajem časnu pionirsku riječ:	[I give my solemn pioneer word]
Da ću marljivo učiti i raditi	[That I will study and work diligently]
Poštovati roditelje i starije,	[That I will respect my parents and elders]
I biti dobar i iskren drug	[And that I will be a loyal and honest friend]
Koji drži datu riječ,	[Who keeps her word]
Da ću voljeti našu samoupravnu domovinu	[That I will love our sovereign country]
Socijalističku Federativnu Republiku Jugoslaviju	[The Socialist Federal Republic of Yugoslavia]
Da ću razvijati bratstvo i jedinstvo	[That I will contribute to the development of brotherhood and unity]
I ideje za koje se borio Tito;	[And the ideas that Tito fought for]
Da ću cijeniti sve ljude svijeta koji žele slobodu i mir.	[That I will respect all people of the world who desire freedom and peace]

While the slogan has been mocked extensively, especially after the war, it represented an ideology of Yugoslavism rooted in the ideal of peaceful multi-faith coexistence that had a significant impact on several generations of people. After the break-up of Yugoslavia, the ideology of Yugoslavism embodied in the slogan continues to live as a memorial form circulating in the Bosnian cultural space. It is sometimes evoked even by younger post-war generations who have not grown up with it. In the face of observable differences, including different ways of speaking, writing, and different religious traditions, *bratstvo i jedinstvo* defined for several generations what it meant to belong to a collective whose members are diverse, and where forms of identity and belonging were not articulated on the bases of religious or cultural purity but on a set of common civic values. As such it continues to denote an alternative social vision to the rigidity of post-Dayton's politics rooted in divisions along lines of nationality.

For Bosnian society, distinctively pluralist for centuries, *Jugoslovenstvo* (Yugoslavism) encapsulated in the concept of *bratstvo i jedinstvo* in its contemporary form is an expression of the Bosnian pluralist mindset and way of life.[25] Bosnia historically played a very special part in the Yugoslav socialist imaginary because "it was the only republic with no clear national majority, and as such, it represented a demographic microcosm of the entire federation."[26] During Tito's presidency, Sarajevo was greatly impacted not only in terms of modernization but also by Tito's anti-nationalist policies. This may hold particular significance for Bosniak populations, since they were recognized as a distinct nationality for the first time within the context of this vision and ideology, in 1963, a status confirmed by the Yugoslav constitution of 1974.[27]

These are the reasons Vahdeta locates the ideological roots of the war in the disregard for common values, and what she means by teaching her son about what "Tito stood for." Vahdeta describes herself as being "free" growing up in Tito's Yugoslavia, a characterization that defies most ideological critiques of socialist life. She utilizes inversely Western rhetoric that has historically labeled the Yugoslav socialist system as lacking in democratic freedoms. Her words expose the fallacy that exists within the easy conflation of democracy with capitalism, and the concurrent implication that a capitalist economy is "naturally" better suited to express and embody democratic ideals, or that it is the only legitimate way to do so. Given that the free market has "reigned supreme" in Bosnia and other parts of the Yugosphere for at least three decades, and that most of the region has been "fully incorporated into the capitalist world" but with a "semi-peripheral role," Vahdeta's claim debunks the market economy's promise to effect well-being and ensure "freedom" understood in a more comprehensive sense, beyond being able to hold elections every four years.

The freedom she references in relation to life in socialist Yugoslavia has to do with a social vision and a sense of personal well-being despite her family's modest wages. Her statement does not surprise me, as I, too, benefited from this social vision. For the average Yugoslav citizen, well-being was defined within a comprehensive state network of social and economic support. This support went beyond salary earnings or what in capitalism is defined as "purchasing power." The support was defined through full, unlimited access to a free and universal health-care system, including guaranteed coverage for all medication and dental care. The system also provided full access to free higher education, organized around academic aptitude and achievement rather than the ability to pay tuition. The state also guaranteed housing for all those who are employed, resulting in very rare examples of homelessness (the first time I encountered homeless people on city streets was upon emigrating to Toronto). The Yugoslav socialist model was also characterized by the freedom to travel during a guaranteed, often month-long vacation period for most employees. Comprehensive and guaranteed reproductive rights and autonomy was guaranteed, including unlimited and free access to abortion and birth control, as well as access to extensive and subsidized daycare services. In terms of

74 Unforgetting and the Politics of Representation

general quality of life, egalitarianism, and the well-being of the greatest number of people, these provisions do not have a match in any of the social welfare systems of the most developed capitalist countries. During socialist Yugoslav times as well as now for many people, Tito represents a system of social and civic values, and not only a reviled political system.[28]

Much more than simply being a form of nostalgia, memories of life in the particular socialist system in the former Yugoslav Federation represent a critique but also an ideology of active resistance to an unsatisfying political and economic present, and a preference for a vision based on shared cultural identity rooted in civic values of tolerance, coexistence, and solidarity.[29] Yugoslavism so understood functions as a political and social subjectivity that is opposed to both nationalism and the uncritical, exploitative adoption of an aggressive capitalist ideology. As such it is of great significance to ongoing local peace and reconciliation processes and the rebuilding of collective identity in the Bosnian Federation, but also in other former Yugoslav countries.

The discourse of *Jugoslovenstvo* in the Bosnian Federation entity is itself becoming a distinct memorial form through which aspects of various pasts— pre-Yugoslav, Yugoslav, and post-Yugoslav Bosnian identities—are contextually interwoven into a multilayered cultural memory system: a dynamic set of socially and interpersonally situated cognitive processes that include habits of mind and microsystems of cooperation and organization that influence thought and the representation of reality.[30] As a discursive memorial form, *Jugoslovenstvo* structures "the collective intellectual activity of a population" and creates a shared cultural space where people "exchange perceptions of reality, make decisions, share memories." Through its evolution and use, like all memorial forms *Jugoslovenstvo* helps "form consensus on what will be remembered (and forgotten)."[31] Its use at the interpersonal level is thus also future-oriented, since it shapes the social fabric, a mode of living and historically rooted patterns of interaction that are based on peaceful coexistence, multicultural curiosity, respect and a practice of solidarity based on the demands of civic life, regardless of nationality. As such the discourse of *bratstvo i jedinstvo* is an important aspect of peacebuilding "from below." At both the individual and collective level, meaningful integration of experience—cultural, political, personal—into the present is a prerequisite for being able to move forward.

In her story Vahdeta articulates faith in the next generation with reference to the political activism of high school students in Jajce, who rallied together for over a year to prevent the opening of a new school to segregate Bosniak students. Students very openly criticized the plan as a political tactic to keep them divided and thus more susceptible to nationalist manipulation. Many faced consequences for choosing to take part in the protest, as some were ostracized by their peers and had to openly disobey their parents for their involvement in resisting the new school, but many also received support from teachers and parents for their participation.[32] Despite the protests and the attention the student-led protest garnered both locally and internationally, the state policy of "two schools under one roof" continues to be implemented in the Bosnian Federation. In official political circles, the issue has acquired the flavor of democratic debates around equity, discrimination, and human rights that recall similar debates in other countries with culturally diverse populations.[33]

The protest remains significant, however, as it sparked a national debate at all levels of society that continues to evolve and produces a wide range of outcomes. In 2019, for example, referencing the Jajce protest, Bosnian media reported on the "fall" of the fence that divided a school yard in Travnik: "this fence has been a long standing material proof of the unacceptable way of life that has been long imposed [on the people of Travnik], a life which, first owing to small scale mixed activities, socialising and friendships, has gradually grown into a life that has always been true here, and which older generations remember: this life is called *suživost* [literally, living with one another] and *zajedništvo* [togetherness, unity]."[34]

In 2021, Nejra Keraljić, the coordinator of the local youth activist branch of the *Centar za Obrazovanje i Druzenje Jajce* (COD) [Center for Education and Friendship in Jajce], commented on the reconciliation process in Jajce with the following:

> We don't have too many problems around this in Jajce because we all live together, we are not divided. The only thing that remains to be a problem is 'the two schools under one roof policy' that applies to primary schools. Over the last two years, the activism of high school students has proven that they are willing to fight against this policy, and for the creation of a single, even if experimental, curriculum that would unite all students. I believe that if they continue this fight, and if they succeed, life in Jajce will be even better.[35]

Keralić's perspective, like Vahdeta's, clearly identify that the official, state-level politics "from above" is often at odds with what goes on "from below," at the level of interpersonal social relations and in civil society, embodied in local perspectives and community organizing. Her frustration with power-hungry politicians who are exploiting for their own personal gain, the post-Dayton tripartite division of Bosnia echoes the frustration of everyone I have spoken to in Bosnian Federation. Vahdeta notes that they only seek "to fire people up," to instill fear of a new and imminent war by inflaming fear of other nationalities who are continually constructed as "the Other."

This perspective is echoed in many of the main Sarajevo dailies, newspapers like *Danas, Dnevni List, Oslobodjenje, Dnevni Avaz*. The dominant discursive framing reiterated in Vahdeta's narrative and emerging in my other conversations is distinctly populist, identifying and openly critiquing corrupt and manipulative political elites who act purely on self-interest and amass

76 Unforgetting and the Politics of Representation

personal wealth and power at the expense of ordinary people who are facing economic and other types of hardship.[36] This populist discourse recognizes the rhetoric of single group nationalism as bankrupt, a lifeless application of existing constitutional terms that fail to be adequately applied, and fails to address the actual will of the people.

As much as it is recognized by many people as lifeless and bankrupt, nationalist discourses nonetheless seem to be able to mobilize voters based on their fear from aggressive, pro-Serb policies enacted by Republika Srpska, whose political allegiance remains to Serbia, rather than to Bosnia. While popular sentiment and much official politics in the Federation entity seeks to transcend ethno-nationalism as a basis for political and social organization, the official politics of Republika Srpska, under the leadership of Milorad Dodik, continued for years after the end of the armed conflict his staunchly ethno-nationalist politics, invoking political support from Serbia, threatening renewed violence, succession, and generally working to undermine the institutions of the state federation.

Ernesto Laclau has argued that socialism is the purest manifestation of populism because it seeks to abolish the power of self-interested elites and emancipate the people from capitalist domination.[37] While there is no clear indication that the current discourse in the media of the Bosnian Federation entity is unambiguously anti-capitalist, the openness with which the media criticizes the ruling elites is unparalleled in any capitalist-based economy. In fact, the unself-conscious use of the phrase "ruling elite" in Bosnian mainstream dailies, and its implicit contrast to the "people," is connected to a socialist conception of political reality, or at least a reality that stands in contrast to the one re/produced in capitalist economies where such terms are conspicuously absent from the public sphere in naming equally alarming trends in wage-gap increase, stark inequities, and crumbling health and welfare systems.[38]

The nation is not only a political project but also a cognitive, affective, and discursive category deployed in everyday practice.[39] The discursive claims that produce personal and collective identities are not simply descriptive of social relations, but they are "simultaneously constitutive of that reality, willing into existence that which they name."[40] Similarly, the achievement and practice of post-war peace, reconciliation and recovery is a complex, heterogeneous, and non-linear process or a condition that exists in constant negotiation and friction as multiple sources of power, including individual agency, in a society coalesce, steep into one another, and engage in mimicry, domination, and accommodation.[41] Forms of remembrance and memorialization shape this condition, as they in turn evolve and are agentively adapted by people in the Bosnian Federation entity, working to build continuities between various pasts and the present, and as a way to chart a future path. This future path is likely not going to mirror the cultural, economic, and peacebuilding frameworks of the EU, nor will it coalesce with Western conceptions of "transition" and reconciliation. It will, instead, be a path that emerges out of the unique individual and

Sarajevo the Beautiful 77

historical experiences of people who have inhabited the region. In describing the city of Sarajevo through a long historical perspective, Karahasan notes that "mixture of languages, faiths, cultures, and peoples living together in such a small place produced a cultural system unique to Bosnia and Herzegovina, and especially to Sarajevo. It was clearly their own, original, and distinctive." The peace and reconciliation that are emerging from the city and its people are also clearly their own, original, and distinctive processes that must be examined on their own terms and within a longer historical perspective dating prior to the recent war.

Vahdeta and I finish our conversation in the evening hours of a beautiful July day in Baščaršija. The aromas of freshly cooked traditional Bosnian food intensify as the restaurants and dessert shops around us prepare in anticipation of an evening wave of visitors. The evening call to prayer fills the air from the several nearby mosques. Having grown up in Yugoslav Macedonia, where Albanian mosques shared space with Orthodox churches, I recognize this as the sound of my childhood. In taking my leave, I try to pay for a small wooden plaque with young Tito's imprinted image, and the short rhyming ditty, *Josip Broz, dobar skroz* [Josip Broz, thoroughly good] from one of the shelves in Vahdeta's shop. The simple irony of the plaque delights me in its unselfconscious expressiveness, and taps into my childhood memories of the photo, ubiquitously present in a variety of media during the 1970s in Yugoslavia. We all know that Josip Broz was not "thoroughly good," but this does not invalidate the complex symbolic meaning of the plaque, and the significance of it being sold in Sarajevo, 37 years after his death, 27 years after the dissolution of the country, and in the aftermath of a bloody war. She refuses the money vigorously and insists that I take it as a present, so that I remember her and our conversation. In an extended gesture of hospitality that is indigenous to the Balkans, tracing its roots in the ancient Greek concept of hospitality, *xenia* (Greek: ξενία), Vahdeta asks that I drop by to see her for another coffee before I leave Sarajevo.

Notes

1 Vahdeta and I discussed all the points in the informed consent form before she signed it. I follow her wishes in terms of how to identify her in her narrative. I explained to her that the ICF was formulated for three distinct groups of people, women survivors of war violence, children born of war, and members of staff in NGOs providing support to the two populations. I also offered her 50Eu as a token of appreciation for her time and willingness to speak to me, which she refused. I didn't really pose any specific questions to her but invited her to speak to me about her experiences during the war; anything that she would like to share with me at that time. I reproduce her words almost in their entirety. The translation from Bosnian is mine.
2 A typical Serbian name.
3 The film Vahdeta references was directed by Danis Tanović and released in 2001. The film takes place during the war in Bosnia and portrays the story of two soldiers

78 Unforgetting and the Politics of Representation

from opposing armies, one fighting in the Army of Bosnia and Herzegovina, and the other fighting on the side of the Bosnian Serbs, who must collaborate in order to survive. The film emphasizes the absurdity of the war in Bosnia and the redundancy of the international troops on the ground in preventing violence.

4 Vahdeta uses the form "Bosna" to refer to the country she lives in, which is what the country is called by its people. Here and elsewhere where people I spoke with refer to Bosna, I have chosen to leave the reference as is, and not to translate it into the English version of the name, Bosnia.

5 Reference to Alija Izebegović, who along with Slobodan Milošević and Franjo Tuđman signed the Dayton Agreement, November 21, 1995, on behalf of Bosnia and Herzegovina.

6 Reference to a student protest in the Jajce vocational high school in 2016 against the Canton's decision to establish a separate school for Bosniak students only, to operate independently and to teach Bosniak students a parallel curriculum, instead of the Croatian one they had been following. The students were unhappy with the lack of consultation, refused to be divided along ethnic lines, and pressed the authorities for a unified curriculum. They succeeded in their demands.

7 The phrase in the original is *truli kapitalizam*, a socialist-inflected catchphrase referring to the profit-driven and exploitative bases of capitalist economy, inherently designed to produce great social inequalities.

8 Vahdeta is referring to the census of 2013.

9 One of the most sensitive accounts of post-war Sarajevo written in English is Fran Markowitz's *Sarajevo: A Bosnian Kaleidoscope* (University of Illinois Press, 2010). Although an anthropological rather than a historical study, the book successfully captures the specific historical blend of influences that make Sarajevo the city that it is even today. Muhamed Filipović's *Ko Smo Mi Bosnjaci?* (Prosperitet, 2007), Robert Donia's *Sarajevo: A Biography* (University of Michigan Press, 2006) and Ivan Lovrenović's *Bosnia: A Cultural History* (Saqui Books in Association with the Bosnian Institute, 2001), are excellent historical accounts of Sarajevo and Bosnia and Herzegovina post 2000, as is Rusmir Mahmutćehajić's collection, *Sarajevo Essays* (State University of New York Press, 2003).

10 Dževad Karahasan, *Sarajevo, Exodus of a City*, translated from the Serbo-Croatian-Bosnian by Slobodan Drakulić (New York: Kodansha International, 1994), 3–5.

11 Suada Kapić, *The Art of Survival: Extreme urban Conditions and Human Resilience based on evidence from the siege of Sarajevo 1992–1996*, (Sarajevo: VIDEOR, 2016), Introduction.

12 FAMA statistics. See FAMA Collection, famacollection.org.

13 Here I draw upon the work of A. Rigney, "Plenitude, Scarcity, and the Circulation of Cultural Memory," *Journal of European Studies* 35.1 (2005), 11–28, 22–23, and "Transforming Memory and the European Project," *New Literary History* 43.4 (2012), 607–628; and Enaken Laanes, "Born Translated Memories: Transcultural Memorial Forms, Domestication, and Foreignisation," *Memory Studies* 14.1 (2021), 41–57, n.p.

14 A. Rigney, "Plenitude, Scarcity, and the Circulation of Cultural Memory," *Journal of European Studies* 35.1 (2005), 11–28, 22–23, and "Transforming Memory and the European Project," *New Literary History* 43.4 (2012), 607–628.

15 Here I draw upon an older understanding of memory in the field of social psychology as seen in Fredric Bartlett's 1932 book, *A Study in Experimental and Social Psychology* (Cambridge University Press, 1932.).

16 Asja Prohić, "Children of War," in ed. Milomir Kovačević Strašni, *Djeca u Ratu* (the Art Gallery of Bosnia and Herzegovina, 2016).

17 "Milomir Kovačević Strašni: Ne bojim se za sudbinu," Selma Boračić-Mršo, Radio Slobodna Evropa, May 8, 2017, accessible at: https://www.slobodnaevropa.org/a/intervju-milomir-kovacevic-strasni/28474603.html.
18 For more on the project see, Rijeka 2020.eu: Artistic interventions in public space Environment of Remembrance – Art as a Resistance to Repression. https://rijeka2020.eu/en/program/times-of-power/artistic-interventions-in-public-space/environment-of-remembrance-art-as-a-resistance-to-repression/. For more on the prison on Goli Otok, see Martin Previšić, Povijest informbiroovskog logora na Golom otoku 1949–1956 [History of the Goli Otok Cominformist Prison Camp 1949–1956.], 2014 (PDF) (in Croatian). Faculty of Humanities and Social Sciences, University of Zagreb, and Martin Previšić, "Broj kažnjenika na Golom otoku i drugim logorima za informbirovce u vrijeme sukoba sa SSSR-om (1948–1956.)" [The Number of Convicts on Goli Otok and Other Internment Camps During the Informbiro Period (1948–1956)] February 2015 (PDF). Historijski zbornik (in Croatian) 66.1 (2015.), 173–193.
19 FAMA, "Guide Through Virtual FAMA Collection," accessible at: https://www.famacollection.org/eng/fama-collection/guide-through-collection/index.htmlGuide Through the Virtual FAMA Collection, accessible at: https://www.famacollection.org/eng/fama-collection/guide-through-collection/index.html.
20 FAMA, "Guide Through Virtual FAMA Collection." Among FAMA Projects and Archives are a comprehensive oral history set of video materials based on interviews of survivors of the siege; a so called, 'survival questionnaire,' the first and only survey conducted in 1996 with reference to the survival experience of ordinary people that collected 4,637 responses, and over 3,000 visual data-units, such as photographs, videos, drawings, animations, map details, and illustrations) depicting different events and topics: from the Siege of Sarajevo; to the Fall of Yugoslavia; from the Negotiations of the Dayton Peace Accords to the History and Making of Kosovo, and the Srebrenica Genocide. FAMA represents the first regional initiative to disseminate knowledge and resources about truth and reconciliation across the countries of the former Yugoslavia.
21 Suada Kapić, "Editorial," The Art of Survival, Videor o.d., 2016.
22 Brady Wagoner, "Introduction: Remembering as a Psychological and Social-Cultural Process," in ed. Brady Wagoner, Handbook of Culture and Memory (Oxford University Press, 2018), 1–17, 5.
23 Wagoner, "Introduction: Remembering as a Psychological and Social-Cultural Process," 6.
24 It has long been asserted in translation studies that passive voice constructions are much more common in English, than, say, in Croatian. See, for example, Božana Kneževi Irena Brdar, "Passive- and Passive-Like Constructions in the Translation of a Croatian Legislative Text into English," Jezikoslovlje 11.1 (2010), 25–51. While not identical to the issue I am pointing to here, this example refers to a tendency in the English to remove or at least obscure agency within its common linguistic structures, through what is referred to as "demoting the agent." Given the global interest in Bosnia and Bosnian women survivors or war violence, as well as children born of war and the growing body of studies of Bosnia in English, the semantic choices we make in those studies based on translated texts will likely be more consistent with English cultural idiomatic usage rather than Bosnian. This in turn has implications for how survivors are represented in English texts for English-speaking audiences, which again, may be different from how survivors self-represent in the original. I am not saying that it is impossible or even uncommon in Bosnia to express a perspective of personal suffering or to identify oneself as a victim. What I am pointing to

80 Unforgetting and the Politics of Representation

is that the language used to discuss concepts of "survivor" and "victim" dichotomy may call up different sets of cultural associations than the self-referential language used by the people who survived the war in Bosnia in the original: the first sometimes obscuring their narrative agency through English idiom; the second, sometimes asserting agency in ways that remain visible only in the original. Poststructuralism has long reminded us that language structures thought and that alternative conceptualizations only become possible for thinking and articulation in alternative language.

25 In 2017, when I spoke to the people whose stories are represented in this book, I did not travel to Republika Srpska, so I am unable to comment on the shapes the discourse of Yugoslavism takes there. Over the years, however, I have spoken to a number of Bosnian Serbs, some of whom currently live in Serbia, who do use the discourse in a very similar, affirmative way, and a form of critique of the present. The nature of the discourse is not static, however, and has been evolving over the years, having been used at different periods with different intentions. Within Serbia, especially during a particular period leading up to the war, Slobodan Milošević propagated the discourse of Yugoslavism to justify his decisions to deploy force and to represent the nature of the conflict as being between those who are "enemies" of Yugoslavia and of Yugoslav values on the one hand, and those who fight to uphold them, on the other, Serbia being cast as one such entity. Subsequent research has revealed that at the time this discourse concealed mainly Serbian nationalist interests and aspirations. See, for example, *Milošević vs Jugoslavija, Knjiga 1. Biblioteka Svedočanstva, Br. 20*, ed. Sonja Biserko (Helsinški odbor za ljudska prava u Srbiji, Beograd 2004). During the war itself, in Serbia there was a scholarly debate regarding the relationship between Serbia and Serbian national identity (*nacionalnost*) and the Yugoslav one. See for example, Ljubodrag Dimić, "Srpski kulturni klub između kulture i politike," *Književnost* 7-8 (1993), 858–903, where the author states: "Bilo bi pogrešno misliti da samo neko ko je prestao da bude Srbin, Hrvat ili Slovenac, može da bude dobar Jugosloven. Naprotiv, samo neko ko je bio i ostao dobar Srbin, dobar Hrvat, ŠiliĆ dobar Slovenac može da bude i dobar Jugosloven" (860). [it would be wrong to assume that only the person who has ceased being a Serb, a Croat, or a Slovene can be a good Yugoslav. On the contrary, only one who remains a Serb, a Croat or a Slovene can be a good Yugoslav" *translation is mine*]. Dimić here seeks to highlight the pluralist conception behind the Yugoslav national identity. See also his, "Jako *srpstvo–jaka Jugoslavija"–izbor članaka iz "Srpskog glasa," glasila Srpskog kulturnog kluba od 1939. do 1940. godine*, ed. Miodrag Jovičić (Beograd: Naučna knjiga, 1991). While it is clear that ethno-nationalist voices won the debate, no study of the recent war, its causes and its aftermath can be complete without a full engagement with the diversity of opinions that existed at the time among scholars and intellectuals, as well as ordinary citizens.

26 Larisa Kurtović, "Yugonostalgia on Wheels: Commemorating Marshal Tito across Post-Yugoslav Borders. Two Ethnographic Tales from Postwar Bosnia-Herzegovina." *Newsletter of the Institute for Slavic, Eastern European and Eurasian Studies*, University of California Berkeley, 28:1 (2011) 2–13, 21–23, 3.

27 See Guy Robinson, et.al., "Remaking Sarajevo: Bosnian Nationalism after the Dayton Accord," *Political Geography* 20 (2001), 957—980, and Robert Donia, *Sarajevo: A Biography* (Ann Arbor: University of Michigan Press, 2006).

28 See Mitja Velikonja, *Titonostalgia: A study of Nostalgia for Josip Broz* (Ljubljana: Peace Institute, 2008).

29 On recent theorizing about Yugoslavism and Yugonostalgia, in addition to Velikonja and Kurtović (above), see Aleksandar Bošković, "Yugonostalgia and Yugoslav Cultural Memory," *Slavic Review* 72.1 (2013), 54–78; Tatjana Petrović,

"Toward an Affective History of Yugoslavia," *Filozofija i društvo* XXVii.3 (2016), 504–520. doi: 10.2298/FID1603504P, and "The Past that Binds Us: Yugonostalgia as the Politics of the Future," in ed. Srdja Pavlović and Marko Živković, *Transcending Fratricide: Political Mythologies, Reconciliations, and the Uncertain Future in the Former Yugoslavia* (Southeast European Integrated Perspectives 9. 1st. ed. Baden-Baden: Nomos: 129–147). I contributed to this area of study recently with Takševa, "Post-war Yugoslavism and Yugonostalgia as Expressions of Multiethnic Solidarity and Tolerance in Bosnia and Herzegovina," *New Diversities* 21.1 (2019), 87–101, based on the same conversations as presented in this book.

30 In this formulation I am borrowing from Merlin Donald's "The Evolutionary Origins of Human Cultural Memory," in ed. Brady Wagoner, *Handbook of Culture and Memory* (Oxford University Press, 2018), 19-40 (20,21).

31 Donald, "The Evolutionary Origins of Human Cultural Memory," 21.

32 Sarah Freeman-Woolpert, "Students Win Major Victory Against Segregation in Bosnia and Herzegovina," *Waging Non Violence*, June 27, 2017, accessible at: https://wagingnonviolence.org/2017/06/students-bosnia-herzegovina-victory-segregation/, For more on the Jajce student protest, see Nebojsa Savija – Valha, "Jajce: The Machine for Production of History: Students Protests against Ethnic Divisions." Technical Report, Nansen Dialogue Centre, Sarajevo, Bosnia and Herzegovina, October 2019; Lidija Pisker, 'Slučaj dvije škole pod jednim krovom" u Jajcu.' (Osservatorio balcani e caucaso transeuropa, 21 June 2017), accessible at: https://www.balcanicaucaso.org/bhs/zone/Bosna-iHercegovina/Slucaj-dvije-skole-pod-jednim-krovom-u-Jajcu-18058.

33 See, for example, Aleksandra Ivanković, Roditeljsko pravo ili segregacija? Dvije škole pod jednim krovom, pred dva suda u dva kantona," [Parental rights or segregation? Two schools under one roof in front of two courts in two cantons] Analitika—Centar za društvena istraživanja. 2017, accessible at: https://www.analitika.ba/bs/publikacije/roditeljsko-pravo-ili-segregacija-dvije-skole-pod-jednim-krovom-pred-dva-suda-u-dva.

34 Translation is mine, from "Travničani oduševljeni: Srušena ograda podjele u školskom dvorištu," *Radiosarajevo.ba* 6 July 2019. The original reads: "Ova ograda dugo je bila materijalni dokaz višegodišnjeg nametnutog i neprihvatljivog načina života koji je, zahvaljujući prvo malim zajedničkim aktivnostima, druženjima i prijateljstvima, prerastao u ono što je uvijek postojalo, a starije generacije pamte u Travniku, a zove se suživot i zajedništvo.".

35 Translation is mine, from the video, "Nejra Keraljić Jajce: Dvije škole pod jednim krovom," CEIRBalkan, Centar za empirijska istraživanja religije. September 10, 2021, accessible at: https://youtu.be/WO57d37ddLQ.

36 On a definition of populist ideologies as they are manifested in established capitalist economies, see Bart Bonikowski, "Three Lessons of Contemporary Populism in Europe and the United States," *Brown Journal of World Affairs* XXIII.I (2016), 9–24. However, Bonikowski discusses populism in the context of capitalist economy and social democratic forms of governance, only briefly acknowledging that populist discourse can be used by both the left and the right wing. Ernesto Laclau, in *On Populist Reason* (Verso, 2007), and in *Post-Marxism, Populism and Critique* demonstrates the relation of populism to democracy in terms that are informed by leftist ideology, and thus provides a more appropriate frame of reference for the type of populism that is evidenced in contemporary Bosnia, as well as in Macedonia and Serbia.

37 Ernesto Laclau, *Politics and Ideology in Marxist Thought: Capitalism, Fascism, Populism* (London: New Left Books, 1977), 172–173, and for an elaboration, in Laclau, *On Populist Reason* (Verso, 2007).

38 See for example, "Canadian Income Inequality: Is Canada becoming more unequal?", *The Conference Board of Canada*, 2022, accessible at: https://www.conferenceboard.ca/hcp/hot-topics/canInequality.aspx, and the Report of the US Government Accountability Office, released in August 2019, "Retirement Security Income and Wealth Disparities Continue through Old Age," accessible at: https://www.gao.gov/assets/gao-19-587.pdf.

39 Bonikowski, Bart. "Nationalism in Settled Times." *Annual review of Sociology* 42.1 (2016), 427–449, 431.

40 J. E. Fox and C. Miller-Idriss, "Everyday Nationhood," *Ethnicities* 8 (2008), 536–563, 538.

41 Here I draw upon and adapt Roger MacGinty and Oliver Richmond's language on hybridity in peacebuilding, as used in "The Fallacy of Constructing Hybrid Political Orders: A reappraisal of the Hybrid Turn in Peacekeeping," *International Peacekeeping* 23.2 (2016), 219–239, 220–221. Their discussion shows the necessity of adopting some version of the postcolonial lens in discussing how hybrid forms of peacekeeping may be implemented in different contexts. While the postcolonial lens does not fully apply to the examination of Bosnia or any of the countries of the former Yugoslavia, a similar imbalance of power exists between so called 'international' or 'foreign' interventions and help measures coming from the developed capitalist economies and states. So, some of this terminology is useful in conceptualizing the relationship of the EU and other members of the international community to Bosnia and other countries in the region when it comes to the terms, conditions and regulatory frameworks that establish normative frameworks in achieving "transition," "reconciliation," or "democracy."

Chapter 5

Growing Up Under Siege

I connected with Merima Omeragić prior to arriving in Bosnia, and we met several times during my stay. Merima is a teacher of language and literature, and describes herself as woman, feminist, Yugoslav, student. In her twenties and since the war, she has been very active in feminist circles in the Yugosphere. Merima introduced me to her friend, Selma Beširević, a journalist for *Dnevni Avaz*, one of the main Bosnian dailies. At the time we spoke, both were in their late twenties. They grew up with memories of the war and a perspective on contemporary Bosnian society all their own. Both were happy to speak with me about what it meant to grow up in Sarajevo during the siege. Their memories of childhood during the war are embedded in their current perceptions of living within the Yugosphere, of the current cultural space, the bankruptcy of ethno-nationalist discourses, as well as an active critique of the current political regime. The way they speak about what it meant to be a child during the siege goes beyond what I have called *unforgetting*, since the things they talk about have never been alienated, denied, or hidden from themselves, but have consciously become constitutive of their own identities, how they think about themselves and others every day. It is clear that they have thought about all of this many times before and have shared the stories in different ways with different audiences. Their memories of having lived through the siege inform how they understand the work that they do in the present, and how other survivors relate to their own past. Their memorial reconstruction of the past in the present resonates with a political power of presence, occupying the space of individual utterance that looks to the future while actively critiquing the political establishment rooted in patriarchal, ethno-nationalist structures. Their words "encroach incrementally to capture the trenches" from the official power base while "erecting springboards to move on."[1]

Selma: *I was six when the war started. I do remember a grenade falling onto my aunt's house where her young baby was sleeping. I remember not being able to breathe, sitting in the dark, in cold, without electricity. I have developed claustrophobia because of having to spend long*

DOI: 10.4324/9781003186168-7

84 Unforgetting and the Politics of Representation

periods of time in small, dark places as a child. When I speak about the war to women from the Mothers of Srebrenica, we both cry. My mother was pregnant during the war—she gave birth to my brother in 1994. I don't understand what they were thinking, making a child during the war. I remember going to school during the war. Our teacher was a Serb. She used to lie on top of us whenever we would hear grenades falling, to protect us. I work for one of the main daily newspapers and we are often assigned topics related to the war and the prosecution of war criminals. It is always very difficult when I must report on those stories, and to contend with insensitive comments that people make in response to some coverage. For instance, do you really think that the 6,000 euros that a woman is awarded by the international court is adequate compensation for the fact that she was raped, for having to remember day in and day out how she had to watch her daughter being raped in front of her, for how all the men in her family were shot and killed?

Merima: *The first memory that we have, people my age, in their late twenties, is from the war. My first job was to help with the records entry for the project dealing with children who were killed during the siege of Sarajevo. Part of my job was to call the parents of the children, those who haven't provided statements. I would call the families and listen to them. I will never forget the story of a father, a man my father's age, he even looked like him a bit. He told me about the winter the children were outside, sledding, when a grenade fell. Both of his children were killed. I remember the way he told the story: I could see that this is a story that he lives with, that keeps spinning inside his head. He told me how he went outside after that to pick up pieces of his children. He said, the way I knew it was him is because he wore a red jacket. After this, the work became increasingly difficult for me. Sometimes people continue to live as if the war never ended. The war lives within people.*

I remember when the factories had stopped working. There was nothing to eat. We didn't have milk or flour. But there was a group of people who had decided that they were going to break into a candy factory, to steal candy for us, the children. I remember one of our neighbors who was among them, on his way back he was dragging a huge dark chocolate slab, probably about a meter wide. My father brought over a gray bag full of candy. So, about a month or two we had candy and chocolate. No flour, but candy. Our teeth deteriorated as a result.

There are other memories that are more difficult. My mother loved playing the piano, and the piano was always installed in the living room of our house. But because our house was up on a hill, and there were always grenades falling and snipers around, a grenade fell and hit the piano directly.

We had nothing to eat. Sometimes we would be fed only once in 24 hours. Mothers were amazing and very inventive. Whatever food they could find, they had to learn how to make it go far, to feed fifteen people and more. All of us together helped one another. This is what I remember. We all helped each other, on our street, in our suburb, in this microcosm that we inhabited at the time we were all united. We shared whatever we had among us, among seven families. My father was in the army, and he was paid in cigarette packs. We used the cigarettes as money. We would go to the market and trade our cigarettes for 10 kilograms of flour, or a kilogram of salt. My parents used the tunnel to get to the market to get food and hygienic products—shampoos and soap—which were difficult to obtain. This is how they used to bring back eggs as well, which is something that I like to recall. It was difficult to transport eggs via the tunnel. So, someone had a great idea to break a carton of eggs into a bottle, which they would then close tightly and used to bring the eggs over to us. How to survive? My mother made pie from rice and lentils and then we would be told that this was a cheese pastry.

I feel emotionally connected to much of the stuff that survived the war with me, and I am not sure that I would be able to part with it. Maybe I will need it, I think. It is my personal experience unlike any other. All of us carry remnants of trauma and some of it surfaces every day, still. For example, I live with a roommate, and I remember the first time she was cleaning up after dinner and made as if she was about to throw out the leftovers. I had to stand up and say, "we will not throw them out," we won't throw away anything. I never throw anything away, especially not food. If I can't eat it, I will give it to cats or dogs on the street, but I will not allow anything to be thrown out. I do realize that there is an irrational component to this thinking, especially when it comes to food that may be past its expiration date, but this is something that I carry from the days of the siege to this day.

We used to stay and cook in the basement of our house. We used to burn old shoes to keep warm. We would also cook on this heat. We also used to burn books. My grandfather used to take books about brotherhood and unity, books from Tito's Yugoslavia, one by one from the shelves, and burn them, swearing under his breath. So, we used the books to warm ourselves up and to cook.

My uncle, who used to be a communist and who grew up in Tito's Yugoslavia, now works in a mosque and is very religious. For some people the war precipitated a complete turnaround from the values and orientation in the former Yugoslavia; for others, the war changed nothing. My parents are Yugo-nostalgic and continue to be so. I grew up in this spirit. My father considers "his people" to be all people on the

Balkans, certainly all people who made up Yugoslavia. The turn to religion, to nationalism, and the far right is a troubling development. There are many variations, however. Based on their own life story, after the war everyone has built an orientation toward the system before the war. I was recently in Macedonia, and wherever I went in Macedonia and whoever I spoke to, as soon as I would tell them that I am from Bosnia, they would be delighted, and would exclaim, you are "ours" [Vi ste naša'—you are ours]. This was very enjoyable. I also spend a lot of time in Belgrade. I have a colleague who is a Kosovar Albanian. We took part in an event where she spoke Albanian, and I spoke Bosnian, and no one batted an eye. We walked down Knez Mihajlova [an old pedestrian and shopping street in Belgrade] in the middle of the night. Unpleasant experiences are rare. I am sure that they happen but nothing unpleasant has happened to me, so I can't speak about it.

Socially and ideologically even, Selma and I are oriented toward arts and culture. In university, it became apparent that people classified themselves according to a particular political orientation. There were those who, unfortunately, you could tell right away, fit into the dominant political perspective—the ethno-nationalist one, which is patriarchal and religious-based. We, on the other hand, belong to the alternative group. When the others go to Friday prayers, we go for a beer. We are divided that way, young people. At the last census, I had to enter a national category. I declared myself "woman." I have a friend who entered "penguin" into the same category.

I noticed that many young people embrace this nationalist ideology because they see an opportunity in it to benefit directly. Given the very high unemployment rate in Bosnia, especially among those who are young and educated, it makes pragmatic sense to embrace the dominant political ideology since there may be opportunities to gain through it. "Divide and conquer" is the motto on which nationalism thrives; it is also a very good way to divert attention from issues that really matter. Why is there so much unemployment, especially among the youth? Why do retirees have a pension that is not sufficient to survive on?

There are stories also that are very specific and that don't fit easily into the categories that people try to place them in. When I was working at the institute for the study of genocide, in 2014, I remember when the Association of Women Victims of War was established in Republika Srpska. I was fascinated to witness how the women survivors were arguing among themselves and failing to express solidarity for one another—they would question the other women about the legitimacy of their stories and experiences. Incredible. I do like to see things around me with a critical eye. There are some problematic types of gatekeeping when it comes to such associations, even here. It seems that often the person who founds and heads the organization gets to say who will become a member and who won't, on criteria that are not always completely transparent. I remember a story about a woman who was from a mixed background, her father was a Croat, and she was Serbian. She was a bus driver before the war, but she continued in this line of work during the war—her route was to drive up and around cities and towns in northern Bosnia and then would come down to Mostar. During the war she even did humanitarian work, procuring gasoline through her own means to continue to drive packets of food, medicine, and other necessities across towns; she also drove people when they were trying to flee. She was first captured by the Croatian army somewhere near Mostar, where they kept her somewhere in some camp for over two months and raped her. Then she was released above Mostar, at Konjice, where the Bosnian Army captured her and raped her. She managed to escape them but then, approaching Sarajevo, she was apprehended by a Serbian army, who called her an Ustaša and who treated her the same. Here in Sarajevo Roma women were also raped, but there isn't much talk about this. This region is not large, but there are so many different groups living within it. It is very complex and difficult to understand for someone coming from the outside. In the end it is unclear who fought whom and why.

Note

1 Asef Bayat, *Life as Politics: How Ordinary People Change the Middle East* (Stanford University Press, 2010), 98.

Part II

I listen…I turn more and more into a big ear, listening all the time to another person. I 'read' voices. A human being is greater than war…A human being is guided by something stronger than history.

Svetlana Alexievich, The Unwomanly Face of War

Chapter 6

Unforgetting the Children Born Because of War

Assessing the numbers of Children who were born because of sexualized violence during the war in Bosnia, or the larger former Yugoslav space affected by war, remains difficult.[1] This is partly due to poorly kept statistical information or a complete lack thereof, and partly due to the continued reluctance of the women survivors to disclose their experiences. After giving birth, the women would often leave the children in the hospitals, so that a significant number of such children grew up alongside those who were orphaned in the war. The authorities would habitually conceal their origins from potential adoptive families and the children would often be adopted without a legal name. The lack of extensive records and the circumstances of war have thus contributed to a lack of legal recognition of their rights and lack of social and global awareness of the challenges faced by this group.

However, the nature of this silence is understudied, especially from the perspective of the women and Children themselves, and the specific socio-cultural context within the entity of the Bosnian Federation. Much of the silence surrounding the Children Born of War, just as the silence of many of the women who survived sexualized and gender-based violence in war, is intentional, and the result of decisions that are only partially related to the women's interiorized sense of shame. Rather than being exclusively a silence attributable to traditional patriarchal values associated with the loss of female chastity and honor, it is a silence that often conceals multiple individual and collective choices that go beyond shame and are, in some cases, politically motivated. In most cases, the hiding was done out of a desire to protect the children from stigma and discrimination and to give them a chance to grow up without being burdened by the knowledge that the truth carries. In Bosnia, this type of silence is sometimes idiomatically referred to as *Čuvati od zlih jezika* [to protect from evil tongues], namely, as protection from potentially hurtful and insensitive comments. In a war where the perpetrators of rape sometimes knew the victim or members of their families, and where in some cases both parties remain living in the same municipality as they did prior to the war, hiding the truth about children born of rape in the community does serve a protective function,

DOI: 10.4324/9781003186168-9

92 Unforgetting and the Politics of Representation

and many women who were pregnant and who gave birth, whether they decided to keep the children or not, have kept this silence out of a desire to protect both themselves and the children. The social and political tendency to simplify experiences of victimization as well as to instrumentalize the discourse of victimhood has often resulted in women being and feeling forever defined, trapped as it were, by a single, war event. Thus, many wish to actively avoid this form of representational reductionism and manage how others see them by simply not sharing that part of their past.

This means that there are Children Born of War rape who still do not know about their origins. However, the mother's desire to conceal the truth from them is not only a self-protective act, but also frequently an act of maternal care. From the perspective of maternal philosophy, maternal practice or "mother work" is not a natural or instinctive activity defined by biological imperatives, but a conscious and thoughtful endeavor focused on meeting the demands of children in three main areas: preservation, nurturance, and training in social acceptability. The decision to not commit infanticide upon giving birth, for example, as some women have done, is itself an act of preservation. The decision to keep and raise a child born because of war rape, regardless of whether the mother decides to disclose or not disclose the details of the conception, engages all aspects of mother work.[2]

And there are Children who do know, who have been told about their origins either by their families or have discovered the truth in some other way, but who themselves choose to remain silent about that knowledge. The general social and cultural tendency to represent them mainly in terms of stigmatization and victimhood also contributes to their unwillingness to share their stories publicly. Unsurprisingly, and like many other people of any gender who have survived torture and victimization related to war, many of the Children prefer for their lives not to be viewed from the perspective of a single dimension defined by their origins and their mothers' wartime experience.

Šemsudin Gegić, the Bosnian filmmaker who directed two docudramas about Alen Muhić, a Child Born of War, may be right to intimate that their numbers may be more numerous than we will ever know:

> children of women who were raped in the war are invisible children because while we stroll around Sarajevo, while we stroll anywhere in the world, we are not aware that we may be passing by children born to mothers who were raped during the war in Bosnia, that they may be living among us.[3]

The type of silence that has surrounded the topic in Bosnia since the war, however, as complex as it is, has not been a total silence, even at a social level. Based on my conversations with two such Children—now young adults—who in their stories reference others, knowledge about the rapes and the children born as a result has been circulating informally within Bosnia both during and since the war. Doctors and nurses who delivered children during the war, as well as other members of staff in the medical facilities where the women received pre- and post-natal care have always known about the issue, but likely remained silent out of respect for the women's and their families' request to protect their privacy.

Rumors could not be prevented, however, and the search for the stories about their origins for many of the Children was initiated through having found themselves on the receiving end of a hurtful remark, or a prejudicial slur. The Children would often be spoken of as "children of the enemy," "children of hatred," or often, "little ćetniks," or a "četnik's," or "ustaša's bastard," if it was known or assumed that the nationality of the perpetrator was Serbian or Croat, respectively, that is, of a nationality different from the mothers'. In shocking examples of victim blaming in the community, their mothers would also sometimes be insulted as "četnik" or "ustaša whore." This naming represents a distinctly mysogynist discursive gesture that combines the ethnification of differences during the war with selective conflation of nationalist politics from different historical periods superimposed on the present.[4]

Gegić's own appearance on national media multiple times over the years to speak about his own interest in the topic, and the two films he directed on the subject are examples of the knowledge making its way into the public sphere and discourse. In 2004, Gegić directed the docudrama *Dječak iz ratnog filma* [A Boy from a War Movie]. The film was among the first documentary voices in Bosnian society to broach the topic of Children Born of War publicly. A blend of documentary and creative performance, the film tells the story of a boy born in Goražde in 1993 to a Bosniak woman who was raped in the nearby town of Foča, and who left the infant—and the town—three days after giving birth.[5] The film, 27 minutes long, features Alen himself, who was ten years old at the time, and who had at that point already experienced being called derogatory names by his peers in school. The film is told through stylized dialogue between the boy and the director, Gegić. The boy, who in the first part of the movie calls himself Edin nicknamed "Pero" [a typical Serbian name], offers to tell the director his idea for a movie based on the story of the raped woman who gives birth to a baby boy in Goražde. In the film we also hear recollections by hospital staff and the manager of the Center for Social Services.

The film also dramatizes the disclosure regarding his origins, the period in Alen's life when he is teased at school for being adopted and called derogatory names. These are the events that precipitate Alen's search for the truth about his origins and questioning of his adoptive parents. Muharem Muhić, the caretaker of the war hospital where Alen was born, is Alen's adopted father, and in the film, he recalls the loving way in which he and his family took Alen and raised him as his own. The film ends with the director inviting the boy, "Edin" to tell him the real identity of the boy in the story. The boy then states, "I am he, the boy with the two names." In fact, Gegić made the film to publicize Alen's story, to help realize Alen's and his adoptive parents' desire to meet his biological parents. In the film, among other things, Alen's adoptive father

94 Unforgetting and the Politics of Representation

Muharem refers to the harassing and exploitative behavior of multiple domestic and foreign journalists who contacted the family for statements and stories without any real human interest in Alen himself.

The action in the film is punctuated by the singing of a traditional Bosnian song, "Dora the slave," whose lyrics date back to sixteenth-century Bosnia under Ottoman rule. The song tells the story of Dora, a girl pregnant likely due to being raped by the feudal lord in whose household she was imprisoned as a servant, and who just as she tries to hang herself gives birth to a baby boy who embodies sainthood in two religious and cultural traditions, a boy who, "before noon is St. Ilija [an Orthodox Serbian saint], and in the afternoon is Hazret [St.] Alija." The song creatively situates Alen's story within a long historical context of sexualized and gender-based violence that is familiar to Bosnia and the Balkan region from a more distant past. The fact that the song is sung from the perspective of Dora herself calls up empathy for her plight, and by extension, empathy for those women who like Alen's birth mother, left their newborns after being impregnated through rape. Although the film deals with a very difficult subject, the combination of dramatization and documentary-style telling succeeds in treating the subject with delicacy and restraint.

Overall, the film portrays Alen as a healthy ten-year-old who is quick to smile, is often mischievous at school but who makes up for it with his brightness and kindness, who likes to watch movies, and who daydreams about his school crush. Speaking about his intention in making the film, Gegić noted,

This film is intended to show children who were left behind that their origins do not spell out the proverbial 'end of the world' for them, and that all light has not been extinguished and darkness created instead. Alen and I have been walking through that darkness and into the light. The film is intended to be a direction as to how it is possible to overcome their issues, and not to be labelled forever as 'children of war', children of perpetrators, or the children of četniks and ustaše.[6]

The film created a big impact at the Sarajevo film festival, and thereafter was shown in Moscow and won an award at the Sofia film festival. It premiered in the same year in the US at the Tribeca Festival, directing the attention of English-speaking audiences to the group of children born of war rape in Bosnia. The promotional blurb, however, refers to it as a short that "explores both the tragedy of the Bosnian nation and the beauty and cruelty of its people."[7] This conceptualization of Bosnia and the region as predicated on extremes that can only be mythologized, exoticized, and sensationalized will be echoed in Angelina Jolie's 2011 war drama about the war in Bosnia, *In the Land of Blood and Honey*. Rather than embodying the "tragedy of the Bosnian nation" the film in fact represented an important first public step in "unforgetting," in making visible this part of recent history and in starting to build a culture of remembrance within Bosnia relating to the recent war. At the time, Gegić's film would not be shown on any official Bosnian TV network. In fact, when in 2017 I asked Gegić about where I could locate the film, his answer indicated that domestic controversy around the film remains. Some of it implicates him as a director and his motivation in making the film, including some wrangling about copyright ownership to circulate it freely. But people had seen it and were talking about it. It made Alen a household name in the town of his birth, if not all of Bosnia and beyond, and contributed to the fight for visibility and de-stigmatization for victims of war rape and the Children themselves.

Two years later, in 2006, Jasmila Žbanić's feature film, *Grbavica* [showing as "The Land of My Dreams" in English], won the Golden Bear Award at the Berlin film festival, and contributed to the further opening of public discussion within Bosnia itself—and internationally—about war rape and children born of war rape. Based on the true story of one of the women who gave birth and raised a child born because of war rape, the film also created a conceptual space that allowed women survivors to build solidarity among themselves and fostered a willingness among some of them to share their stories with others who had similar experiences.

The generation of children whose stories it represented were at the time already in their early teenage years. The film centers on the protagonist, young Sara, who learns that she was born because of the rape her mother endured during the war. The film builds cinematic empathy for the complex mother-daughter relationship, informed by ambivalence, that is, strong alternating feelings of love and hatred the mother and the daughter experience in the context of their close relationship. The film centers on disclosure and its effects on the daughter, as well as her ultimate acceptance and assimilation of the new knowledge into a positive self-concept and forgiveness for her mother. Additionally, however, the film explores the subjective experience of war-related sexual violence on the women who survived it, opening a public space to acknowledge what happened, and the aftermath of the violence for many survivors.

The silence and invisibility of Children Born of War has been, in fact, an official silence—the silence of the state and of state institutions that have been reluctant to recognize the children as a special legal category and to foster the creation of extended networks of social support for the women, the children, and adoptive families. The official tri-partite division among the three constituent peoples of Bosnia fixed through the Dayton Accord and operating across all official systems and frameworks has contributed to the reluctance to initiate a public discourse about the children of war. For years after the war, the constitutional delineation between "us" and "them," "victims" and "aggressors" has been animating all official Bosnian politics, nurturing, and seeking to re/construct an imagined sense of clear "unity" based on ethno-national belonging. The Children Born of War, through their genetic make-up, complicate and deconstruct such understanding of national belonging, since they carry within them and personify both "us" and "them."[8]

96 Unforgetting and the Politics of Representation

Mixed unions, that is, unions between members of different nationalities were common in the former Yugoslavia, my own identity being an example of this. The post–World War II strategy of the League of Communists of Yugoslavia (LCY) "was neither to abolish national identity nor to discourage participation in political life based on nationality" but instead to "elevate the Yugoslav state to a political status exceeding that of any nationality."[9] This strategy resulted in the relegation of cultural and religious differences to the area of lifestyle rather than political economy, thus encouraging mobility and mixing among people of different backgrounds. The aim of this multilayered model, based on the idea of "brotherhood and unity," was to "disaggregate differences of region, gender, religion, nationality, class, in order to unify those differences on a supranational level."[10] What facilitated the implementation of this model is that most people on the territories of the former Yugoslavia are of Slavic origin, people with common ancestry, closely related languages, sharing a similar culture in dress, food, and lifestyle, that is, of common ethnicity.[11] In other words, the Yugoslav federal structure, in addition to the multilayered model of "brotherhood and unity" provided an official framework for identity that did not depend on nationality but was supranational, based on a set of civic values. The identities of Children Born of War, especially in cases where the rape involved a perpetrator and a victim from different nationalities, appear thus to symbolize the violent war itself. But by the same token their identities can be understood as symbolic of a potential road map for creating a civic national identity rather than one based on an imagined sense of pure nationality. Their increasing visibility in the Bosnian cultural sphere has steadily called attention to the constructed character of "ethnification" of differences as well as the limitations of nation-building based on essentialized biological identities.

In 2014, another child born of war rape, Lejla Damon, appeared on Bosnian media. Although many of her statements to the media were released in English, her connection to Bosnia has been relevant for developing an internal public discourse relating to Children Born of War. Her story and subsequent activist work as reported in the Bosnian media has been part of the collective "unforgetting" and has contributed to making the children born of war and their biological mothers more visible. Although Lejla does not speak Bosnian, having been smuggled out of the country upon birth and adopted by a British journalist couple, many of her interviews and statements have been translated for Bosnian audiences.[12] Over time, Lejla developed constructive and agentive strategies that helped her express and understand the complex reality behind her identity, and her birth mother's decision to give her up for adoption. One of those strategies was to become involved in numerous activist and non-profit organizations, advocating for the rights of women who experienced sexual violence and the Children Born of War. From early on she had developed an empathetic perspective on her birth mother's decision to give her up, being able to justify the raped women's right to negative emotions and to understand the events of the war and her birth mother's experience within a broader context.

Unforgetting the Children Born Because of War   97

In describing the recent meeting with her birth mother for Balkan Insight, Lejla shows public admiration for the woman's resilience as well as empathetic understanding of the short- and long-term experience of trauma that marked her subsequent life: "The strength of that woman, just to keep going...She's not well physically, and emotionally I'm sure it's the same, but the strength to continue—and the strength to see me—that takes so much. I think she's an amazing person, and she is a complete inspiration and a role model."[13]

Gegić's second film based on Alen Muhić's story, *Stupica nevidljivog djeteta / An Invisible Child's Trap* premiered in 2015 in the Goražde Cultural Center as part of the project Oral BIH History, run by the Institute for Research of Crimes against Humanity and International Law in Sarajevo. Unlike Gegić's first docudrama, the film was widely publicized over Bosnian media, attracting a great deal of support among the Bosnian public.[14] Since the release of the first film, not only had Alen been quite forthcoming about his motivation to make the second film to help locate his biological parents, but all of the other events and releases I outline above were already circulating in the Bosnian public, creating an existing sphere of discourse around the issues. This design was successful, since he was contacted by his biological mother after she heard about the film in the US, where she has been living since the war. She and Alen did meet, which was of great importance to him in fulfilling his desire to learn the details of his origins.

He was also able to locate his biological father, Radmilo Vuković. During the war, Vuković was a member of the Army of Republika Srpska indicted for war crimes against civilian populations in Foca that took place in the summer of 1992. The Bosnian prosecution also brought up charges of rape relating to Muhić's biological mother who testified as a witness at the trial. Vuković was sentenced to five and a half years in prison but was released shortly thereafter, although a subsequent DNA test confirmed his paternity. His release and acquittal represent an example of a patriarchal and misogynist bias within the legal system. His defense claimed that he and the defendant knew each other and, moreover, that they were in a relationship, thus invalidating the defendant's claim of violence. Even though the defendant denied the existence of a relationship, her words were not enough to ascertain, without legal doubt, that she was indeed raped. Discovering the truth about his origins and being able to name both of his biological parents brought a sense of positive closure for Alen Muhić. In a statement he gave to *Ramski Vijesnik* in 2018, he asserted the way in which he sees himself and the agentive way in which he faced prejudice:

> *I have and will continue to fight against stigma. What I don't understand is why it is the victims who are being stigmatized and not the perpetrators? I think the biggest issues is that victims remain silent. I do know however that they do so because the community assigns blame for what happened to them. It is my desire that all victims speak out, and through speaking out to leave behind the trope of the victim, so that we can fight together against prejudice. They have no reason to feel ashamed—they are not to blame for what happened. We need*

98 Unforgetting and the Politics of Representation

> *to blame the perpetrators, rather than the victims. I know that I am not the only one as a child of war, and I hope that others will start to speak out freely, without fear. Keeping the silence perpetuates stigmatization.... I did not agree to be forever locked into the image of the victim, to always be in a state of helplessness. I am a fighter by nature. I love people, and I love life. I forgive everyone for what I went through. I don't hate anyone. In life, the person who overcomes hatred is the real winner.*[15]

In an interview to N1 BiH, a daily online news outlet, Armin Omerović, the actor who plays Muhić in the second film, stated,

> *Alen is the hero of our generation; he is the hero of all of us and we can all learn from him what it means to be brave, determined, and full of integrity. It was an honour to share the screen with him.*[16]

In some of the early statements about his birth mother and in the context of his personal struggle to solve the puzzle about his own identity, Alen appears to mirror the patriarchal sentiment of traditional Bosnian society that assigns blame to mothers who abandon their children, even in circumstances when those children may be the product of rape. However, over the years, and over the course of his active searching for answers, his understanding has shifted and matured. Even though he and his birth mother do not keep in touch regularly, in our conversation he said, "Thank God, we spoke, we met, she saw her grandchild, my son ... She suffered a lot."

From this point on, there are several events over the course of the following three years that significantly increase visibility for Children Born of War within the Bosnian federation entity at least, moving the agenda forward in terms of their legal recognition. In the same year, 2015, Alen was among several other Children Born of War who founded the Sarajevo-based *Udruženje Zaboravljena Djeca Rata/Association Forgotten Children of War*. Among the founders were several female human rights Bosnian activists, including Amra Delić, a neuropsychiatrist from Tuzla researching children born because of war. Ute Baur-Timmerbrink's 2015 book *Wir Besatzungskinder: Tochter und Söhne alliierter Soldaten erzählen* [We, the Children of the Occupation: Narratives of the Sons and Daughters of Allied Soldiers] was promptly translated into Bosnian the following year. The book details the stories of around 250,000 children born to local German and Austrian mothers at the end of World War II by fathers who were members of the Allied forces that occupied former Nazi-held territories, soldiers from the US, the Soviet Union, Great Britain, and France, and whose stories were a taboo for over 70 years. Delić, having been immersed in work with the Children in Bosnia for some time at this point, hosted the launch of the translated edition, ensuring extensive local media presence.

In 2018, Ajna Jusič, a feminist, psychologist, and a Child of War, took on the leadership of the Association. Her presence and vision have shaped the values and the work of the Association since, turning it into a powerful voice for political change and recognition for Children Born of War in Bosnia, but also in the region and globally. Since 2018 the Association has been a very important presence in the local and international sphere supporting the agenda of children born of war globally and leading the advocacy for their legal recognition and social visibility and acceptance. Their message is contextualized within the process of reconciliation, transitional justice, peaceful transethnic and multifaith coexistence, and non-violence in the region. In personal terms, drawing upon her own challenges growing up as a Child Born of War, and her first-hand knowledge of the issues affecting this group whether they were raised by their birth mother or not, Jusić has empowered herself while working tirelessly to empower others.

The Association Forgotten Children of War follows Ingvill C. Mochmann's definition of Children Born of War, according to which such children are those who would not have been born if there had been no war.[17] In the work of the Association, this category of children comprises three broad categories: children whose (a) fathers are/were members of an opposing/enemy army, that is, members of a different ethno-nationalist group compared to the mothers, (b) whose fathers are/were members of stationed or temporary peacekeeping troupes (for example, UNPROFOR, IFOR, SFOR), or (c) whose fathers are/were foreign humanitarian aid workers while the mother was local.[18] This is an encompassing approach, as it implies that there are significant similarities in the experiences of people who were born in the three identified scenarios, although not all may involve instances of rape and sexualized violence legally defined. Although it is significant to remain sensitive to the intersectional differences among people who belong to one of these three groups or a combination of two out of three, all three groups face similar obstacles in Bosnian society when it comes to systemic forms of prejudice. While only those Children belonging to the first group may be able to acquire the status of civil victim of war, especially if the designation is limited to the mother having achieved such status under existing laws, the broad definition acknowledges the shared social dimensions of the experience of a Child Born Because of War.[19]

In the spring of 2021, supported by the International Organization for Migration, Mission in Bosnia and Herzegovina, the Association partnered with the Museum of War Childhood and the Wings of Hope Foundation to document the experiences of Children Born of War, and of survivors of conflict-related sexual violence who were minors at the time. The aim of the project was to raise awareness among the wider public, calling attention to the current position of these people within Bosnian society. By documenting and exhibiting their personal stories, the project contributed to the fight against the stigma and discrimination that the survivors and children born of war still face today.

The collaboration continued, resulting in an exhibit conceptualized by Ajna Jusić i Mirna Omerćausević entitled, "'Progovara(j)mo' Breaking Free: Izložba o djeci rodjenoj zbog rata u Bosni i Herzegovini" [Exhibit about the children born because of war in Bosnia and Herzegovina], which first opened in the fall of 2021 in Sarajevo. The exhibit was shown in Belgrade as well, organized by Inicijativa mladih za ljudska prava—YIHR Srbija [Youth Initiative for Human Rights Serbia], Žene U Crnom Srbija [Women in Black Serbia] and the Autonomni ženski centar [Independent Women's Centre Serbia]. The exhibit comprised large black-and-white photographs of children born of war, members of the Association Forgotten Children of War, and their mothers, a record of their testimonies spoken by actors, and finally, a video project that brings together the photos and the stories.

The exhibit was informed by the transforming trauma into art concept, encouraging and facilitating social dialogue through the creation of a safe space for the Children Born of War to face society with their identities and narratives. Even though the Children's experiences do contain a shared dimension, each story is different. Traumatic events are experienced differently by different people, although psychological and psychiatric conceptions of trauma may be able to identify typical responses. By combining the photos of the Children with the photos of their mothers, and with their individual stories, the exhibit highlights that no two experiences are the same and that each account is specific to a specific person. At the same time, this artistic revisioning reveals that despite those differences, all members of the group Children Born of War have faced similar challenges both personally, in their own search for and struggle with their identity, as well as socially, through prejudice and ostracism that marked their childhood. In some cases, those challenges were further compounded by the effects of secondary trauma and having grown up with mothers who were severely traumatized themselves, and who were themselves contending with the work of raising a child born of war rape with varying degrees of support. In some manifestations, the exhibit invited the Children themselves to draw a visual representation of themselves on canvas and mark the areas of their body that feel trauma. As Jusić pointed out recently at a research workshop in Innsbruck where we co-presented material from this chapter, the work of the exhibit was immensely significant. It was significant not only for the people of Sarajevo in terms of building collective awareness around this group of citizens, but for the Children themselves, as this was the first time they were invited to physically represent their traumatic experiences and represent them in relation to their own bodies. As such, taking part in preparing and mounting the exhibit represented a key step in their own process of *unforgetting* and recovery.

In this sense the exhibit, and other similar events the Association organizes and promotes, function as a restorative processes aiming to facilitate reconnection, reconciliation, and peace on multiple levels. Among the main goals of the exhibition was raising awareness and promoting reflection among audiences of their own discriminatory practices that make the fight for justice even more difficult on the territories of the former Yugoslavia. The success of the exhibit has depended on combining the visual arts and creative expression with a powerful vision of social justice. Through this combination the exhibit helped express experiences that are too difficult to put into words, and articulate aspects of trauma that are felt to be "unspeakable," thus helping with the successful processing of intense, difficult emotions.

A combination of music, documentary storytelling, and performance in relation to the Children Born of War rape in Bosnia is also utilized in the documentary dance theater piece "U ime oca/ In the Name of the Father." The work premiered on March 20, 2019, at Tuzla National Theater in Bosnia, directed by Darrel Toulon, and it was devised with the cast of young Actors from Tuzla using transcriptions of interviews made with Bosnian Children Born of War. The piece is "situated at the crossroads of performative community arts and politically relevant immersive theater, informed by academic research"; it "capitalizes on the theater as a forum for dialogue by breaking through the 4th wall and inviting interaction and conversation between audience and performers."[20]

The benefits of combining these elements are well known in literature dealing with the role the creative arts play in trauma and healing and enhancing well-being, for individuals and for communities. Studies have shown that music can calm neural activity in the brain, which may lead to reductions in anxiety, helping restore effective functioning in the immune system.[21] Movement-based creative expression focuses on nonverbal, primarily physical, forms of expression as psychotherapeutic or healing tools that help relieve anxiety and stress the movement of mind and body in a creative way.[22] Given that the theater piece was also performed in Belgrade, Serbia, as well as different locations in Croatia, when asked to comment on whether she and other performers fear when they travel across the region to perform, Jusić pointed out:

> We are afraid, of course. Every child of war fears if the place where they are travelling to may be the place where the perpetrator, their biological father, walks freely. It is natural that we feel some fear. However, there is no such fear that would overpower our motivation and the desire to perform this piece anywhere in the world. We stand on the stage proudly, and our message to everyone is that rape as a weapon of war must stop, and when that happens, we can begin to speak about us, human beings who have arrived in this world because of it. Yes, we will perform it anywhere.[23]

In the case of the Children Born because of War, the healing capacity of narrating difficult truths through art is of great benefit in their journey of personal recovery, restoring their faith in the possibility of being and feeling socially accepted. It is also of great benefit to the larger community whose members learn through artistic engagement more positive, inclusive, and non-discriminatory way to express the truth about the Children, their origins, and the recent war. In this context, artistic expression plays a key role in fostering the peace process on many different levels in a holistic sense. As cultural productions that aim to raise awareness of the category of Children Born of War and the issues that affect them in a collective setting, such events play an important role in the healing of cultural trauma and the loss of social cohesion effected by the war. By presenting the audience with a new narrative about the Children and their mothers, a new way of seeing in the context of post-war rebuilding, they effect a temporal process that works to repair the social fabric ruptured by war.

The Association has actively advocated for eradicating prejudice and discrimination toward Children Born of War, but also toward women who have experienced sexualized and other forms of gender-based violence, and all those who are marginalized by heteropatriarchy. The Association describes itself as "a visibility instigator for those who have been invisible," a human rights organization whose key values include solidarity with women who have experienced sexualized and gender-based violence, zero tolerance for any form of violence against women, equal treatment, and equal rights for all marginalized groups.[24] Among their main goals is to advocate for educational support for Children Born of War, as well as for access to social and psychological counseling and support. In articulating their identity as a human rights organization, the Association explicitly draws upon feminist tenets in stating that "a woman is never to blame for the violence she experiences," "violence against women can never be used as a strategy of war," and "women's bodies are not a territory to be conquered on the way to war victory." Their principles—"openness, diversity, tolerance and democracy"—arise from these values and their activities have been geared toward empowering women survivors and children born because of war through an outcome-driven agenda.[25]

In a 2019 statement to UN Women, Jusić's voice came to resonate with the authority of her own personal experience as she spoke on behalf of others in the Association: "We do not want to be invisible; we want to be treated equally. I am Generation Equality: I am a child born out of wartime rape."[26] The equality that Jusić refers to means that she seeks legal recognition for Children Born Because of War, and access to services and supports that have been made available to other civilian groups affected by war, such as male veterans, the children of *šahidi* (a term mainly reserved for male members of the Bosnian army who lost their lives in the war) and other groups legally recognized as "civil victims of war." More recently she claimed that no transitional process of justice within Bosnia and beyond will not be complete until the children born because of war receive full legal recognition.[27]

The enabling circle of helping others to help oneself, evident from the life trajectories of all three children born of war, has broader political implications as well. Their willingness to speak out about their origins, and to engage in activism and other types of publicly minded action aimed to raise awareness around the issues affecting women survivors of war rape and the Children Born of War, further contributes to the de-stigmatization of these populations in the cultural sphere. Their public visibility problematizes and deconstructs the official silence and residual shame surrounding rape in war and its consequences as specifically gendered crime. Their vocal critique of the stigma surrounding both women and Children, and of the oppressive or non-existent policies and support, helps destabilize existing gendered stereotypes about women survivors and their Children as "broken," as well as empower others among them.

Speaking in the fall of 2022 to representatives of the EU Parliament on the topic, "We are not weapons of war," Jusić categorically reframed understanding of Children Born of War, rejecting negative stereotypes, and putting forward a new, matrilineal self-definition: "My identity is based on being my mother's child, and everyone must acknowledge this. We are not and we will never be defined as children of the enemy."[28] She also rejected being characterized as a "child without a father" since this is a label predicated on a patriarchal, deficit understanding of their identity, one that automatically reduces the role of mothers, as well as stigmatizes those women who are sole-support parents, even outside the war rape context. While she reiterated that Children Born of War continue to experience "systemic invisibility," she argued that their issues need to be seen in the broader context of patriarchal prejudice and discrimination against those who are for whatever reason perceived as "different" from the majority. In decisively stressing the primacy of the mother as centrally constitutive in the identity of the Children Born because of War, Jusić's message is unambiguously feminist. In her characterization of the nature of discrimination faced by Children Born of War in terms of minority and majority, and the ways to end them, she clearly situates this category of people within the fold of larger social groups: that of Bosnia's youth, or all citizens of Bosnia and Herzegovina.

Through the activism of the Association and their entry into public discourses of peace, reconciliation, and human rights, the category of Children Born of War in Bosnia has emerged into a visible political, and since recently, legal category. Through their very identity, as well as their agentive self-definition, they have come into public view with the aim to reconfigure civic identity and actively effect change. In this sense, they are among the most radical political elements in contemporary Bosnian society

For example, their recent leadership of the project "Symbols of the lost past" sought to engage youth aged 18–25 in dialogue around their own experiences relating to the war while learning about the experiences of women who fought in the war, as well as women who survived rape during the war and children born of war through their own personal narratives. The stated aim of the project was to highlight the positive role of women in building a culture of memory. This goal stood in contrast to the historical masculinist and patriarchal bias in the official culture of memory of Bosnia, one based on the cult of the soldier/hero and the honoring only of "our" victims of war. The project also involved students' laying flowers on the memorial sites marking the deaths of children in war, in Sarajevo and the city of East Sarajevo, the capital of

Republika Srpska, regardless of their nationality. Part of the initiative was the creation of a short documentary film, "Djeca, Mir, Život" [Children, Peace, Life] with the purpose of creating a shared narrative about how the past is remembered across the post-Yugoslav region. The film production was supported by the Reconciliation Network of the Regional Commission (RECOM), a cross-national regional organization focused on extra-judicial mechanisms for the establishment and public disclosure of facts about war crimes and other gross human rights violations and promoting the values of cross-regional justice and peacebuilding.[29]

The Association collaborates closely with youth and women's organization across the region, and often works with high school students in helping develop awareness around meaningful peacebuilding and human rights within the entity of the Bosnian Federation. It has also partnered with individuals and organizations from across all entities in Bosnia and Herzegovina, Serbia, and Croatia, as well as other European countries to create educational materials, such as short films and regional exhibitions, that are focused on raising awareness of children born of war and sexual violence in war. True to her feminist committment, Jusić has emphasized that the only way to build peace is through solidarity: "No one group of people who are seeking legal recognition and are fighting for equity and human rights can build peace alone. We can build peace and achieve results when we work together. If there is one group that is left behind in the peacebuilding process, this means that peace is not being built on solid foundations."[30]

This multimodal approach to peacebuilding and the healing of individual and social traumatic wounds unites peacebuilding, memory, trauma, and imagination as it looks toward the future.[31] The activism of the Association continues to situate the category of Children Born of War within the broader context of youth culture of Bosnia and Herzegovina, and the issues affecting youth within larger political currents and global phenomena. In a 2022 issue of the media platform Balkan Perspectives #19, devoted to youth culture in the western Balkans and the facilitation of debate and dialogue on the process of facing the past, reconciliation, and peacebuilding, Jusić writes:

We live in a world of old wars and fast migrations, where it is increasingly more common that people from anywhere in the world come to live side by side. To maintain the peace in such a world and such a place, everyone must experience both equality and prosperity. Prosperity in the case of Bosnia and Herzegovina, unfortunately, is frequently absent, while separatism has acquired serious dimensions. The current politics of Bosnia and Herzegovina, regardless of which nationality propagates it, characterizes people primarily according to ethnic, religious, and tribal categories of identity. The only goal of such politics is ethnic secessionism and national purity. History teaches us that this form of government always leads to conflict and war. We have felt it and can vouch that it is true…In the current political landscape, where the recent war still represents the most important social event for the country, our youth is constantly exposed to twisted interpretations of the past, that is, they are exposed to the interpretations of the past propagated by political leadership who in fact block the peacebuilding process. The alternative to such government is and must be the building of a culture of living together. We can celebrate our differences and look upon differences as a form of human resources and wealth, an asset in social and cultural development. A precondition for this desirable social order is the acceptance and respect of the identities of all individuals, regardless of how 'different' they are. Realizing opportunities for decision making, personal as well as collective, is a necessity for young people in Bosnia.[32]

In May 2022, on behalf of the Association, Ajna Jusić accepted the Večernjakov Pečat Award for humanitarian work, an annual award issued by the eponymous Bosnian community organization and one that enjoys great social popularity within the country. Acknowledging the work that Jusić had done on behalf of the Association Forgotten Children of War, the award also signals the extent to which issues affecting Children Born Because of War have become visible to the Bosnian public, and their willingness to recognize them as socially and politically significant. This award comes two years after the Serbian foundation *Jelena Šantić* awarded the Association their own regional award, to recognize and affirm their artistic and activist contribution to building peace, tolerance, understanding and solidarity in the region.

The increased visibility of the Association and their political influence has recently resulted in two significant legal changes. Since May 31, 2021, the Sarajevo municipality Stari Grad no longer requires declaring the name of the father on municipal forms. The new forms require only the "name of one parent or guardian" instead. One of the common challenges faced by Children Born Because of War, and one linked to their continued stigmatization, has been the fact that since the war, most forms at every level of government have required the names of both parents, mother, and father. While under the Association's definition some Children who are categorized as being born because of war may know the identities and names of their fathers, those who are children born of war rape usually do not. This has presented a challenge for many when completing forms and applications by exposing them to insensitive or disparaging remarks. Several other municipalities have indicated that they are considering making the change, showing promise that changes will be adopted at a broader level. The recent change benefits members of the Association directly but it also benefits Bosnian society overall. Pre-war Yugoslav laws and policies did not require the name of mother and father on any forms. The change in this requirement represented, in the argument of the Association, a clear indication of the re-traditionalization of gender roles that has taken place since the war. Reverting to older, Yugoslav policies requiring the name of one parent on official forms more accurately reflect the gender-conscious changes in the understanding of family that have taken place over the last several decades in global contexts.

106 Unforgetting and the Politics of Representation

Jelena Čajić, a member of the Association and a child born of war rape in Bijeljina, felt emboldened by the change to comment on her experience in public. In a short reportage following the legal change, Jelena remarked:

> *I always felt that I was different and that there is more to my story. I came across a document in my mother's house that prompted me to ask questions, at which point my mother, aunt and grandmother told me about my origins. What followed were very difficult years when I blamed myself for what had happened to my mother in the war. This traumatic cycle is very heavy emotionally, at some points even completely destructive. Today I believe that it is very important to speak openly about these experiences, the war, sexual violence, so that other children do not have to go through what I had to go through growing up. Since I was in primary school, I had been made to feel embarrassed in front of everyone, being asked about why I don't know the name of my father and having to explain everything repeatedly to various people. This is completely unnecessary information for a clerk or an administrative support person. This is why we started the initiative, "Name of one parent/guardian." ...When I first met other children born because of war, after becoming a member of the Association and after I met Ajna Jusić, who greeted me with 'sister', I felt like I belong, it felt like being a member of a community, among people who want to help me and to whom I want to help.[33]*

The Association's advocacy, in collaboration with the Bosnian Office of TRIAL International, and other government agencies and NGOs, recently resulted in another significant legal change for Children Born of War rape, a change that has been in the making for more than eight years. In the summer of 2022, the government of the Brčko District adopted a law that recognizes civil victims of war, with the explicit acknowledgment of children born because of war rape as being part of this civic category. A draft law passed unanimously by the Parliament of the Federation of Bosnia and Herzegovina on July 26, 2022, was open for public debate for a period of 45 days, after which the Brčko District adopted it first, followed by the legal adoption by the entity of the Federation as well. For the first time in Bosnian history Children Born of Wartime Rape specifically are recognized as civilian victims of war, along with all other civilian victims, including individuals who have experienced sexual violence during war. The legal framework establishes the basic principles of legal protection for civilian victims of war and their definitions, as well as the specific scope of supports and services which they are entitled to claim. Because it is adopted at the highest level, the framework also obliges all government agencies within the two entities to adjust and revise their policies to reflect the changed status for this group. For many individuals, challenges remain relating to the proof required to claim this status. Also, the category of children born of forced marriages is not included in the recognition, something that the

Association continues to work toward. Despite these challenges, the new law represents a legal precedent locally and for Europe, and it is among the first recognitions of this kind at the global level.[34] As of yet, within the state of Bosnia and Herzegovina it is only Republika Srpska that remains as the one entity that has not been willing to take part in these conversations and reforms.

Acknowledging Children Born of War as a legal category represents a legal validation of the experiences of women who have given birth to children born because of war rape. The public form of acknowledgment also has the potential to motivate many women to disclose to their children the truth about their origins, something that many continue to keep hidden. It is also a validation of the children themselves under one part of Bosnian law, and a visible legal marker of their existence. By clearly situating their own life histories within larger political and social narratives of war, peace, sexual violence, gendered relations, and patriarchy, the Association has given a new voice to a category of Bosnian citizens who have been largely silent and disenfranchised.

In March 2021, the Serbian Youth Initiative for Human Rights (YIHR) in Belgrade invited Ajna Jusić to speak on the questions, "Are post-Yugoslav societies future oriented? If not, why not?" The topic was defined through the lens of "lost multiculturalism that characterized the former Yugoslavia" and current political manipulations implicated in the continuation of the politics of violence.[35] Among other things, Jusić reiterated the Association's unique contribution to peacebuilding in the region:

We can build meaningful peace as a society only when we have faced the terrors of the past war. This process, however, must start with individuals. For example, we have mapped the places in Bosnia where systematic and mass rapes of women took place during the war. But there are many women who were raped individually, and many of them have not had the opportunity to return to the place of this crime to face it and begin to achieve closure in their own personal journey of healing and looking forward. We cannot build a better society while being blind. All those who have experienced pain and victimization during the war, regardless of their nationality, must be allowed and encouraged to face the terror of their own past before moving forward, in all post-Yugoslav spaces. Only then can we begin the work of healing, and peace. Until everyone faces their own traumatic experience, we cannot move away from it, and cannot attain peace, as individuals, and as collectives. In Bosnia, for example, we must begin this work from the foundation up, since our very constitution is discriminatory, and propagates discrimination.

Our Association is unique in its perspective on how to attain peace—by situating it in a broader context of human rights—and this perspective is our gift to world. We are not here only to receive charitable donations. We are actively gifting our perspective and our activism to the rest of the world where conflict exists. If Bosnia succeeds in solving the issue of children born because of war, we can truly become a blueprint for post-conflict recovery and the achievement of sustainable peace. In all post-Yugoslav spaces, we must work to create a culture of mutual respect and dialogue to overcome dominant ethnonationalist narratives. People from different sides need to come together and exchange views and experiences. In Bosnia alone, there are still people who live in divided Mostar and who haven't crossed to the other side of the city that 'belongs' to the other nationality. Women who have survived war in the federation are not given opportunities to speak with women who survived rape in Republika Srpska. This is unheard of. This is wrong. Change at all levels must come from recognizing that ethnonationalist politics does not work. That so many young lives were senselessly lost in the war because of ethnonationalist politics. Ethnonationalism has not resulted in anything positive, on the contrary: it has made life worse for everyone and continues to do so. We must stand up and say, 'I have had enough of this. I want better.' Youth needs to lead the way to dialogue, and many in Bosnia do, although they are not given enough opportunities.

Regional collaboration is of key importance. Our Association leads in creating spaces and opportunities for dialogue through our artistic engagements, the play, the exhibits. Art represents a form of dialogue, especially since through it we combine our own experiences, sadness included, with engaging the audience in dialogue around this experience, which they begin to feel, too. Activism and art come together and are interactive, dialogue-creating. These are spaces of dialogue that allow people to start thinking—what if we could have this sort of dialogue more often? What if we could have it on a regional or global level? These are spaces that allow for the generation of empathy and an empathetic response toward the experience of another human being. I cannot begin to express how it feels, the responses of the public we have received after they see our play and the exhibit. Those are the times when I have experienced what it may be like to live in the future, when we are understood, accepted, respected. The times when we feel that we belong. What we feel when we encounter the people who have seen the play and the exhibit, these are the most beautiful moments of our lives. Art has the capacity to elicit empathy in people.[36]

Here and elsewhere, Jusić emphasizes embodiment as a basis for peacebuilding, one that challenges dominant and official sites of meaning-production and replaces them with the recognition of alternative ways of knowing that validate individual experience and voice.[37] Rather than being only reports of private experience, such narratives are also fully elaborated interpretations—or what may be called cases, examples, or exemplars—of experience.[38] As such, they play an important role in "the spatial distribution of social remembering," an active cultural process and a social conversation that participates in constructing "narrative alternatives" to stereotypical conception about Children Born Because of War and their place in society, as well as peace and recovery at the broader level.[39]

The work of the Association is of key significance to the ongoing development of local epistemologies of peace. Through their projects and involvement in the political, public sphere, they foster an embodied form of peacebuilding and a culture of memory defined by remembrance and recovery across different nationalities. Their activism is reshaping larger social discourses about Children Born because of War, leading to greater de-stigmatization and recognition. At the same time, through the cross-nationality position they occupy within Bosnian society, they are uniquely equipped to critique as well as deconstruct the institutionalization of ethno-nationalism within the post-Dayton Bosnian context. Since recently, in continuing their advocacy for social visibility and for broadening the basis of legal recognition, the Association has argued that Children Born of War represent Bosnia's cultural and historical heritage that must not be erased or made invisible. In making this political claim, the Children claim a central role not only in terms of what counts as collective memory relating to the war, but also in terms of nation building and Bosnia's future.

Notes

1 According to a statistic reported by the local NGO "Women Victims of War on April 11, 2015, on Face TV, a Bosnian commercial HDTV channel based in Sarajevo they have 61 children born of war on their records, although they speculate that this number is likely significantly higher based on how many Bosnian women were raped. Most recently, the chapter "Bosnia: A New Dimension of Genocidal Rape and Its Children" in ed. Sabine Lee's book, *Children Born of War in the Twentieth Century* (Manchester University Press, 2017) provides a summary of estimates regarding the numbers of children born because of gender-based and sexualized violence during the recent war The numbers remain difficult to pinpoint with certainty. The President on the Association Zaborravljena Djeca Rata recently noted in a private conversation with the author that they have around 30 members, but the Association mainly operates on the basis of self-identification, which means that these numbers tend to fluctuate.
2 I have written about this perspective in relation to several examples from Bosnia in, Takševa, "Raising Children Born of Wartime Rape in Bosnia," in ed. Takševa and Sgoutas, *Mothers Under Fire: Mothering in Conflict Areas* (Demeter Press, 2105), 155–177.
3 Cited in Emina Žuna, "Djeca mržnje i njihove majke," *MediaCentar_Online*, Dec 22, 2014, accessible at: https://www.media.ba/bs/mediametar/djeca-mrznje-i-njihove-majke (translation mine).
4 Rape in war and forced impregnation has a long history predating the war in the former Yugoslavia. For a recent historical summary, see Sabine Lee's book, *Children Born of War in the Twentieth Century* (Manchester University Press, 2017). For the specific cultural and nationality-based context for the violence inflicted on Bosniak women particularly, and the use of forced impregnation, see Tatjana Takševa, "Genocidal Rape, Enforced Impregnation, and the Discourse of Serbian National Identity," *CLCWeb: Comparative Literature and Culture* 17.3 (2015), doi: 10.7771/1481-4374.2638.
5 Since May 2020, the film is publicly available and can be accessed here: https://youtu.be/DI5ZND6yN_Y/.

110 Unforgetting and the Politics of Representation

6 Cited in Žuna.
7 See the caption on the Tribeca Film Festival web-pages, accessible at: https://tribecafilm. com/festival/archive/512ce2ab1c7d76e046000a74-boy-from-a-war-movie. There has been extensive media coverage of Muhić's story as well over the years. See for example, "The Bosnian war baby still searching for answers, 20 years on" by Andrew Anthony, *The Guardian*, July 12, 2015. In the summer of 2021, young students from Albania, Bosnia and Herzegovina, Montenegro, North Macedonia, and Serbia interviewed twenty people who survived traumatic experiences during the war in the former Yugoslavia for the Youth Memory Transfer Project, and Alen Muhić was among them. The interviews are accessible at: https://youtu.be/7PQkNC5mdGQ; Jonathan Custeau and Jessica Garneau, "Enfants nes du viol: Des victimes invisibles de la guerre de Bosnie" by, *La Voixdel'Est Numerique*, August 24, 2022.
8 See Takševa and Schwartz, "Hybridity, Ethnicity and Nationhood: Legacies of Interethnic War, Wartime Rape, and the Potential for Bridging the Ethnic Divide in Post-Conflict Bosnia," *National Identities* 20.5 (2017): 463–480. doi: 10.1080/14608944.2017.1298580. Also see, Takševa, "Negotiating Identities in Post-conflict Bosnia and Herzegovina: Self, Ethnicity, and Nationhood in Adolescents Born of Wartime Rape," in ed. Tarama P. Trošt and Danilo Mandić, *Changing Youth Values in Southeast Europe: Beyond Ethnicity* (Routledge, 2017), 19–38.
9 Randy Hodson, Dusko Sekulic and Garth Massey, "National Tolerance in the Former Yugoslavia," *American Journal of Sociology* 99.6 (1994): 1534–1558, 1538.
10 Zala Volčič, "Scenes From the Last Yugoslav Generation: The Long March From Yugo-Utopia to Nationalisms." *Cultural Dynamics* 19 (2007), 67–89, 69.
11 Hodson, Sekulic and Massey, "National Tolerance in the Former Yugoslavia," 1541.
12 The interview that introduced Lejla Damon to Bosnian audiences, and from which I quote, was published by BBC news on June 10, 2014, as "My Mum Would 'Strangle Me' Because She Was Raped." Accessible at: https://www.bbc.com/news/newsbeat-27775008. There are numerous stories about Lejla Damon in the media. See for example, "Wartime Rape in Bosnia: A Daughter's Search for Truth," BIRN, by Eleanor Rose Londo, July 19, 2018, "How Rape Has Become a Weapon of War," an ABC NL video interview with filmmaker Teresa Turiera (May 19, 2022), https://youtu.be/9GLzywE27gw; "There's Still Someone in the Woods," a documentary film by Teresa Turiera-Puigbò and Erol Ileri (2020). The film was followed by an eponymous exhibit in Jersey City u New Yorku 23. aprila–28 Aprila 2022, and features the stories of several other children of war, including Alen and Ajna.
   After the exhibit the audience was invited to take part in a discussion on the topic 'rape as a weapon of war.
   "Mlada Britanka: Majka mi je silovana u koncentracijskim logorima u BiH," Večeni List Hrvatska (June 11, 2014); "U.K. woman shares family's Bosnian war story of rejection, reunion," by Joe Lofaro, CBC News Ottawa (March 15, 2018), a story that was written during Lejla's visit to the University of Ottawa, to attend a workshop organized by my research team and I as part of the project "Children of the Enemy: Narrative Constructions of Identity Following Wartime Rape and Transgenerational Trauma in Post-WWII Germany and Post-Conflict Bosnia." This event provided Lejla with the opportunity to meet children born of war rape to German mothers, women who were raped by members of the Allied forces at the end of World War II. Being able to take part in and witness these encounters and conversations was a true privilege, the memory of which I will always cherish.
13 Eleanor Rose, "Wartime Rape in Bosnia: A Daughter's Search for Truth," Balkan Insight, Jul 19, 2018, accessible at: https://balkaninsight.com/2018/07/19/wartime-rape-in-bosnia-a-daughter-s-search-for-truth-07-17-2018/.
14 See for example, E.A., "Na snimanju jedne od najpotresnijih priča: Zbog filma o Alenu Muhiću ne spavam noćima," November 28, 2014, KlixBiH, accessible at:

Unforgetting the Children Born Because of War 111

https://www.klix.ba/vijesti/bih/na-snimanju-jedne-od-najpotresnijih-prica-zbog-filma-o-alenu-muhicu-ne-spavam-nocima/141128008.

15 Editors, "Alen je oprostio svima: 'Otac mi je srpski vojnik koji je silovao moju majku, ali nikoga ne mrzim i sretan sam'," August 5, 2018, Ramski Vijesnik, accessible at: https://ramski-vjesnik.ba/clanak/alen-je-oprostio-svima-otac-mi-je-srpski-vojnik-koji-je-silovao-moju-majku-ali-nikoga-ne-mrzim-i-sretan-sam/107369/ (translation is mine).

16 Anadolija, "Održana premijera filma: Alen Muhić je heroj generacije," Mar 24 March, 2015, N1BiH, accessible at: https://ba.n1info.com/vijesti/a32991-odrzana-premijera-filma-alen-muhic-je-heroj-generacije/. Translation is mine. Over the years, Muhić's public statements show a developing perspective in terms of his perception on his biological mother. While there are some early statements where it seems that he has adopted the patriarchal views of Bosnian society which assign blame to mothers who abandon their children, even sometimes in circumstances of rape, his later statements show that his understanding of the context and circumstances of women who were raped during the war—including that of his biological mother's—has shifted toward forgiveness. In his case, what appeared to present a difficulty for him, is the claim that his biological parents had known each other even before the war, and that they had even been in a relationship, which made him question his biological mothers' decision to leave him behind. Finding out who his biological parents are, and learning more about the great numbers of women in Bosnia who were raped and brutalized in various ways during the war, and about the social prejudice that they continue to face after the war contributed to him being able to situate his mother's experiences and decision in a broader context.

17 See, Mochmann, IngvillC. "Children Born of War–A Decade of International and Interdisciplinary Research." Historical Social Research/HistorischeSozialforschung 42.1 (2017), 320–346.

18 On the specific nature of the definition of the category 'children born of war' in the context of Bosnia and Herzegovina, see the following scholarly exchange: Amra Delić, Philipp Kuwert, and Heide Glaesmer, "Should the Definition of the Term 'Children Born of War' and Vulnerabilities of Children From Recent Conflict and Postconflict Settings Be Broadened?," *Acta Medica Academica* 46.1 (2017), 67–69. doi: 10.5644/ama2006-124.191, and Tatjana Takseva, "Response to Whether the Definition of the Term 'children Born of War' and Vulnerabilities of Children From Recent Conflict and Post-conflict Settings Should Be Broadened," *Acta Medica Academica* 46.2 (2017). doi: 10.5644/ama2006-124.XX.

19 See Tatjana Takseva, "Response to Whether the Definition of the Term 'Children Born of War' and Vulnerabilities of Children From Recent Conflict and Post-conflict Settings Should Be Broadened," 177–179.

20 This is how the piece was described on the Film Programme web pages of the University of Leeds, in the series, Transforming Conflict and Displacement through the Arts and Humanities, accessible at: https://changingthestory.leeds.ac.uk/transforming-conflict-and-displacement-through-the-arts-and-humanities-film-programme/u-ime-oca-in-the-name-of-the-father-2019/.

21 Heather L. Stuckey and Jeremy Nobel. "The Connection Between Art, Healing, and Public Health: A Review of Current Literature." *American Journal of Public Health* 100.2 (2010), 254–263. doi:10.2105/AJPH.2008.156497 (n.p).

22 Fran Levy, *Dance Movement Therapy: A Healing Art* (Virginia: National Dance Association, 1988); Nena Močnik, "(Un)canning the Victims: Embodied Research Practice and Ethnodrama in Response to War-Rape Legacy in Bosnia-Herzegovina," *Liminalities: A Journal of Performance Studies* 14.3 (2018), 23–39, 23.

23 Facebook, The Association Forgotten Children of War, @zaboravljenadjecarata, March 28, 2022, 12:30 pm, accessed on Oct 25, 2022 (translation is mine).

112 Unforgetting and the Politics of Representation

24 See "Ključne vrijednosti i principi rada (ZDR), accessible at: https://zdr.ba/kljucne-vrijednosti-i-principi/,(translation is mine).

25 See "Ključne vrijednosti i principi rada (ZDR), accessible at,: https://zdr.ba/kljucne-vrijednosti-i-principi/,(translation is mine).

26 UN Women, "I am Generation Equality: 'I am a child born out of wartime rape'," November18,2019,accessibleat:https://www.unwomen.org/en/news/stories/2019/11/i-am-generation-equality-ajna-jusic-forgotten-children-of-war.

27 Ajna Jusić, "Research Workshop: Children Born of War and Process of State and Nation Building," University of Innsbruck, May 22, 2024.

28 Facebook, The Association Forgotten Children of War, @zaboravljenadjecarata, Sep 17, 2022., 8:11 am, accessed on October 25, 2022 (translation is mine).

29 RECOM Reconciliation Network, "A Brief History of the RECOM process," accessible at: https://www.recom.link/en/a-brief-history-of-the-recom-process/.

30 Facebook, YIHR Serbia, http://www.yihr.rs/, "Razgovor sa Ajnom Jusić: Era međuljudskog dijaloga," Live Recording, March 16, 2021, 8 am, accessed on Oct 27, 2022.

31 Here I draw upon the relationship between trauma and the arts discussed in Stephen K. Levine's book, *Trauma, Tragedy, Therapy: The Arts and Human Suffering* (Jessica Kingsley Publishers,2009), 16–17.

32 Ajna Jusić, "Generacija 'Mladi'," Balkan.Perspectives #19 BHCS, *Mladi i suočavanje sa prošlošću na Zapadnom Balkanu*, (2022), accessible at: https://dwp-balkan.org/bs/balkan-perspectives-19-bhcs/?fbclid=IwAR2kvjImK5vWoWmHNWrgjKm9nuCyMHNG4WqAueL8aQuQ_h_lC7bWoDhOpzM.

33 Marija Arnautović, "Djeca rodjena zbog rata: 'Ime jednog roditelja'," reportage for *Slobodna Evropa*, May 28, 2021, accessible at: https://www.slobodnaevropa.org/a/udruzenje-zaboravljena-djeca-rata-inicijativa-ime-jednog-roditelja/30305660.html (translation is mine).

34 "Children Born as Result of War Get Their First Legal Recognition in BiH," *N1 Sarajevo*, July 15, 2022, accessible at: https://ba.n1info.com/english/news/children-born-as-result-of-war-get-their-first-legal-recognition-in-bih/; and, Arman Fazlić, "BiH: Djeca rođena iz čina seksualnog nasilja u ratu prepoznata kao civilne žrtve rata novim entitetskim zakonom," *Osservatorio Balcani e Caucaso Transeuropa*, August 23, 2023, accessible at, https://www.balcanicaucaso.org/bhs/zone/Bosna-i-Hercegovina/BiH-Djeca-rodena-iz-cina-seksualnog-nasilja-u-ratu-prepoznata-kao-civilne-zrtve-rata-novim-entitetskim-zakonom-226738.

35 Facebook, YIHR Serbia, http://www.yihr.rs/, "Razgovor sa Ajnom Jusić: Era međuljudskog dijaloga," Live Recording, March 16, 2021, 8 am, accessed on October 27, 2022. https://fb.watch/gqA86XTkEa/.

36 These are selections from the live recording that I have made myself and translated them. Ajna's entire talk is 1hour and 32 minutes long.

37 See for example, Sharlene Nagy Hesse-Biber, *Handbook of Feminist Research: Theory and Practice*, 2nd ed. (Sage, 2012).

38 D. Jean Clandinin and Jerry Rosiek. *Handbook of Narrative Inquiry: Mapping a Methodology* (Thousand Oaks, CA: SAGE Publications, Inc., 2007). Sage Research Methods, April 18, 2023. doi: 10.4135/9781452226552.

39 Jens Brockmeier, "From Memory as Archive to Remembering as Conversation," in ed. Brady Wagoner, *Handbook of Culture and Memory* (Oxford University Press, 2018), 41–64, 60–61.

Chapter 7

What Does It Mean to Be a Child Born Because of War?

What follows are excerpts from the narratives of three children of war, two women (S.W. and L.) and one man (A.), who shared their stories with me in 2017, when they were all in their late twenties. One grew up with her birth mother in Bosnia, while two were adopted: one in the city of his birth (A.), and the other (L.), by a family abroad.[1]

Growing up not knowing

S.W.: *My identification documents have been a problem because there are fields to be filled in and one of those fields asks for the father's name, and that is the problem. In my student card, since 2010, I am only required to enter the name of one parent, and this is fine. Problems arise when the father's name is required and in those cases I either write my mother's name or put a dash. I mostly just put a dash. People cannot accept the fact I write the name of my mother instead of my father's name. I had an issue in high school, with one of the professors in my first year of high school who asked me the name of my father. At that moment I was deeply embarrassed that I did not know. Everyone was laughing at me, asking how it was possible for me to not know, but I did not. I do not blame them as they were only children. That is how I realized that something was not right, since before this it was my mother who would complete the paperwork required for me to enroll in school. Even when you look at my birth certificate it is just a dash that stands in place of the father's name. I did not take my stepfather's last name. If I do, I must stop what I am doing now, and it is also legally connected to my mother's pension somehow, I am not exactly sure how, but she receives her pension based on having me as a dependent. If I take my stepfather's last name it all changes, we lose it all.*

My issues were connected to the issues that my mother had to deal with. Disability pension reviews happen every three to five years. For each review she needs a new assessment from a psychiatrist or a psychologist… Every review triggers our trauma. That is how our government operates. My personal problems are connected to not being able to apply for scholarships

DOI: 10.4324/9781003186168-10

since I do not fit into any category for which they are offered. I apply as a child with only one parent, which I am, with a father "unknown." I try to explain about what my mother went through, but people do not understand. The forms contain only one category for a child with only one parent, which is a child of a "Shahid," someone who was killed in the war while fighting (meaning one parent died in the fight, it can be mother too). People do not understand my situation and it is very rare that a scholarship is given for my category. I also must search specifically for those opportunities that I can apply for based on my social status and low income. There was only one institution that offered scholarships under my category, which is BBI or Bosna Bank International, an Arabic bank, and they are the only one who have offered this option for a scholarship in my category. Their categories contain: child of Shahid, child of demobilized fighter, and child of civil victim of war. I personally do not use term "victim," I prefer to say "survivor." You are obliged by law to write "civilian victim of war" and that is the official category they are registered under.

***

L: *I don't know anything about my biological father. I don't think I will ever know anything, and I don't think I care, honestly. I don't think about it much. But when I do think about it, the thought that we might be living on the same planet completely infuriates me. The fact that we are breathing the same air. I thought about it so many times, wondering whether my birth mother knew who it was. I highly doubt that she does, but even if she did, I am not sure that any justice can be had. It seems that there is no punishment for the perpetrators. He may have moved on and obviously my birth mom has not. It is awful and so frustrating to think that the perpetrators may be living an easy life and are on Facebook.*

Searching for pieces of the origin story

S. W.: *The main trigger for my knowledge about my origins was a middle school teacher who asked me about my father's name. I was struck by how unbelievable it is that I did not know the answer. I knew that my stepfather is not my biological father. That question suddenly stopped me dead in my tracks. I think that if this question was not posed to me at that time, I might have gone in a different direction altogether. I do not know when my mother would have chosen to tell me. If I met this teacher now, I would thank him for asking me that question. Now I would be able to answer the question because I subsequently found out who my father is. This is how detailed my quest has been. I worked with mother on that. I know a lot of information about my father and that is very lucky. Mother knows the name of the family, and the first and last name of my biological father. Thousands of women do not have that information...*

What Does It Mean to Be a Child Born Because of War? 115

That search was long and difficult. I did find out details from my mother, but before we had a conversation about this, I had searched through some of her paperwork and found her medical test results. I knew that she went to the psychologist regularly, and I just put two and two together but decided to stay quiet. At the time, I had no idea how to deal with it all. I was supposed to be kicked out of school…I did not even attend school as I should have since my identification papers were always a problem, which for me always represented the main issue. I started counselling. I even lived with a foster family for a period.

It was very difficult for my mother and me. My stepfather knew about my origin, but my mother was not ready to tell me. She never lied to me. She would always just say that there will come a time when we speak about that. She delayed telling me because she was waiting for me to grow up a little, to be able to handle it better. I happen to know several women who now have a real need to tell their children about their origins, but they have no way to start the conversation…These experiences are very diverse. I am personally convinced that I know only about 40 percent of all that there is to know…It is all very diverse, the women and their children, and their lives in general. The tricky thing was that I grew up and learned the truth much sooner than mother expected. Also, I had to know; at 14 I felt the need to know, so I had to find out on my own.

***

A.: *I found out that I was adopted and about my background when I was seven or eight years old, while playing soccer in the backyard. I got into an argument with a friend since I claimed I was the one who scored a goal. We argued about who gave more goals and such childish stuff. In the skirmish I pushed him to the side, but he was older than me and I guess because he resented that I managed to push him in front of everyone, he blurted out that I was adopted and that I was found in a dumpster. I went home in tears. I told my father what happened—my adopted father, even though in my eyes he is my real parent, and that will never change. My adoptive father then told me who my real father is, but he did not give any names, including the name of my biological mother. He just said she lives somewhere in United States and that my biological father is also somewhere abroad. At this time my adoptive parents hid the truth from me. They did tell me they were not my biological parents, but that they love me and see me as their own child. I did not make much of it back then until I was in fourth grade in elementary school, when again while playing I found out some parts of the remaining truth from another boy, Anel. Anel told me that there were conversations about me in his household, and that those conversations involved knowledge of my biological mother's identity. Apparently, my biological father is from the same town as well, and the two of them worked for the same company. That is how I found out about that.*

116 Unforgetting and the Politics of Representation

Then I came home and told this to my father and mother, and then they told me the names of my biological parents. I also found out that after leaving Bosnia my biological mother got married, and that she has two sons who are living with her in the USA. At that time, I found this information very hurtful since she left me and had other children. It appeared to my child's mind that she clearly does not love me, and at the time I hated her. I also felt anger toward the people who adopted me. These feelings have changed completely since then, but at that time, this was how I felt about it all. It mattered to me very much. I kept wondering about where they are, and whether they would accept me. But I had to reconcile with all of that and simply stay with my adopted family.

***

L.: I did not know anything about my adoption until I was seven. We were in IT class and for some reason we had to enter the day and time of birth into a software platform. I asked my mother about this, and because she was unable to provide this answer, she told me that I was adopted. She also told me the reason why I was adopted and about the war in Bosnia.

I was 16 when my parents told me what my birth mom's name was. I googled it and I found a journal article that was published around that time. I did not tell my parents about what I found, but from this article, I knew exactly what happened. That year my parents did tell me everything. They gave me my whole file, along with court documents, when I was 18. For my birthday they bought me and my boyfriend at the time tickets to go to Sarajevo. They told me that they had met my birth mother and that it took several years to finalize the adoption formally. So, it felt like my I am starting my life again at the age of 18, finding out about myself, learning about the war in Bosnia… even though I knew I was adopted, this part of it was new. Since then, I have not stopped learning about it. If my parents had told me any sooner, I would have probably been very self destructive and would have found it very difficult. It still made me feel very strange, because rape is the worst thing that can happen and then you are told that your life is the product of that, and you are also told about how much your parents loved you—it felt very strange, you know?

I am now nearly 25 and it took me all this time to accept this about myself, as something that just is. A few years ago, I went to a summit on sexual violence, and spoke about my origins. This is when the story came out in public. I was still not sure what it meant, either to me, or to other people. I remember people approaching me after that, people who emigrated or fled from Bosnia, or who survived the war thanking me for speaking about it. This felt very good, as I still have friends here in the UK who don't know where Bosnia is on the map.

The burden of knowing

S. W.: After I found out who I am and how I arrived in this world I had such a difficult period. When I found out I became very closed off and withdrew into my own world. I was torn thinking that my mother did not love me. I distanced myself from her and could not speak to her about that. I went to counselling. A lot happened before my mother, and I finally sat down to talk. I only see now how important all that work was for me, and how meaningful. I got in touch with women who survived all of that and we worked together a lot, we took many workshops together, I attended many of their meetings. It took years for me to accept this situation, and my origins. This was a challenge for me, something that I must fight for. I know that it can be very difficult for my mother because she does love me. I needed a lot of time to understand that my mother loves me and that I am her all and that she is my all. I always found it easy to connect and communicate with women who survived violence and it was easy to talk openly about it with them. We are in touch even today and some of them still call me when they need someone to talk to.

My mother and I started visiting the psychologist together and started working on all that together. We were going through it together even though we never really talked about it directly at the time. Then we decided to share the burden, as it were. I wanted my stepfather to become part of this process and he joined the counselling. This was helpful as gradually we were able to speak to one another more openly. Mother and I talk about all of it now over coffee…

***

In my case my birth mother, I think, really hated me. I was able to find some information about her attending art therapy school, where she had said that I was the same as man that raped her and she did not want me. She could not even look at me, she said on video that was made via this art school. In terms of how this information impacts me, it's difficult to say, it's strange. On some level I feel like it is what it is. On another, this is who I am, but this knowledge cannot define who I am. You cannot go through life failing or not doing things because you were born from a situation like this, or because you are adopted. When you look around and get to know people, there are stories that are worse than this one. This background cannot be an excuse for not doing well. Do not get me wrong, I do feel self-conscious because there are things about myself that I don't know, and people ask questions. Although I have had a very normal upbringing in the UK, my knowledge of my origins will continue to impact my life going forward.

118　Unforgetting and the Politics of Representation

When I found out about my origins, it was difficult. Although some of it was probably due to being a teenager. It is interesting though, to think about nature and nurture. I have the same body language as my [adoptive] mom, like that is why we annoy each other [laughter]. It is like we are the same people, and that is because I have been raised by her from such a young age. They experienced a lot of uncertainty until the adoption was finalized. They were not sure if they are going to be allowed to keep me. They fought to keep me. Obviously, I do not have kids, so I genuinely do not know what it feels like, all the emotions and parenting and stuff like that. But I do feel lucky to have my parents. They have said to me that the one thing they regret is that I didn't have the opportunity to learn Bosnian growing up. Maybe one day I will learn it.

I also know that my birth mom does not have the allowance of a civil victim of war and did not know it existed because you just do not talk about it. To receive it she must go in front of a panel and describe to a set of strangers how and when she was raped, trying to justify it so to be seen as eligible for this allowance, and to open herself up to the possibility that she will be told she is not eligible. What is it that makes you eligible? Things like that are so insensitive. And really, where do you send the pain? Because you sit there and you get upset and then you get angry, and then what? The perpetrators are still walking around free, with new families, new kids, new wives, new houses. The hardest thing for me is to think about the difficult life that my birth mom has had. It is she, and women like her, who have had a difficult life, not me. When I talk to the press, I am always asked how I feel about my background, whether life has been difficult for me. And I always have to say, no, not really. I cannot be selfish, especially when compared to what other members of the Association [Forgotten Children of War] had to go through. I didn't have to deal with a system that does not really care. I have had two parents who absolutely love me and support every choice I made, whether it was the right or wrong one, who stood by me no matter what.

***

A.:　　*I know that my mother suffered a great deal. Now, if she was raped or not, she knows that best, she, and my biological father. She says she was raped. When I met him, he said he did not even know her. Later he admitted to the judge that he did it. Then he said they were in a relationship before the war, that they worked in the same company, and that during the war each went to their own separate side…He admitted to raping her and not allowing her to abort even though she did not want to raise a child, so she rejected me in the end... There are many stories, and I still don't know the truth. I think that she was raped. They would not go to court if this was not the case. I don't really know. However, there were a lot of witnesses planted from Radmilo's side, Muslims. They were offered 5,000 convertible marks [KM, Bosnian currency], which in today's standard would be as much as having 50,000 KM in your pocket. They were bribed and that is why Radmilo is a free man today even though he admitted in court that he did rape her and that he will admit me as his son and that he will help me financially. He never did any of those things. I saw the miserable conditions he lives in... His biggest punishment is that his wife, professor of the Serbian language, left him, his daughter left him too, he is alone. Then I saw what kind of person he is, that he is nothing as a person, and I did not want to comment any longer. Even though I could see that we look alike. It was as if I saw myself 23 years ahead. I took a lot of his genes physiologically, but I hope not psychologically.*

His brother, Marko Vuković was the director of Foča Hospital, a surgeon, famous as a Partisan during WWII. Everyone in their family were Partisans. Partisans and Chetniks could not stand each other. I do not know why Radmilo took to that other side, to fight against the people. Because Partisans were Croats, Serbs and Muslims and Slovenes and Macedonians, all fought against Germans. I am saying, I still don't know the whole truth: maybe he did not rape her, maybe they were dating. But I do think it was rape since there were witnesses who said that he did rape her. What struck me also is that my mother's sister says she was also raped but it was never proved. There are a thousand games being played there and no one tells the truth. But as I said, I did fulfill my goal, met my mother, met my father. Whether it was on the big screen or not is less important. I never searched for media attention for its own sake. I wish that the attention I received over the years was because of being good at sports, or for being a great artist, rather than on account of my life story, since these are sensitive topics and when we talk about them, we should talk about them respectfully, and not with stupidity: this one was raped, this one was not. Those are things that need a long time to be accepted and understood. Once they are said, there is no going back, as the saying goes.

I always stood up for myself

S. W.: My mother says I was always very determined and interested in a cause. I did argue a lot and wanted to have it my own way. I started to engage in activism when I was starting to search for my own identity. I am involved in feminist activism because I know that there are so many other women,

women like my mother, who experienced sexual violence. I am a feminist but do not minimize anything in terms of gender and suffering. Three years ago, I started creating my own database of men who experienced sexual violence during the war. There is not much public dialogue about men who are survivors.

***

I am aware that there are many problems for women survivors of sexual violence there, that some have not been treated for trauma, that the children are not being acknowledged. I went back to Bosnia, and what struck me is that people who did awful things during the war are now living next door to survivors. How is a child of war supposed to receive any support in those circumstances? It is very difficult. This is why I do feel lucky to be where I am, in a different country. But I feel a very strong connection to Bosnia—it is a very big part of my life. In recent months, I felt that I want to do more from here, from where I am.

I feel that something must change, Bosnia cannot keep on going on like this. There should be more open conversation about the war. I am not saying that everyone should talk about the war all the time, but some things have not even been acknowledged. There is still some tension among the different ethnicities. And you know, how are you supposed to move forward if you do not even acknowledge what happened in the past? There is now a hotel that is made just outside Sarajevo out of a building where rapes and other atrocities took place during the war.[2] This is very disrespectful.

I am campaigning with a charity—I want to raise awareness about the women who have experienced sexual violence and about the children of war. It has been 25 years since I was born, and this is a positive story. There is six (6) of us, all from different countries, Uganda, Sierra Leone, Bosnia, Syria. I haven't told them yet about traveling to meet my birth mom. I want it to be done in the right way.

Even though I have had a very normal life I feel a strong connection to Bosnia, and I want to know about what is going on and how people are feeling. I cannot just ignore what happened. I choose not to ignore it, although it would be easy to do. When I go to Bosnia it feels like a second home, and I feel very comfortable there. I love the culture and atmosphere in Sarajevo in particular.

***

A.:   *You see, as a child, I was always ready to enter a fight, and I always stood up for myself. I don't know how and why, but conversations often ended in a fight. But I never fought with younger kids, only with older ones, and I always won those fights. I was the winner at the end and even though I got*

What Does It Mean to Be a Child Born Because of War? 121

badly bruised I still ended up a winner. That is how I managed to deal with some things. I saw how rotten people are, that they want to harm others on purpose and that taught me how to deal with my life story. Later I learned more constructive ways of dealing with unpleasant characters, but while I was attending high school it was quite difficult. When I was about 18, I went out with my friends to a club one night, and there was a guy that lived near our house and knew my story. He was intoxicated and approached me. He addressed me as Pera [common Serbian first name], which was a provocation, and I did not want to talk to him any longer. I was fed up and punched him. After that, I have had no problems since everybody knew that I was nice, but that I can erupt at times.

When I was a child, I had a dark complexion, and first I was very plump and then I went very thin—the same has been for them, too. I took on a lot of mother's genes. And when it comes to her husband I would honestly like... I do not think I am afraid of anyone but God and that is how it is going to stay for good. People tell me not to dare to say things like that publicly—well I do dare, and I want to tell them. That is why I say that my idol is Ivan Pernar[3] [laughter] because he goes against the system and follows the truth while everyone else is silent.

If people are listening, if they respond in a positive manner, I will speak out. I will continue to give interviews because I want to achieve justice, so that things come out in the open. I am also sorry for the mothers who lost their children. I am sorry for the children who lost their parents, who grew up in orphanages and in the streets. That some of those children could have been good soccer players, politicians, economists, psychologists, but that they may have been limited by their circumstances, by having grown up in orphanages. What hurts me the most is that we have been killing one another amongst ourselves, our own people. Only the war profiteers benefited from the war, and from the current circumstance.

***

L.: *In the future I do see myself living in Bosnia. I would like to live there, or at least keep coming back to it. The work of raising awareness for women survivors of war rape will not cease. When I told my dad about how much work there is to be done in terms of activism, he said "well, you better make a start." The possibility of contributing in this regard is exciting, but it will be so frustrating when I am still saying the same stuff in five years time and nobody is doing anything about it. But I suppose that is politics, is it not?*

A nice childhood

S.W.: *When I think back, I had a nice childhood. My mother tells me I always asked a lot of questions, about why some women have a man with them and why we do not have a man with us. I do not remember I asked that, but I do remember that I went with mother for her to attend some meetings and they took pictures of me which I did not like... I did not want my pictures to be taken. When it comes to Medica, I never questioned anything about it, I was born there, and those women were like mothers to me so I could not wait for us to go there. While I was a child it never occurred to me to question our presence there. There were other children there and I used to play with them.*

But then mother met my stepfather when I was seven. When I was in second grade in elementary school my mother got married and that was okay. My stepfather and I connected right away. He used to bring me diggers and little cars to play with. I always liked cars, I never really liked dolls. We got along well right from the start. My mother was very choosy, and he is the only boyfriend she ever introduced to me. I was so lucky, being so young, to have him around during my elementary school education, to help me with homework, to be my father, to bring me up. This was a proper upbringing for me since the second grade. I found a real father figure in him. But I never call him 'dad'; I don't know why. He has cute nicknames though. It is part of my luck in life that he is such a good man and that I met him so early in my life. And I think I learnt what courage means from him, as well as some other psychological traits, as I would from a father. Other things I picked up from my mother, so it all balanced from both sides. I played soccer with him and played with barbie dolls after we came home. We went everywhere together as a family.

Even though I am a child born of war, I am really one of the luckiest. And this is a big difference, when you hear me speaking and if you heard some of my friends. I grew up in Medica, surrounded by all the help that the center had to offer. When I found out about my origins, I was lucky to be in and near Medica and to have had help every time when I felt bad and needed help. Only a small number of people had access to those services, and I did. I am a favorite in Medica too since I was the first child born there. I am also the first child of war to register in the Women Victims of War association, too. It is the silver lining in my circumstances to be accepted within my mother's family.

Also, I feel accepted by my stepfather's family. When grandmother (my stepfather's mother) says she will give 10 KM to each child after her pension arrives, I also get those 10 KM. I mean there is no difference between me and her other grandchildren. It is a very nice family. They are a little on the quiet side, and his brothers are quite religious, so perhaps this makes sense. When it comes to mother's side of family, I was always the favorite.

My mother is also very lucky because she married a man who knew about what happened to her during the war, who understand it, and who accepted it. He accepted me, too, and I looked at him like he is my own

What Does It Mean to Be a Child Born Because of War? 123

father. He did turn out to be a perfect dad. Many women with similar experience started having problems the moment they revealed what happened to them to their partners. I used to have at least five moms when I was a child. Even though I came to this world the way I did, everything was focused on me, and even now, I do receive a lot of attention.

My mother means everything to me. She was always like a lioness fighting on my behalf, and in my defense whenever people would ask about me and my background. She used to tell me that if she hated me, she would never fight for me as she did, and that she would not have stuck with me through so many challenges that we tackled together. She was always there for me. I had problems in elementary school. In the school I transferred to after mother got married everyone called me "the brat." That was my nickname at school, and I took it to be part of my identity, but my mother would come to school and fight with the world, and never let me feel like I am different and that I do not belong. She wanted people to understand that I was also a child like all other children and that I am worth it just like everyone else, and that she is also worth it even though I will not be able to answer questions about why she has a child and is not married. Everything that happened to me in school I used to tell her right away. She used to sense some of the things I was going through at school even when I didn't say anything. And she always protected me. Medica protected me too.

***

A.: *My adoptive family has always treated me the same as they do their biological children. They have two daughters. They also have grandchildren. I never felt neglected, and they gave me all the love they gave to their own children and grandchildren. Not just them, but my sisters as well. I was closer to my younger sister since she was born a year after they adopted me; we are close in age; we grew up together. The older one got married and moved out. She has two grown children now. The hardest things I had to deal with—discovering about my origins, but also other things, first love, first poems—somehow, I got through it all with her beside me. She was my shoulder to cry on, she was the one I celebrated successes with. I will never forget any of that. She looked on me as a younger brother and not as someone who is adopted, so she is close to my heart even though I have a very close relationship with my older sister as well. My younger sister and I are close also because we both encountered problems along the way. I always saw it as my task to try to help her deal with her problems, the way she helped me with mine. When she was going through a hard time, I suffered together with her as I understood things she went through in life. And I talked to her more.*

124 Unforgetting and the Politics of Representation

My older sister taught in the elementary school I attended, so she was familiar with everything, and she was there when I found out I was adopted. She also knew about my fights, about my weak grades, and about my good grades. That meant my parents got to know about what happened in school very quickly too, via telephone, from her. At the time, through my child's eyes, her approach to this made me feel that she is betraying me, but I think she had my best interest at heart. My younger sister always had my back when I was involved in fights, she protected me in front of our father, and kept my secrets.

What helped me accept and understand the knowledge about my origins is the love I was given by my adopted family while growing up, the kind of love that made me forget that I was adopted. They indulged me a lot—seaside holidays, driving license, getting motorcycle, that is why I never felt it. I felt it more when my other sister got married and it was difficult to me to be growing up with both my parents watching closely over me, since they are rather old fashioned and care about reputation. They are careful not to insult anyone, not to incite anyone to insult them, since they are very honest people, they really are. They were always my support, and they will always be. They stood by me for so many years and there is no chance for me to turn my back on them now. Thank God I never had to see a social worker, a psychologist, neuropsychiatrist… They have a healthy family, so I was able to accept and understand some things in a healthy way. My childhood was nice, my wishes were attended to. Although the news about the adoption was difficult for me, I still managed. And my relationship with my adoptive mother is the same as if she were the one who gave birth to me, she is my mother, that has been her attitude toward me and that is how I see her. She never left me out if she went to buy something for my sisters, there was always equal love. It was the same with my father. My adopted mother went through a lot. She argued with people and with neighbors for everything to come out into the open, so that there are no secrets about me. She is a hero for me. She and father. Really, they are heroes.

***

L.: *I have been with my adoptive parents since birth, since I was nine days old. So, our connection is very close. During the war, my mom was a camerawoman, my dad was a journalist. They filmed together during the Bosnian war, and this is how they found me. I was born on Christmas Day 1992, and they were filming a piece about a baby being born on Christmas Day in the war. The clip would have been about 30 seconds long, but this is how they came to meet me and my birth mom at the time. She made it very clear that at the time she did not want to have anything to do with me. Whether that was her choice entirely or it was also her family's choice, I don't really know. But I am very grateful to her for letting them adopt me because through that, she gave me everything. My childhood was amazing. I was an only child until the age of seven, when my parents adopted my brother and sister who are twins. I had a great childhood.*

Of nationality and identity

S.W.: I happen to know the identity of my father. I do know a lot, as I searched for a lot of details, but I never had need to, you know…I can't say that I ever wanted revenge, but I did have moments when I really hated him… I spent a lot of time trying to heal from this emotion, to realize that I cannot continue to feel hatred, that I cannot lay down in the evening full of hatred and wake up in the morning with the same feeling inside me. My mother always told me I should not hate and that if you hate, it is the same as if you hated yourself. That makes me realize only now the type of upbringing she gave me from the start. She never allowed me to hate based on differences between people. I am grateful for my mother's dedication to raise me with those values. I always had friends who are not Muslim; some were Croatian, some were Serbian, and some were Roma. I was always open-minded about this. My mother inculcated that in me. She never limited me to socializing with only one group, and we do have a lot of nationalistic types who are full of hatred around here. Maybe not in Sarajevo, in the city, but if you go to smaller towns, you will understand what I am talking about, you will see how it really is. But she never told me that this is a problem for us, she never forbade me to socialize with someone because his name is Saša [typical Serbian name].

My best friend, Jovana, is Serbian and she and I are all to each other. She is from Zvornik. I always mention her because we became friends in university, we became close through mutual feminist understanding; I have my story and she has hers, her father was killed during the war. Each one of us could have a cause for hatred but we do not feel hatred. Upbringing is important, regardless of ethnicity. That is my attitude. For me, ethnicity is not relevant. For example, women from Republika Srpska received their legal status as civil victims of war around 2000, but they are still not receiving a pension. We are still waiting to see what will happen with that. I cannot say that nothing happened to these women in Republika Srpska. I cannot say that my mother suffered more just because she is Muslim compared to some woman who is not Muslim. I cannot say it is harder for me than for my friend in Banja Luka—we were born in the same way, on the same day, on two different sides. It is being said that we have different blood. There is no difference between him and me and I cannot say that it is harder for me. I still think that a sense of ethnic difference is instilled in children, I do not know. I was never taught like that. But I do not judge parents who raise their children like that. I cannot do that. My mother had psychological support and help from the start and that is important.

I cannot be judgmental toward a woman who has three children and her husband died in war because of his ethnicity. That is her revolt, she judges everyone, she was left alone with three children. I take that as an example. It all depends on the people who have been affected, especially older people who survived the war. I cannot talk about how it was in Sarajevo that year during the siege. I do not know that. I myself was not there to live through it. I see movies, I read accounts about this. I trust the accounts more than movies.

Here in Sarajevo, we are multiethnic and multinational, and we really are. We have Bosniaks, Croats, Serbs, Jews, Roma. We are all here in the same city, but still, we have Sarajevo and then we have East Sarajevo. East Sarajevo is Serbian Sarajevo, and this proves that all is not well. Even still, you could be walking along, and one moment you are in the Federation and the next you step into Republika Srpska. I have a friend who lives in Dobrinja, and there is this big line that divides the territory right next to the apartment building where she lives, and we have nothing else to talk about. People do not pay attention to that, but it troubles me. When I am asked about it, I always say that we cannot have a real conversation if there is a border running between her kitchen and living room. This is even more pronounced when you go to another town where there are 2 percent of Serbs and 98 percent of Muslims.

When I was on my way back from Srebrenica, coming back from the annual event commemorating the massacre against Bosniak men and boys, our bus was stoned. I was praying for us to pass safely and quickly. We were going through Vlasenica which is small Serbian town that we must pass through to get to Srebrenica. We were sitting on the bus and there were stones raining all over the bus. I am not sure how we will overcome this. Right now, there is a lot of political manipulation. I attend political rallies, especially before elections, and whenever I hear something stupid, I write it down. We shouldn't be discussing issues that concerns us all, like unemployment, only before the elections. The topic of any political rally should not be that we are such "great" Muslims...I have attended these rallies, especially when the government of Bakir Izetbegovic offers 10 KM to attend them. I go because I am interested in observing how it all works. That is the only way we can understand what to do. Since as soon as we come to elections, they start talking about how we are "great" Bosniaks and Muslims. Indeed, there were more Bosniaks who suffered in great numbers, but we cannot always make this the basis of all political campaigns. We cannot continue to speak of ourselves as if we are the only victims. We were not the only ones. Similarly, when you go to Republika Srpska to listen to Dodik, you realize that he is doing the same thing speaking to Serbs. Recently on the news he announced that Srebrenica will be captured again, and there was an argument whether the mayor of Srebrenica should be a Bosniak or someone from Republika Srpska.

These are political and legal manipulations. And there is social psychology that explains it all. People just live in hope, and each day they hope something will change, but they do not change their voting choices. Things do not change. Even if I were to run as a candidate, things would not change. Every year there is someone new on a political scene and each year the same old people win. A vote costs 50 KM in this country. Some time ago my grandmother received a package that was sent to her by the local SDA [Stranka Demokratske Akcije, "Party of Democratic Action"] candidate as "help for pensioners." The package was full of flour, coffee, sugar. I do not blame those who give up. I understand that. I understand that we do not have same foundation and the same perspective. I understand why a friend of mine will sit all day in a coffee shop, and why I will spend that day making rounds and arguing. Often people ask why there are not more activists, but we are here. We are here but still our numbers are small compared to those who are not motivated to fight for change.

It all begins in the same way, that is how war started. There is less than a month since Dodik threatened that they will secede. People are afraid. We read about how guns are on the ready. My grandmother says she will vote for SDA if that means there will be no shooting. People will do anything just to prevent another war. I think about this a lot, and it is such a mess. It is possible to work with young people, but institutional divisions are what they are. You can work a lot with young people here in Sarajevo but what can you do with a young village girl who has grown up in an exclusively Muslim community, where there is only one side represented and presented? They are not used to anything different.

***

A.:   *I have never been a nationalist. All people are the same to me: we share the language, air, food, we drink the same water. I am a Muslim because my adopted family is Muslim. If my adopted family was Croatian, I might be a Catholic, maybe Orthodox, or Buddhist, it all depends on who adopted me. However, I adjusted to this environment because my Muslim family is here, and I accepted their beliefs the same as Milorad Dodik accepted his family's Orthodox faith. We are not guilty for the religion that we were raised in. But I never cared if someone was a Muslim, or Serb, Croat, Albanian, I always try to have good relations with everyone. I do not like to talk about the war in general because it reminds me of my origins, which made my life quite complicated. Thank God, everything ended well.*

   My view is that everyone who was born in Bosnia is Bosnian. So be it Serbian, Muslim, or Catholic Bosnian he is still just a Bosnian, however you look at it. I would love for it to be this way, but according to current politics this is not possible. Politicians exploit the nationality card. If you are Orthodox you cannot work in certain companies, and this circumstance

128   Unforgetting and the Politics of Representation

is something that just worsens the situation in Bosnia and Herzegovina. This is totally idiotic. If current politics were not like that, life here would be much nicer. This was supposed to be discussed right away after the war, not after two decades, and in the context of deep divisions between people. In my opinion, only people who are very primitive can uphold nationalist politics. Maybe if my family was nationalistic, I would be too. Nationalist views cannot be created out of nowhere and nothing. They must have roots. First there must be a root, then a tree and then the fruit; there cannot be fruit right away.

All of us would be much better if Tito's era returned...My father liked Tito. He has always been communist. And he always says that before there was no war, and it was as Tito said it had to be. Before, if you swore at Tito, you would go to prison. Today you can swear at the late Alija [Izetbegović], and Bakir [his son], and politics in general, and you can start a fight in the street and police does not come near you. What's the use in swearing and such freedom of speech? I wish those old times were back since there was order then. Yugoslavia was one country with many different people in it, and still it managed to go without war. When Tito was in charge the different peoples did not fight, argue, wage wars against each other, slaughter each other. At the time, the state fought against Chetniks. Today it is the opposite of all that. Today we are fighting against our own country. That is why I would like Tito's era to come back. There was employment for everyone. Youth worked, did not waste time, there were not so many gambling spots. We have accepted a Western system, like each person is going to be "somebody," but we end up as nobodies. I read a lot of books about Tito, so I feel free to talk about that. I do not talk about what I do not know.

Here in Goražde, there are not many who would like to talk about Tito's Yugoslavia. But there are many youth who refer to the past as a joke, and do not take it seriously. It is said that youth should lead the world, but now only old politicians run politics in Bosnia and Herzegovina. Not 20, 23-year-olds. The politicians are people who profited during the war and who were planted by the SDA party to rule Bosnia and Herzegovina and that is the reason for things being as they are. Those are bribed diplomats. There is a story about the University of Tuzla, that you can get your diploma tomorrow, with express delivery if you pay for it enough. Everything is in vain since our state is like that.

I have many good friends who are Serbs. There is Sinisa, Mihajlo, Nemanja, Vojislav. There are plenty of them. They do not really want to talk about it all. Or if we talk, then we talk openly: you are Serb and that is it, I am Muslim, that is it. They don't seem to care much about Dodik. Maybe this is because they live here in this town with us and are used to us... I have a friend named Bojan, all the way since elementary school we used to praise Allah and God together. When he comes over, he praises

Allah, maybe because he grew up like that with me and learned all of those phrases and it stayed with him.

It doesn't help that the schools are segregated. I have a few Orthodox neighbors who were not allowed to go to school during the war here in Goražde where the majority population is Muslim, so they had to be sent to Kopače, Višegrad. However, today this is not as prevalent in Goražde. There are more Serbs over here now, and their children go to school here and there are no issues about that nor do they have problems at school. For example, my wife went to university in Foča where there are 90 percent Serbs and 10 percent Muslims in the surrounding villages. At the beginning there were some provocations, but later people got used to it. In the northeast it is the worst—there they are nationalists. The biggest number of war profiteers and war criminals live in Foča, Višegrad, Čajniče. Goražde is the only town in Bosnia where you must go through Republika Srpska to enter the Federation.

In Goražde schools are not segregated any longer. But I read that there was a plan in Jajce to build a multiethnic school and that everyone will be going to school together. Good for them. It would be good if there were more schools like that. Absence of justice kills a person. I do not think people will put up with all of this much longer. There will be no peace until the ruling elite keeps Bosnia divided into three separate parts. Bosnia was always inhabited by Croats and Serbs and Muslims, that will never change. How are we going to be taken seriously by the EU if we cannot agree among ourselves?

***

L.: *In terms of national and ethnic identity, I hope to get a Bosnian passport. I want one because it is a part of who I am, and it is strangely important to me. Bosnia is my second home. I don't know whether it's possible to declare oneself British Bosnian. I am not sure how to fit the two. So, I am British, I was born in Bosnia, but I don't have a Bosnian passport yet. I feel like the passport gives me and would give me the nationality.*

I want to change something

L.: *We do share a bond, us, children born of war. This bond was present even when we met for the first time within the Association. We just sat and looked at each other. There were 15 of us. I used to retell that story to my mother for days. We are all different, but we are also the same in a way, with the kind of lives we have been leading. There were some who came from the Federation, some from Republika Srpska. There are those who would not come, who are not ready for that. I thought it would be sad when 15 of us meet for the first time in the same room, but we even managed to laugh, to exchange experiences about problems we face in our municipalities, and we felt understood by each other. When I spoke with Alen [Muhić] for the first time, he told me he understood me, and I knew he did.*

You can do a lot if you are connected to people.

At this point I feel like I don't really have to come to terms with anything any longer. It is what it is. I enjoyed meeting the members of the Association. It was liberating to be able to make jokes and laugh about our origins and the situations this creates. But these are jokes that we can make between us only. If anyone else tried to joke about it, they would be crossing the line. But we laugh about it, like it is just normal, you know. Meeting them was important because I have never met anyone else with my background before. There is no one else like that in my group of friends. But to have someone with the same background, and to be able to say to them how wrong everything is, how I want to change something, is very meaningful. Though the Association I learned about the stories of other women survivors and understood how difficult it has been for them.

I would love to tell other children of war that it is all going to be okay, but then I think back to that bus journey and those towns that some of those kids are living in, and for them, I do not know. I wish we could form a community or some place on the internet, where everyone can just come. I believe there are so many of us out there, and some do not even know where they came from or about their origins. There is very little support out there, and it would be good for everyone to know that they are not alone. Because even I felt a little alone before I met Ajna [Jusić]. It is easy to feel that you are the only person in the world with that kind of story. And obviously each story is not going to be the same, but it is the fact that there are other people out there that you can talk to and have a great night with, have a drink and a chat with, and that it doesn't feel strange to talk about it or not talk about it. Just to have a community to socialize with and feel safe. I know that there are associations that try to create that community, but their reach is not broad enough. And sometimes there is a big story about that in the news, but usually it disappears from the spotlight. How many such children are out there? People want to move on, people want to forget about that as a form of coping, but it is also a form of denial.

But having such a community is important and almost cathartic for me. Also, my hoping to help women survivors in Bosnia will in turn help me. You discover things about yourself and others by helping, and in turn you are being helped, and that is very therapeutic. Sometimes I do know there are things that I just cannot even deal with, as there are many aspects of their experience that are so difficult to comprehend.

I remember my first interview for War Child was with the Evening Standard. It was the most surreal experience. I had just finished training in the Foreign Office because I was a youth delegate, and part of the training was just about how to be sensitive to other people's feelings. I remember how strange it was to be coming home on the tube after the interview was published, and a close-up of my face was all over the newspaper pages. So, I am standing there on the tube looking through the glass watching people read my story. And was so conscious of the fact that if any of those people simply looked up, they would have recognized me. And that was my first interview when it all began. And I was and still am cautious with the media as I want to make sure that my family is OK, that my birth mom is OK. Sometimes I think that publicity is a good in that it brings awareness for people and maybe encourages others to step forward and tell their story. But sometimes it is overwhelming. It is difficult when your life becomes so talked about and it sometimes makes me feel self-centered, the fact that my story is public knowledge. Sometimes others have a hard time grasping some things, and then it becomes difficult to have a meaningful conversation. And this has happened frequently, even with people close to me. And then there are times when I would like to tell something to someone and be understood and this is simply too outside of their own interest and experience that it becomes impossible to communicate. It is difficult to form a relationship—this is how it feels sometimes. Sometimes I feel extremely old.

Notes

1 All three interlocutors were responding to the same set of questions below, initially developed as part of the collaborative SSRCH funded project, "Children of the Enemy": Narrative Constructions of Identity Following Wartime Rape and Transgenerational Trauma in Post-WWII Germany and Post-Conflict Bosnia" (2016). Agatha Schwartz with the University of Ottawa was principal investigator, with co-investigators, in addition to me, Christabelle Sethna and Mythili Rajiva, both with the University of Ottawa. As with my other interlocutors, some chose to respond to the questions one by one, while others approached it more as a free-flowing conversation, with me occasionally directing the conversation toward one of the questions, often rephrased.

1 Could you say something about yourself? (How old are you, what is your educational background, what is/was your profession (depending on the age)? Are/were you married; do you have any children/grandchildren?).
2 How would you describe your childhood?
3 When and how did you find out the truth about your origins?
4 How did this information impact your life and your definition of who you are?
5 Has this information affected your relationship with your mother/your family/ your children?
6 Did you receive any support from your family, community, or government?
7 What kind of support do you think is important to provide for others in a similar situation?
8 (if the person has a family and children of their own) Does your partner/do your children know that you are a child of war rape? If so, has this affected their feelings about their identity?

132 Unforgetting and the Politics of Representation

  9 How do you think about your national or ethnic identity?
 10 Would you say that you have come to terms with your personal identity? What has helped you in this process?
 11 (only for Bosnian subject): Do you see a future for yourself in Bosnia?
 12 Do you have a message for other children of rape, in your country or elsewhere?
 13 Is there anything else that you would like to share about you as a person, about your mother/family, about your experience in general?

2 The reference here is to Vilina Vlas, a resort in Višegrad that was appropriated by the White Eagles, a Serbian paramilitary group, and used as their headquarters as well as a rape camp. In 1994, A UN Report concluded that at least 200 women and girls were raped and otherwise brutalized in this locale. Some survivor testimonies about what took place in Vilina Vlas are recorded in the 2009 Judgment for the ICTY Trial of Milan Lukić and Srdoje Lukić, In-Trial Chamber III Case No, IT-98-32/1-T, accessible at: https://www.icty.org/en/case/milan_lukic_sredoje_lukic. Many of the women held captive there were either killed, or they took their own lives because of the torture. From *the Final Report of the Commission of Experts Established Pursuant to Security Council Resolution 780 (1992)*, accessible at, https://www.siracusainstitute.org/app/wp-content/uploads/2017/01/Final-report-of-the-Commission-of-Experts-on-former-Yugoslavia-1993-94.pdf). After the war, the tourist authorities of Republika Srpska opened the facility as a spa and a rehabilitation center. This was followed by a petition launched by survivors and activist groups urging Google to "remove Vilina Vlas (as a tourist site)" from its search engine and its map tool. By May 2021, over 28,000 signatures were collected. However, the location remains visible on Google Maps.

3 At the time of the interview, Pernar was an elected member of the Croatian Parliament, and the founder of the Alliance for Change party, which later became Živi Zid ('Human Shield'), a populist party whose platform stood in opposition to the then right- wing Croatian government. Pernar advocated secularism, in contrast to the government's nationalist adherence to the Catholic church and pointed out that Croatia as well as Serbia is guilty of genocide. The party platform included revival of Croatian agriculture thorough reform of the judiciary and public administration; lustration of the corrupt staff; free health care and education. His position on the politics of ethnic hatred included the statement: "…imagine that I walked around Banja Luka and that I offered every Serb who walked by me a knife and told him that he could kill me because I'm a Croat and that no one would punish or judge him … I am certain that 99% of them would not do that, which means that Serbs are not a genocidal people." *Al Jazeera Balkans* (Nov 19, 2016), "Pernar: U Jasenovcu bio genocid, Oluja je etničko čišćenje" (in Croatian), accessible at: https://balkans.aljazeera.net/news/balkan/2016/11/19/pernar-u-jasenovcu-bio-genocid-oluja-je-etnicko-ciscenje.

Part III

As I delve more deeply into the boundless world of war, everything else becomes slightly faded, more ordinary than the ordinary...Now I understand the solitude of the human being who comes back from there. As if from another planet or from another world. This human being has a knowledge that others do not have, that can be obtained only there, close to death.

Svetlana Alexievich, The Unwomanly Face of War

Chapter 8

The Space of Dialogue
Women Who Lived Through Violence

I met with seven women between the ages of 40 and 55 who survived war rape and other forms of brutalization. Six of them are Bosniak, one is Croatian. All of them were very young when the violence took place: three of them were 15 and 16 at the time, with the rapes being their first sexual experience. Only one of them was married at the time; her husband was also captured and taken to a different concentration camp.

Four of them were raped by Serb militias. One of them was raped by members of the Croat army, while another was raped by both Croat and Serb militias. Five of them were raped by multiple men, multiple times, over extended periods of time. One of them was captured and raped likely by members of the Bosnian Army; she and her family live in a village where they as Croats are a minority, and where the majority group is Bosniak. The perpetrators were masked, but she surmises that they would not have had much reason to hide their faces unless they were worried about being easily recognized. She was 13 at the time.

Three of them gave birth to children conceived because of rape. Two of them raised the children; one of them gave her daughter up for adoption upon giving birth but was in the process of reconnecting with her at the time we spoke. She has been bedridden for years, spoke with difficulty, and asked that her therapist be present during the conversation. She is one who presses a gift into my hands after our conversation in her apartment, and tells me, 'ti si naša' [you are one of us]'.

For one of them, the experience unfolded in a context of captivity: the perpetrator claimed he loved her, and kept her captive for two years, which protected her against being raped by others. She was 18 at the time. She is one who invites me to her house, and this is how I met all the other members of the family, her husband, and two younger children. Her son, the one who was born because of her war experience, was at work when I visited. His mother wished that I could have met him. She speaks of him with great pride.

Three of the women had a great deal of experience speaking with journalists and researchers over the years, since they were among those who started

DOI: 10.4324/9781003186168-12

speaking out early after the war. Four of them did not have such experience speaking with others or publicly, and this was the first time they spoke to a researcher. One of them had not spoken about her experience to anyone since testifying in the Hague at the ICTY, an experience she found alienating and dehumanizing. All of them—even those who had experience in sharing their story—indicated that they had spent several days preparing for the meeting psychologically. Some of them had witnessed the brutalization of close members of the family and their murder. For two of them, the burden of these memories and knowledge represented a greater trauma than the one resulting through harm to their own body. Although I offered to show them a pre-published versions of the research that would be created through their stories, they declined. One of them articulated quite clearly that she agreed to speak with me because I assured her that the research I publish would not be translated into Bosnian. I realized that the very act of agreeing to speak with me represented an act of courage and agency, a process of *unforgetting*, every time anew.

I also met with Munira Subašić, president of the "Mothers of Srebrenica Movement" and Žepa Enclaves, and Esma D., the coordinator of SEKA Goražde. The "Mothers of Srebrenica" organization was registered a year after the war ended, in 1996. At the beginning, their aim was to find out the truth about children who were imprisoned, taken away, and missing from when Srebrenica fell.[1] After a few years of searching, it was discovered that they were all dead. This non-governmental organization then began the work of exhumation, identification, and prosecution of people responsible for the crimes. Part of their work has been to provide care and support for those children who had lost one or both parents in the war, as well as support for women who had lost their children as well as their entire families. Some of the children were placed in orphanages, some with their extended family and friends and some went abroad. Munira spoke proudly of the organization's extensive membership database, comprising 8,116 members whose details were shared only with ICTY. The NGO continues to collaborate with the Division of the Court of Bosnia and Herzegovina. Munira herself lost her son in the genocide, a boy of 16 at the time, whose bones she found, exhumed, and then reburied. Although now in her seventies, her grief and the memories of the events are still fresh. Her drive for justice is great, and her energy is indefatigable. What astounded me the most, however, is the absence of hatred in her perspective and her lucid commitment to peace and reconciliation. For her and for Esma, the work of *unforgetting* has a social dimension that has been seamlessly woven into their everyday lives, and closely linked with the advocacy they led on behalf of others and the organization.

Esma D.'s narrative appears in the following chapter in full. While she is also a woman who experienced violence during war, the nature of that violence was different in that she was not raped or tortured, nor had she lost close family members in the war herself, but she took up arms and volunteered to go to

The Space of Dialogue 137

the front lines as a fighter. In this sense, her agency manifests in a different way from the agency of the women who survived rape and other forms of torture, or those who lost close family members. Rather than being on the receiving end of direct violence, Esma D. is one who has inflicted direct violence on others in the same war, in addition to having experienced the mental anguish associated with living through war and the effects of post-traumatic stress disorder experienced by ex-combatants in post-conflict settings.

I was fortunate to be able to offer modest financial compensation to the women as a token of gratitude for their participation. All except Munira and Esma accepted. Those who had more extensive experience speaking with journalists and researchers were very open about the fact that they would not be spending two hours of their day speaking about their war experience without any financial compensation. This should not be easily interpreted as a form of self-commodification, or a simple transactional approach to sharing their narrative. On the contrary: they had learned from experience that there is value to the stories they hold, and their approach developed in response to how they were initially treated by others. They related having given their stories away freely, naively, assuming that they were being asked to tell them by people who truly cared about what happened to them. But they related ending up feeling used and exploited when they felt that the stories were extracted from them and utilized as a commodity, that there was no real interest in them as human beings. What troubled them is that many researchers and journalists approached the meeting in an extractive manner, neglecting or outright denying the inter-subjective, relational nature of the exchange, and the dialogic context that they assumed would be involved in sharing a personal story about rape in war with a stranger. As one of the women said, "what bothers me the most is that they didn't care enough to send me a card, to say hello, ever." Asking to be paid for their time and accepting this modest monetary compensation was, therefore, a way to assert their agency over their choice to speak, and to assign a very practical, commodified value to their stories. Munira was fully versed in speaking with researchers and media. In fact, my conversation with her was paused when journalists from a local news station arrived at her office, inviting her to comment on a recent local verdict. She invited me in turn to remain to hear it. Esma spoke from the perspective of a particular type of survivor of war, one who has been engaged in healing and helping herself overcome traumatic experiences while also actively helping others with the same process.

The stories of two of the women who survived rape and raised children born of war rape served as a basis for, respectively, the film *Grbavica: The Land of My Dreams* directed by Jasmila Žbanić in 2006, and the book written in German by Alexandra Cavelius, *Leila, ein bosnisches Mädchen* [Leila, a Girl from Bosnia] in 2000. For both women, with each subsequent telling, the distance between the experience itself and the teller increased, leading to increasing coherence and control over the self-narrative. Each survivor has in this case achieved

138   Unforgetting and the Politics of Representation

"ownership" of her own story as a story that she has told many times, and now can make an autonomous decision about what she wants to do with it, depending on present circumstances.[2]

The other four women had significantly less experience speaking about the war. One of them was curious what it would feel like to speak to a researcher as opposed to her therapist whom she had been seeing regularly. Another was distinctly motivated by the desire for "her little voice" as she called it, to be recorded, feeling that she has not been given sufficient opportunities for this over the years. One of them, the oldest among them and a skilled artisan who spends much of her time creating beautiful objects by painting on wood, felt curious about who I am and thought that it might be nice to speak with someone like me. One of them, who lives in a small village near Sarajevo confessed to feeling lonely, only recently having realized that she may be entitled to some support and medications, and in being presented with the opportunity to speak with me welcomed both the money and the opportunity for friendly dialogue. She was very keen to meet me, and proud to show me around her modest farm, promising that if I come back to see her next time, we will roast a lamb on the spit on her land.

All women approached our meeting and the ensuing interaction as a conversation, a dialogue. I was called upon to share details about myself as a person, a woman, a mother, and then lastly as a researcher. Several approached the questions as part of my "research needs," and the work that we would "need to get through." I would show them my list of questions and invite them not so much to answer them but to speak to them in any way they wish, without worrying about the order. Some of them chose to answer in order, others didn't.[3]

In most cases I would leave the piece of paper on the table in front of us, so that it is visible and accessible in case they would like to speak to them directly. In the few cases where the women chose to answer the questions in order, the real conversation would begin after we had gone through "the work" of answering the questions and could then move into a more relaxed chat about many things, present and past, our families, our goals, and aspirations. In some cases we shared a meal, and much of this after-talk unfolded over food and drink. Several yet did not look at the questions at all and demanded my full conversational presence and responsiveness as they narrated their memories and present experience. Their stories and approaches to the past as well as the present reflect the intersectional diversity of their experiences, pointing to the limitations of analyses that tend to homogenize them as a group.

Each conversation represented both a confirmation and a re-inscription of each woman's authorial, storytelling agency and her own healing path. Each woman ascribed explicit value to the act of narration that is of benefit to themselves. None of them—even the one who has been bed-ridden for 19 years— were fully at ease with the self-concept of a victim. Although all women articulated past and present challenges, all of them exhibited remarkable

The Space of Dialogue 139

resilience and agency. Examples of agency are numerous throughout their stories and range from actively seeking justice through participating in criminal trials, to recognizing that the time has come to seek out professional help with managing symptoms of trauma on their own, in some case for more than a decade.

Occasionally through their stories they refer to their own decisions to speak or not to speak about their past, as well as to other women they are aware of who may have decided not to speak to anyone. In all cases the motivation for speaking and for remaining silent are complex. When it comes to remaining silent, that choice is never to be equated with complete victimization or passivity. In some cases, the women indicate that silence may be a deliberate and strategic choice, precisely to avoid being trapped in the image of the victim. Many of them do not want to be defined by a single incident, which is how the label "victim" is often operationalized in various legal systems, as well as socially. Speaking out about one's experience or being found out as having been raped during the war can invite a range of responses from others, most commonly victim blaming or pity—neither response being adequate or acceptable to the women.

In addition to the personal nature of their narratives, and the individual benefits the act of narration may or may not have on each one of them, their memories of war experience and their orientation toward the present bear upon collective epistemologies of peace, justice, and recovery. Olivera Simić points out that "[t]he listening to truth narratives also implies bearing 'witness to the testimony' by which the responsibility for finding justice is shared."[4] As the researcher, and a woman with a family background connected to the culture of my collocutors, I share in this responsibility. However, making their stories visible through publication extends that responsibility to all other readers, at all levels. Everyone who takes the time to read their narratives becomes a witness to their testimony, sharing in the responsibility for finding justice.

The women's truth narratives also redefine the meaning and scope of justice in important ways. Justice in a judiciary sense, as public punishment or correction for those who have perpetrated criminal acts, is of key importance to some of the women, but not to all. Two of them in particular are openly ambivalent toward the institutionalized aspects of the criminal justice system. Their ambivalence stems from having testified at court and having experienced the process as either only partially satisfactory, or not satisfactory at all. In such cases, women point to the fact that some but not all perpetrators are sentenced, and even when they are sentenced, the causes and effects of harm remain.

In one instance, a woman who testified decided to do so only to try to achieve justice for her father and brother who were murdered during the war, which she sees as the real and greater tragedy compared to her experience of being raped multiple times at the age of 16. The process to which she was subjected as a witness was also something that she wished she had been better

140 Unforgetting and the Politics of Representation

prepared for, not having realized that the truth of her claims will be actively debunked and attacked by the defense. For another woman, the positive judicial outcome of an individual trial pales in comparison with the lack of protection she received as a witness, and her knowing that many perpetrators still reside in the same community as their victims.

The women's notions of justice, therefore, are always situated within specific embodied contexts and cannot be understood exclusively in relation to internationally defined transitional justice frameworks and state-centric approaches. This does not mean that they see the harm that was done to them and their families as private, and not deserving of public attention. But it does mean that justice must be reflected in social interactions and structural arrangements, sets of conditions that integrate the individual with the collective, and go beyond simplistic and paternalistic conceptions of victimization and suffering, and legal and judicial frameworks.

Their stories and perspectives, and their decision to share them through research also have implications for how we understand the ecologies of peace and peacebuilding. Peace and recovery are as much individual processes as they are collective.[5] Resisting dominant social and politicized constructions of victimhood is a form of agency and assertion of a more complex self-concept that participates in redefining the terms of healing and recovery. As women who not only lived through the war but who were directly brutalized because of it, their critique of official narratives of war and the politics of victimhood is a significant form of resistance. This resistance has as much to do with advocating for specific types of formal recognition, and financial and housing stability for women who have survived war-related sexualized violence, as it does with long-term psychological support and a more informed conception of what it means to be a woman who has survived sexual and gender-based violence during war.

Their stories also deconstruct easy assertions about nationality and nationalist politics in contemporary Bosnia, at least within the Federation entity, and its putative internal relevance as a social vision. While each one was targeted due to her nationality during the war, all but one indicates that this experience has altered their understanding of who they are as people, how they choose their friends, how they get along with their neighbors, or how they think about politics and the future of Bosnia. In this way their perspectives highlight the power and agency that each woman exercises within current structures and her particular social and cultural matrix, as well as how each challenges those structures and matrices while embodying the fundamental principle of peaceful, nonviolent action.

Notes

1 Srebrenica was in the epicenter of war at least from 1993, if not earlier. The fall of Srebrenica took place between July 11 and July 22, 1995, when over 8000 unarmed civilians, mainly men and boys, were executed by the Bosnian Serb Army led by

The Space of Dialogue 141

Ratko Mladić. The genocidal intention is manifest not only in the numbers of those who were murdered, but also in the deliberate targeting of members of a single nationality in a concerted effort to reduce or eliminate their population in particular areas. Detailed accounts regarding the fall of Srebrenica exist, most notably among the publications of the Institute for Research of Crimes Against Humanity and International Law at Sarajevo University (Accessible at: http://www.institut-genocid.unsa.ba/pub.html), and Edina Bećirević's 2009 scholarly study based on her doctoral dissertation research, *Na Drini Genocid* (Genocide on the Drina [my translation], a title that in the original hauntingly echoes the title of Ivo Andrić's novel Na Drini Ćuprija/The Bridge on the Drina. As well, a number of survivor memoirs have been published, and works by Bosnian authors that include survivor narratives, such as, *Samrtno Srebrenicko Ljeto '95* (Deathly Summer in Srebrenica '95 [my translation], by the "Women of Tuzla" Association (Accessible in Bosnian at, https://bosnamuslimmedia.files.wordpress.com/2008/04/samrtno-srebrenicko-ljeto-1995.pdf); Emir Suljagić's, 2005 book, *Postcards from the Grave*; Hasan Nuhanović's, 2007 book, *Under the UN Flag: The International Community and the Srebrenica Genocide*, and Adnan Rondić's 2015 book, *Živjeti Srebrenicu* (To Live Srebrenica [my translation]), among others. A detailed description of events, including the involvement –and culpability—of UN peace keeping forces also exists in the Report of the UN Secretary-General Pursuant to General Assembly Resolution 53/35: The Fall of Srebrenica (15, November 1999). The Report is accessible to the public in several languages, including English, here: https://digitallibrary.un.org/record/372298?ln=en (Accessed on October 26, 2021).

2 For some of the basic tenets of narrative therapy as applied to trauma contexts, see Michael White, *Re-Authoring Lives: Interviews and Essays* (Adelaide, South Australia: Dulwich Centre Publications, 1995), and *Maps of Narrative Practice* (New York: WW Norton & Company, 2007), as well as his "Trauma and Narrative Therapy, Part I and Part II," workshop videorecording, https://dulwichcentre.com.au/narrative-therapy-ezine/trauma-and-narrative-therapy/. Also see, Valerie Raoul, *Unfitting Stories: Narrative Approaches to Disease, Disability, and Trauma* (Waterloo, ON: Wilfrid Laurier University Press, 2007), and Ana Penjak and Michael Heitkemper-Yates, eds. *The Practice of Narrative: Storytelling in a Global Context* (Oxford, England: Inter-Disciplinary Press, 2016).

3 These are the questions that I shared with the women before we met:

1 Could you say something about yourself? (How old are you, what is your educational background, what is/was your profession (depending on the age)? Are/were you married, do you have any children/grandchildren?).
2 How would you describe your life before the war?
3 Would you like to say something about the ways in which the war (to be specified whether WWII or the war in former Yugoslavia) has affected your life and the life of your family?
4 Did you or anybody close to you experience any violence during the war, sexual or other?
5 Could you describe this experience?
6 In what ways has this experience affected your life/ the life of your family?
7 Have you talked about this experience before and to whom? If not, why was there silence over this experience? If yes, has talking about it helped you to come to terms with it?
8 Has anybody in your family had a pregnancy/child resulting from the rape(s)?
9 Do you know what happened to this child or to other children of rape?
10 Did you receive any support from your family, community, or government?
11 What kind of support do you think is important to provide for others who have lived similar experiences?

142   Unforgetting and the Politics of Representation

If a child of rape is involved—questions for the mother:

1 How did you decide to keep your child?
2 What were some of the reasons that motivated you? How do you feel about the decision now?
3 Describe what motherhood means to you.
4 What was the most difficult thing about motherhood for you?
5 How has your family/community reacted to the fact that you kept your child?
6 Does your child know the truth about her/his origins? If yes, how did you tell her/him the truth?
7 Is there anything else that you would like to share about you as a person, as a mother, and about your experience in general?

The limitations of this study, as in the case of the children born because of war, is that it represents the voices of a small, self-selected group in the entity of the Bosnian Federation. The group was not entirely self-selected either, as in the case of both groups I had to rely on the leadership of the NGOs and their discretion to share or not share my call for participation with groups or individual under their care. A level of this discretion likely involved their own assessment and screening of who may or may not be interested in speaking with me, and who has or has not had other opportunities to engage in such conversations with a researcher before, as well as their assessment of the relative benefits that such a conversation may bring the individual survivor.

4 Simić, "Drinking Coffee in Bosnia: Listening to Stories of Wartime Violence and Rape." *Journal of International Women's Studies* 18.4 (2017), 321–328, 325.
5 My positioning of peace and peacebuilding as an ecology that integrates the personal and the public, the individual and the collective in the context of embodied individual identity is consistent with some recent approaches in critical feminist peacebuilding, such as, for example, in Maureen P. Flaherty, Thomas G. Matyók, Sean Byrne and Hamdesa Tuso, *Gender and Peacebuilding: All Hands Required* (Lexington Books, 2015).

Chapter 9

The Vulnerable and the Brave, in Their Own Words

Remembering the past

S.: *I grew up in a big family. My parents had eight children…. Mine was a patriarchal, rural family where it was unheard of that a girl goes to high school—girls went to primary school only because it was required by law. When the war started in this area, our town was divided between two sides along the railway tracks. Above the railway, there were Croatia army barracks, Croatian flags were flying, and the bars were for the members of the Croatian army headquarters. So, everything above that line was theirs, and this side of the city was ours [Bosniak].*

There are mixed marriages in my family. Even though my father was very traditional, he never told me that I wasn't allowed to…Blaža, my friend from school, used to sleep over at our place and my father loved her dearly. My family never told me to dislike her because her name was Blaženka, you see. My father wasn't prejudiced in such a way, because that wasn't something you would pay attention to, at least not in my family. We practiced our religion, but our home was open to everyone. And so, by chance, I ran into this woman who said, "let's have a coffee, let's have a coffee…" They had probably already embraced that extremism because later I heard that she was in the Croatian army and had been to the front lines. This was probably some kind of trophy for them, taking in as many Muslims as they could to ruin their lives. Maybe that was also the case in our army. I don't know, I wasn't there, but it was a dirty war. It didn't matter if you were destroying a woman, a child, or an elder. What mattered was that you destroyed the other. And so, in my case, that woman had set me up and they took me away.

After they left, when I regained my consciousness, I was completely naked. They left me in a forest. There were five of them. They probably thought I was dead. I stumbled across a light, and it was a Croat house. An old woman came out, wearing the traditional Croat dress. When she heard that I was Muslim, she ran out and gave me a white blouse, a very large one. "Put this on," she said, "and run back to the forest, you've come again among Croats." And so I walked.

DOI: 10.4324/9781003186168-13

Among those five men, I only recognized one. I know I've seen him before and I later found out his name. The rest of them, judging by their accent, they weren't from Bosnia. I think they probably came from Croatia. They were not from my town because I know those people, I've lived with them. So, after that, I told my sister, mother, father, and brothers what happened to me. Everyone took it very hard, but my brothers were crushed.

After that, you know, you somehow live with that. For me it was harder, it seems … I mean, there's physical pain, you survive a great physical pain, you recover physically, it goes away. It is only afterwards that you … At the given moment you have no idea what had happened, you only feel a certain pain, and then, you are slowly returning to normality, but there are those looks on the faces of your parents, your sister, and your brother…If something similar were to happen to my daughter, I wouldn't know how to get closer to her, how to help her, what to tell her, you understand? They didn't know how, they'd just look at me and cry. Finding out that I was pregnant was what really crushed me. It never crossed my mind that I could be pregnant or that I could give birth to a child.

***

L.O.:   *I graduated from elementary school and because my father was an alcoholic, I agreed with my mother to go to her parents, so I went to Bihać where my grandparents lived, and there I started first year of medical high school. I was 18. And then the war broke out. Then communication with my mother stopped and we could not talk to each other for a long time. Somehow, I do not remember that period well. I know everyone was afraid because war broke out. I was still unaware what that actually meant, to be in war, nor when I would be able to go home. I was waiting for the phones to start working again so that I could talk to my mother, and I did not expect at all that something big was about to happen. Then, one morning I was woken by a thundering noise. I thought it was a thunderstorm, but it was the sound of grenades and only then I got really scared and realized we were in war. That was the first time I heard the sound of war. I cannot recall how much time passed exactly but I got captured by the paramilitary unit commanded by Fikret Abdić. They sold me to the Serbs and that is how it all began. I was not held in prisoners' camps the entire time but was moved around and spent some time in various houses. I spent three years as a prisoner. It was six years later that I returned to my hometown, to see and speak to my mother for the first time since leaving for Bihać.*

***

The Vulnerable and the Brave, in Their Own Words 145

Azra: My life before the war was a typical Yugoslavian story. Mine was a Bosniak family. My father is from Bosnia and my mother from Croatia. My mother was employed before she got married but stopped working after she got married and looked after us children. My father worked. It was a typical Bosnian story, we lived well, my sister went to study, I planned to study as well. When the war started, I was in my third year in high school, I was 17. Something like that. I was able to cross from Višegrad to Visoko [near Sarajevo] when the fighting started. The war interrupted everything. And because of that interruption… for so many, many, many years I was unable to continue with my life. I tried, I tried to study, I really tried, it took a very long time, but it did not get a bit better. The Yugoslav army simply came and occupied the town where I lived. They came first, then the White Eagles and then after them the domestic paramilitary formations. We were captured in the city. We could not leave, we were trapped. My father managed to escape somehow; my mother, myself, and my younger sister remained. My older sister was in Zenica, where she was a student. They would come and take someone every night, and every night we heard the sounds of someone nearby being taken away. We were under house arrest as it were, we were hiding so that they would not know we were there. They literally took over the city and screams could be heard all the time. Then one night, we were hiding with a little girl whose parents managed to escape, and she came to stay with her sister who lived in the same building as us. She went to the same school that I attended. We were hiding, and then they came and abducted us. The took us to a hotel, me, my sister, and this friend.[1] This is where they kept imprisoned women. The little girl and my sister never came back. I have never heard anything about my sister again. I was 17, she was 15. I am still mourning for my sister. All that I went through, I think I would agree to go through it all 60 more times just for her to come back. Or I wish she was the one who managed to escape, to leave, and I the one who stayed behind.

I was held in the hotel for two nights. At some points I could hear another woman's name being called. I heard sounds, I heard screams. But I didn't see them. Because it was a hotel, there were women at the reception area. The soldier who was the leader of the White Eagles took me back to the apartment, and threatened me not to go out anywhere, telling me he will return my sister home. I was naïve and believed him. However, my mother was afraid and arranged for me to escape. That always bothered me. Maybe I should have stayed as he asked, maybe he would have returned my sister. But he probably wouldn't…He would have come back again to take me—that happened to some other people. Later we did hear that he came back, that he was looking for me, he, and his formation. But I somehow managed to leave. There were convoys in the area, and I managed to cross to the free territory.

I lived in my own, emotionless world and I was not ready for men nor for friends. I was feeling tightness within me. I also did not know how to set boundaries, how to defend myself. I had missed out on all socializing, and I didn't know how to behave around others. I was closed off. I felt an enormous pressure when I would go out with someone, it was not a positive experience. Then I wasted a lot of energy trying to hide it all, so that it cannot be seen and noticed, but it was noticeable. For lack of experience, I did not know how to judge a situation. I did not know how to carry myself. I only started getting better three to four years ago. I missed motherhood, I missed. I never shared the details of my experience with my sister or my parents; I don't want to stress them with those details. I tried to minimize it, so that it does not hurt them. Because the loss they suffered hurts them, and I did not want to add to it. They do know what happened, but they never found out the details.

***

Selma: *I got married the spring the war started, in May 1992. I have two sons.*

    When the shooting started, we all escaped to a nearby basement, which was full of people, Serbs and Croats and Muslims, people in mixed marriages. After two, three days of hiding, the military started going through apartments, collecting men. That is how they took my father-in-law and my husband away. They came inside with a gun and kicked all men outside, in slippers and short sleeved t-shirt, without any luggage, told them to line up in front of the building. Men's hands were tied behind their back; they had to keep their head down. They were taking only men of Muslim nationality. And that is when my husband was taken away to imprisonment. He went through all camps around Sarajevo during those nine months. And I stayed with my mother-in-law in the apartment and then they took us. We were imprisoned in the local sport hall, and we had to sleep there, on the concrete floor, with smashed glass all over. We were kept there for seven months. My mother left on a bus one day before the war started. They provided a few buses, and she took one of them directly to Pazarić. We stayed behind, and after that it was no longer possible to leave.

    The worst was that we did not recognize any of those uniformed people. And they were coming every day to look for us and harass us. They go into your place with a shotgun and shoot all over the walls "get out of here, what are you doing here, why did not you go with your people, we do not need you here, all of these people should be shot dead." We went through that every day until they forced us in that sports hall, that camp. And they were coming over there as well, in uniforms, not army uniforms, but completely black ones. Just black. That was terrible. They organized exchanges for us and if the exchange was not successful, they returned us to that camp. And then I heard someone was looking for me, and that

The Vulnerable and the Brave, in Their Own Words 147

they will bring another woman in exchange. I was ordered to go. My mother-in-law stayed behind, with my brother-in-law who was still a child. They did not take him to the camp with the other men. I was petrified with fear. I didn't know where I would be taken. In front of the building there was a white VW Golf. "Mrs please go in and sit down," I was told. Two men sat on the back seat around me. That was horrible. They had huge moustaches that extended up to their ears. I wanted to run away but I knew that if I had turned around and start running, they would kill me. They had guns. That car ride was the most difficult thing I survived. They dragged me through the woods, saying they were taking me to the exchange. And they stopped the car. We were in the woods, and it was night. They told me to get out of the car. That is the last thing that happened I remember clearly, those four men, who then did whatever they wanted.

What happened destroyed my life. No one can cure that. Because I was trying to fight them off, they tied my hands behind my back. I was screaming, crying, screaming. When it all was done, they pointed to a road down the hill and said, "run down there, run, your people are waiting for you over there." I ran and ran and ran until I reached my people. There were other women who were there and who started walking where I had come from. But I did not talk about it to anyone. I was quiet about it all these years. It has stayed inside of me. Do you believe me when I say that it cannot be cured?

***

S.Š.: *I am 38. This is my second marriage. I am in my second marriage for 13 years already. Life was difficult before the war. Life has always been difficult. We lived in the countryside. Mother and father lived mostly from agriculture. Children did not have any possibilities, none. I had just finished grade five (5) when the shooting started. I was 13 (13). I got married in 1997 after the war, when I was in my second year of high school, then got divorced and remarried. It was '92 and I heard on the news that Sarajevo was under siege. Very soon the war started here as well. We thought it might not, but it did. War—I would never wish it on anyone.*

Members of the Muslim army captured us, locked us in houses, in basements, in vans, they drove us around and were deciding whether to kill us or not. At one point they drove us to a gas chamber but then returned us. They wanted to kill us but then changed their mind. They said they had their own peasants and will kill them instead. So they spared us, did not kill us, even though they wanted to. At first, they decided they would not, so they kept us locked up in houses. They did not have enough food. They called us Ustaše and decided they will not feed us.[2] When they released us, we brought food from our houses to people who stayed captured so that they have something to eat. We were among the women and children who were released; they kept the men imprisoned.

I am worried about talking about this, since my parents must return to a village that is inhabited mostly by Muslims; I don't want them to be harassed. The worst was when they were coming in the evening with socks over their faces and they would turn the house upside down and did a lot of things. They asked for money, put a shotgun to my older sister's throat, saying they would kill her, first rape her and then kill her [crying]. They raped me as well in the same house. My parents were there. They locked us in a van and drove us around, there is nothing that they didn't do with us, kick us with their legs...This lasted a year and a half. They just kept coming to our house. We couldn't escape because we were behind barricades. Grenades, bombs, you cannot walk around when it was all a mine field. After a while we managed to cross to the neighboring village where we were able to get on a bus. Mother had left already. If we stayed, they would have killed us for sure. We could not put up with that any longer, with raping and beatings. They would come at night, turn the light off, and have socks to cover their heads so you do not see who it is. You can see only fingertips, everything black, and you can see the mouth, otherwise it is masked military suit and a shotgun. I believe they were Muslims because they were the majority in the village where we lived, it is all Muslims over here.

No one asked anything; if you needed anything or how you felt. I was very young. I was hungry and thirsty all the time. We had kept some potatoes. The military took all our food, all the flour, they asked for baked goods and took everything away and we were left with nothing. We were hungry. That is how it was the whole time. If you had an animal to slaughter you did—some they took away, some we managed to save for ourselves. My sister has been incapacitated since. She is well now, all things considered, but she must take pills all the time, because she has the army in her thoughts, you cannot forget that. The army stays in your head.

Everyone hides what happened to them. No one will go out in public with what happened to them. I remember one girl, when they forced us to go north of our houses. They locked one girl in something like a storage closet and there was one soldier guarding the door. I wanted to enter that closet and the soldier told me not to go there, there was a soldier inside with her, and this one was guarding the door. I saw she was locked in there. What they did to her that I do not know. There were all sort of things going on. They lock you in a room and then soldiers come with socks over their heads and you see nothing, you do not see who they are. I reckon that these are neighbors of ours because they had to hide their faces.

***

The Vulnerable and the Brave, in Their Own Words   149

Sena: *I was born in 1973, so I was 19 when the war started. I lived in the village with my parents, brother, and sister until 1992. And after they took my father and brother away, I went through agony in Višegrad, going from house to house, running away, hiding. They came and took me away, and they returned me. Then they took me away again and returned me. Do you happen to have a tissue?*

So that is how that period went on, between May and August, until we managed to leave. Every time they came to take me, they took my sister-in-law as well. And I know about many girls, when we were captured in one school, I saw it, it was visible, they took them and returned them and so on. I have not spoken to my sister-in-law about that period since. I cannot. I wanted to cut myself off from everything, from family.

We tried to move to Višegrad several times, but we failed. And then they… We tried to leave with a convoy, me, my mother, and sister. My brother, father, and sister-in-law were going to try to escape in another way. However, we did not make it. Then, during the attempt to cross the border with Serbia, they caught us and separated us and took my father and brother away. They never came back. They were exhumed, my father in 2001 and my brother in 2013. After the war, my mother and I have never spoken about my father and brother, nor do I mention their name in front of her. That is so painful. When my father was being identified, I was in labor, so it turned out I could not be present and that haunted me for years afterward. Why couldn't I protect my mother? And when my brother was being identified, I was there and then I felt much better. Somehow, I cannot let them go, I wish I could do it, but I cannot.

I was barely 20 years old when all of that happened to me.

I learned to live again in Medica. It was like when someone teaches you to walk again. That is how it was. Because you forgot to walk, and you had to learn to walk again.

***

Munira: *I know that the dead cannot come back. But I have grandchildren and I care for them. I want for my grandchildren to make friends with all citizens of Bosnia and Herzegovina and the whole world, but they must know that there are good people and bad people. Not people who are rich, not people who are of a specific religious orientation, not people of a specific color or race, but only people who are good and those who are bad. Because that is how it must be. If we go down another road, then we have done nothing, we just wasted all those years fighting, wasted our time, our nerves… There you go.*

150   Unforgetting and the Politics of Representation

I cannot understand, I am saying, I found my child... but how to take two bones in a casket, to carry two bones in a casket...This is more than sadness. I can only scream to the sky. And you look at these two bones, and you think, you gave birth to him with a head, arms, and legs, normal, seen him become a man, and then you find him, you bury him. Well, I did not find him...I changed greatly when it happened, when I found those two bones. I did not have feelings of hatred before, since hatred is weakness, but I feel that something is waking up in me, and I am afraid, so...

During the war my son was in grade ten. He turned 16 during the war. But it does not matter how old he was, if he was 50 or five, he is my son. Here there is another mother, they killed her son at 14, she buried him, but she could not find her husband, she is alone now. I mean even Kadira who lost two underage sons, or Hatidja, or Samura from Bajramović, who buried three sons and a husband. So many children. And then when they start talking that they were only killing people who were of fighting age—it is not true, they killed women, children, babies, the elderly. For example, Amida's husband was born in 1906 and was not even capable to say his own name, not to mention to serve in the military. And there are so many cases like that.

When it comes to women who were raped, I will tell you something. Our women are private. If one tells you once, she will not tell it to anyone ever again. Around two years ago we had a case of a woman who came here and told me to lock the door, told me she was raped, and that she cannot keep it inside and deal with it any longer. She made a pie and came here, started crying and we talked, and she showed us scars from cigarette burns. She spoke about this then, 20 years after it had happened, and she never came back again. I speak to her on the phone sometimes. In fact, I just called her a couple of days ago asking her to go with us to visit Prijedor. She said she could not because she feels ashamed. She feels ashamed because she told us. She said it was the biggest mistake of her life to tell me, but she could not keep it inside any longer and when she told us she was crying, crying, crying, we cried. I would never tell on her, never tell her name, that is how it is. Then there are women who talk sometimes and sometimes if they are asked, they will say yes, and other times they will say no.

I personally know only one woman who gave birth to a child after being raped. I went to visit her once because of a death in the family. You know, the boy is very sweet. A young man. And then she told me something she could not say to anyone. That is that there are moments when she does not love him. Then I felt sorrier for that child than the mother. You know, he does not know the truth.

While it may be important to tell the truth, the truth will cause suffering for that generation of children. I believe that many children, if they found out the truth, would be disappointed. I do not think there is a child

The Vulnerable and the Brave, in Their Own Words 151

who could carry what we could carry. Take my example. In my lifetime, in Srebrenica, in Sarajevo I lost a brother, a husband, a son, two sisters, a father, my mother (who died of natural causes), two of my husband's brothers, an uncle and his son. And that is the family. I lost a sister-in-law, my brother's wife, and their daughter, my niece, as well as her husband, and I cannot remember more. I am trying to say that, when you must deal with all those losses, to look for the remains of all of those people...different people deal with this differently. Some of us deal with it well, we carry it well. Others deal with it by not wanting to mention those who died, ever. And there are those who cannot stop crying, who are not well, and you can see it.

I just visited my daughter-in-law who does not have legs. She lost both legs in Sarajevo. Yet, she gets around the house, tells me to sit down, and she is preparing everything, does not allow me to make coffee or anything, she climbs the chair. I almost blurted, let me do this. How she struggles. And she put two curlers in her hair. That touched me more than if she had said nasty things about my parents. She wants to be pretty. Two curlers. She does not have a man; she does not have anything. I ask her if she washed her hair and she says no, she just wanted to curl her hair. When I left her house, I felt tired, as if there were no life left in me any longer.

Not everyone cries, or screams

Azra: *When I arrived in Medica I was 17. It was as if suddenly I became numb, frozen. Mourning for my sister, everything that happened to me, all of that was pushed into the background and became buried deep inside me. I took it all and pushed it somewhere, as if none of it happened to me. This went so far that I felt nothing when someone was telling me about my own sexual abuse. Nothing could touch me. All I could feel was grief for my sister. I became distanced from it all. It lasted for so long, that frozen state. I dragged it around for a couple of years. I was trying. I graduated from high school since I had only one more year to go. I was trying to pick up my interrupted life by attending university, but it did not go well. It is not that I was not good at studying, but it was always very difficult for me.*

I simply had no emotions. And I did not see this as a problem. I just mourned my sister. And that was the reason that all of that was hard for me. When I felt unwell, I would not connect it to what happened to me. I thought I maybe suffer from a genetic illness that runs in my family, so I went to investigate my family history, but as far as my parents knew, no one in our family had such an illness. This was the extent to which I had distanced myself from my own experience. I became totally separated from my own emotions.

152   Unforgetting and the Politics of Representation

And then, when I was about 26 or 27, all of it traveled up to the surface, all of that that was buried deep inside of me. And then I was not well at all for a few years. I was not well psychologically. It simply started. It started with obsessive, forceful thoughts. In my head swarmed a million thoughts, and a feeling of fear. I could not be still any longer, I felt like I will go outside of my own body. Like I was going outside of my own body, I could not stand to be inside of my own body. When I started working with the psychologist, I was even told that this state is often a symptom of trauma, and a mechanism of coping with it. I started suffering from depression and feelings of guilt. But over time, I started realizing what was going on, and I started feeling better. Once I could see and acknowledge this connection, I started with that process of grieving. And this process if not finished even today. Because of this, I think it is very important that I relate to other women survivors that not everyone reacts the same way. Not everyone cries, or screams. This is important to know especially when society pressures women to take on the role of victim. It is important to be informed, to know that trauma can result in different dissociative states.

It lasted for about four years. So, at least nine to ten years of my life were somehow erased, they slipped through, I did not succeed in anything during those ten years. I did not manage to finish university even though I really wanted to. But slowly, somehow, I managed to get better, I realized that ten years passed, and I did not accomplish anything, anything at all. I am sad because of that. Of course, there is always something to be grateful for. I am healthy. But there is not a day that passes...I mean there are still crises, but I will always be thankful to that psychologist who helped me to start functioning normally in some basic way, so that I am not afraid of this and that, and that I don't self- harm, because I engaged in repeated self-harm. And when I look at it all now, in retrospect, I tell myself I cannot regret those ten years, that I need to remember how I felt during those years with all the difficulties and suffering.

Mother because of war

S.:   I was 22 when I gave birth. Can you imagine, never in my life, I mean, when I speak about it with other women who had gone through that experience... In my case, for long while afterward I had scars, and I was bleeding. Because of the shock your brain probably prevents you from thinking about reality or everyday things. You are only thinking about what had happened.

When I found out I was pregnant, I didn't have the slightest intention to keep the child. As I've told you, my sister and my mother brought me to that war hospital in our town. There was a female gynecologist on duty there. When we arrived, the wounded from all over the place were being brought there. When we were seen by Dr. Azra, she examined me and confirmed that

I was already in an advanced stage of pregnancy. I didn't say a word to her, it was my sister and my mom who were begging her, pleading with her to end my pregnancy. We had no money, yet my mom was offering gold, anything that she owned. The doctor wouldn't hear of it. She said, "What's the matter with you, women? Can't you see that we have nothing for the wounded? We have nothing, how could I terminate a pregnancy."

When I gave birth to S, I really didn't think, not even within the smallest part of my being, that I would keep her. It was out of the question. I prayed that the child is a girl, not a male who will grow up to be a criminal. A girl wouldn't commit a crime.

When they first wanted to bring her for me see her, I said that I didn't want to, so they didn't bring her. They brought her to me in the morning so I could nurse her. One glance at her, and, no way, it's out of the question. I asked to be taken back to Medica. When I arrived to Medica, they had prepared a room that used to be an office. They had put on a sign, called it a nursery. They put her there, because at the time there was an outbreak of jaundice and they quarantined me there too.

It is said that motherhood awakens within us instinctively. But I had no feeling whatsoever. I cried, tossed, and turned. Understand, there was no help. I'd call for the nurse to plead, "please take her away, she's crying, I want to sleep." They kept bringing her to me. "If you love her so much, take her yourselves, I don't want her," I would say. They kept urging me to try nursing her, but I wouldn't hear of it. A little time would pass, and they'd be at it again, "Please, she'll die, please, just until the documents are ready." I kept saying "no" to everyone. But then I got mastitis and had to treat it with penicillin. The nurse would plead with me to hold the child. All the other women there would come to see the baby, they loved her. The baby was almost three months old, and I was still refusing to even change her clothes.

Once, the nurse asked me to help her out and rock the baby to sleep. So, I placed the baby on my knees and fell asleep in the meantime. The baby slipped through my knees; her tiny legs upward, blue in the face. So, the psychologist took me to her office to sign the papers. I took the papers, without reading them, I was ready to sign them. She advised me to consult my family before signing. I wasn't sure how to get in touch with them. They had not heard from me since I left my town that day, three months and three days before. They assumed that I had committed suicide or had died. No one had any idea where I was, what had happened to me. They had sent a radio message and I messaged my brother telling him that I was alive. No word whether I had given birth or had an abortion, absolutely nothing. Then, one day, I was told that I have visitors. My first instinct is to say that there's no one who'd come for me, no one whatsoever, I feel utterly alone. And when I saw my brother and my sister...

154 Unforgetting and the Politics of Representation

How thin and starved they were. At home they had nothing to eat, so when they sat down and saw the white bread that we were eating, my sister mechanically took some bread and put it in her purse, to take back with her. As soon as I opened the door, my sister mechanically went to S.'s cot and took her into her arms. She turned around and said to my brother, "She is ours." He just lowered himself on the edge of the sofa. And so, we stepped outside, and the psychologist told them everything. My brother said, "No matter where you leave her," he said, "we'll always know she's ours. Don't sign anything. We'll go back home, talk to our parents and be in touch."

And so, they went back home. Soon after that, some three days later, my father came to see me. "My daughter, don't give her up. She is ours, after all. Don't give her up; if you did, I'd look for her all over the world." It's interesting that after the visit from my sister and brother, after my dad's words, I automatically started looking at the child differently. I guess, deep down, I was afraid, unsure about how I would think of her once I left Medica, who would I turn to, on whose door would I knock with her? And then I started learning how to be a mother, how to dress her, how to take care of her.

Medica had really helped me a lot. S. was three and a half years old, and we were still there. So, really, we didn't suffer during the war. On my return, my father met us in the street, in front of all the neighbors. That was the greatest "elan," wind at my back, because I was afraid how he would deal with our neighbors. Imagine arriving in a village such as ours with a child, an unmarried young woman is bringing a child with her. In front of everyone, he said, "my dear Brena"—at the time Brena was in the news.[3] "She's mine," he said and took her into his arms. And inside our home, he had made a rocking crib for her with his own hands. When I realized how much they loved her, nobody else mattered. What mattered to me was that my family loved her.

***

Alma: *I am from Kotor Varoš. I am forty-one (41). I was born in 1976. I don't have an occupation. When the war started, I had completed only one year of high school. I was forced to flee. I have very good memories of my childhood in my town before the war. During the war we became refuges and UNPROFOR members from Geneva conveyed us to Travnik. However, I was separated from my parents at the checkpoint, and detained by Croats who raped me. They managed to find us, and detain us, myself and five other young women. I didn't know them; I took no notice. I was sent back to Travnik and was detained there. They said they'd transfer me to a kitchen in Mostar. When I was released, I came*

The Vulnerable and the Brave, in Their Own Words   155

to some cottages where commanders were housed. There were five commanders. So, I ended up in the cottages near Lašva. At that time, Lašva was about to fall. I was in a buffer zone in a conflict between Croats and Bosniaks.

Let me tell you a story. I went to pick up some flour. Mediha and I crossed the buffer zone. We had no idea that soldiers were there. I mean, we saw soldiers and everything, but it made no sense. Us against them? It wasn't like that before; we were all one people. The folks of Kotor Varoš, I never suspected that they would harm me so badly. One of the men raped me and then asked the other one to do the same. "Do it, you want to? I'd shoot you in the forehead right now, and, as for her, I'd take her if she wanted me to, even if only in a retirement home." And then he left the room. The one who raped me, his name was Marko, and he was not from my town.

I was released after five days because I was saved by a major. He said, "I know her father," so they shoved me into the attic. My father was employed by a military firm at the time. All the other five women were raped. He managed to take me up to the attic. I'd rather not…He was horrible. I was by myself and could hear everything. Since that experience, I became aggressive, rude, you name it. I have a daughter, the result of those rapes. I have a daughter I haven't spoken to for three years. [When she found out about her origins] she told me, just like in that movie, "Grbavica," "Whore, you don't know who my father is."

I was only 16 at the time. I only found out that I am pregnant in my third month. I was without resources. I was aware that I was carrying a fetus, that the child was mine alone, that it didn't matter how it came, that I was alone, without my parents, without anyone. I didn't know if the war would ever end. So, to reject one's child… They asked me in Medica if I'd give up my child for adoption. I said no. That's how it was. I was in Medica for two years, and then I ran away. I couldn't understand why everyone liked me at Medica, gave me food, while elsewhere others were taking it away from me. I simply couldn't understand. I could have had an abortion, but a part of me wanted that child and I didn't know how much longer the war would last.

*** *

L.O.:   *I know that there are other women who have raised children born of war, but my case is specific when it comes to pregnancy since my son's father saved my life in a way. The end of war was approaching, and the Dayton Peace Agreement was already signed, so they just shot and killed all the prisoners in camps, including women. My son's father offered me to go with him and save my life in that way. Each time I need to talk about*

156 Unforgetting and the Politics of Representation

> *that it gets difficult for me. I do not want to say that it was rape but on the other side I cannot say that it was not rape. I used to think he was a nice man, better than bad, but now I am thinking that if you want to save someone you do not have to make them a baby, you do not have to sleep with them, you do not have to fulfil your urges. That is how I see it now. At the time and out of fear for my life I did not even think if that was evil or not. Only after I saw my belly growing, I realized I was pregnant. I had no idea that I could be pregnant before that, I felt nothing. I felt no love, no disgust, I felt nothing; I was numb. I thought that children are supposed to be loved and I did not understand why I did not feel that; I was afraid I will not be able to love this child. I thought I will not have any feeling for him. I had no idea if it was going to be a boy or a girl. The pregnancy itself went well, I had no problems, no complications which is strange considering the fact I was pronounced clinically dead after I gave birth; I was very anemic and my iron levels were significantly below normal, even though I did not feel that during the pregnancy. I gave birth in 1996. The Dayton Peace Agreement was already signed. I remember that they took him away after he was born. I had no desire to see him, considering how I felt and that I was not well. I remember being woken up by a terrible fever. I remember I was falling to darkness and the next thing I know they woke me up after two days telling me I went into clinical death and that I was okay now. Then they asked me if I wanted to see the child and I said I did, and then they brought him over. He seemed so strange, I do not know, like he was not mine. He grew close to my heart immediately after I saw him for the first time. He was sweet and cute and gentle, and I wished not to give him away to anyone ever again.*

On what it means to mother a child born of war

> *S.:* *My daughter is my reason for living and something most sacred. Without her, I wouldn't be who I am, and yet, you know, because of her I'll never forget, just one look… She is my greatest regret…I regret the most in life that… I don't regret it, yet I can't explain to you that feeling.[4] I should have given her up for adoption, maybe her life would have been different. She would have never found out how she had come to life. I think it was so selfish of me to want to fulfil myself as a mother rather than give her up and have a nice life. She is someone I can't live without, and, at the same time, something that has prevented me from forgetting, all my life.*
>
> *If I didn't have her, I would have never been a mother. I cannot have more children. If I didn't have her, I'd die, and yet, the fact that I have her… You know, I am a burden to her…I've always been standing in her way as an obstacle. God knows what I would do without her, I'd have no life. I mean, if she weren't there, I would have probably ended my own life*

even though this runs counter to my religious upbringing. I would look at her and tell myself that I have a reason for living. And yet, she is also a constant reminder to me. As they say, when a parent makes a mistake, it's the children who pay the price. I keep wondering whether I made a mistake. I kept saying to myself, God, it's my fault, why was I at that place at that time, why did I trust people? She's now paying the price, but what can I do? Nothing. I can't help her, but she seeks no help. My God, maybe it was meant to be. She is such a good person, always looking out for others, isn't she? It's not that I'm bragging, but she's so nice.

Being able to talk to her openly as I do means that I have everything in her—a friend, a sister, a brother, a daughter. Now she is my everything. Thank God, I didn't give her up.

***

L.O.: *It was much easier with these other two children, they did not have the same problems in school, the experience of raising them is not even close to how it all felt with Zoran, everything is somehow different. However, now after all of that is behind us and he is all grown up and as soon as he turns up at the door, I feel proud and glad. There you go. I do not know, maybe because we succeeded together, that we went through all of that together and I feel he fought with me. He is stable and brave when it comes to many things. We moved here from Zenica in 1998 when Zoran was two already.*

He was born in Republika Srpska. I was with his father when he was born. I did not have anywhere else to go. I did not know anything about my family as we had lost contact. Nor did they know anything about me. Zoran's biological father fell in love with me. And loves me. That is what he says. He never got married afterward. We do have contact now. Z is in touch with him. However, I came here on a UNHCR truck when I found out about my parents, and I did not want to return over there again. He felt differently about that. I felt guilty for a while, for taking the child and not wanting to live with him, like I destroyed his life. I felt guilt for a long time. I thought I was evil, even though I was imprisoned while being there. This is because he was always saying how he loves me, how he loves the child, and I thought that is how it was. Now I think that if he was such a good man and had considered the fact that I was 18, he could have offered me shelter until we found my parents so I can go home. I did not have to birth children to anyone.

My mother took me in and accepted me back. When it comes to community, there were a lot of refugees over here at that time. The story was that I brought a Serbian bastard, a Chetnik's child. Others took pity on me and yet others told me I do not belong here and the best thing for me is to sort out paperwork and flee the country. Some said I would not be

158 Unforgetting and the Politics of Representation

able to survive there. There were a lot of different reactions. We had some family friends on my mother's side, and they supported me. Some people asked why I need this child and why I brought him with me, some suggested I give him to the orphanage claiming he will destroy my life. And so on…My response was always that it was my decision to make. I did not argue a lot. I was quiet when they were around. I kept to myself mostly. I did not socialize a lot. Nor did I have friends.

I am very proud of my son. It is very noticeable that I feel this way and my friends and family say I exaggerate sometimes. I am too proud of him considering what he and I went through. I did not even know how to feed him when he was little, so I gave beans and egg to a three-month-old baby. We did not have a lot to eat. And he survived all that. He was never ill. He never got any vaccinations until we came here of course. His name is Zoran. That is scandalous here.[5] When we first arrived, SDA[6] held power and they suggested to change my child's name and that he should not be named Zoran. However, I liked his name even though it was not me who gave it to him, he was named by his grandma over there, that man's mother, she wanted him to be Zoran. That is such a nice name, like dawn, like something new. We went through a lot together, but I always tried to ensure that he doesn't feel like he was different.

He is a bit of an adventurous type. One thing that is hard on me is the fact that he fell in love with a Muslim girl from a neighboring village, who was raised in that tradition. They love each other but her parents cannot know she is dating him. That is what hurts me the most.

***

Alma: *So, well…I kept the child so that I would have someone of my own with me. But I used to beat the baby. In a bout of anger. It wasn't the child's fault. And the baby was so cute. My God, how cute Lejla was as a baby. Everyone in Medica loved her. She'd go to Mirha's [therapist] office and play there. Mirha would give her a little train, just so I don't beat her. I think [she] kept taking her away from me so I wouldn't beat her. Yes. I was there with her for about two years. I grew tired of it. They had strict mealtimes. They'd always call you out if you made a mistake, and I always made mistakes. And so on and so forth.*

I wasn't working on my trauma then. I simply didn't want anyone to touch my wound. Always the same question. Are you ready? I wasn't ready. I'd just stand up and leave the room. Or I'd bungle something, anything, just so there's something to do. And when they'd give me a task, do you think I'd complete it? No way. And when I'd go out with my child, I'd tell her, don't call me mom, I'm your aunt. When we left Medica, we moved to an abandoned apartment, because at the time you could move into abandoned apartments. And then I tried to find a job but

The Vulnerable and the Brave, in Their Own Words   159

had no success. I had another daughter, but I didn't get along with the man, the way he was, sick, wretched. I wasn't ready for therapy. Luckily, I met my current husband. I was helpless. He's twenty years my senior, but...What happened, happened.

I started drinking. Social workers took my children away. I gave up on myself. It made no difference to me. Alive or dead, I wasn't interested in anything. I lost Lejla, I lost everything. Despite everything, I don't know if I loved her or hated her, she was important to me. One moment I'd love her and the next one I'd hate her. ... Maybe it's for the best that they took her away. She wasn't speaking to me for three years. She couldn't understand...Lejla herself has the same attitude I used to have. It probably affected her as a child because children do remember. She remembers when I beat her, for example.

How to tell the truth

S.:   *When my daughter came of school age, she'd turn to me, asking, "Mom, why is everyone calling me an Ustasha bastard? Mom, what is a bastard? Mom, why won't that girl play with me? Why? Her mom told her not to play with me because I am a bastard." And, when she started grade one, in the neighboring village, what a mess it was... She didn't understand why she's marked, why she's being shoved, or excluded.*

I got married when my daughter was in grade three (3). And then she would ask, "tell me about the war, where were you during the war?" So once, the two of us were sitting and I asked, "what would you do, honey, if your mom was, imagine, if your mom was raped and gave birth to you because of it?" She said, "I'd kill myself right away, if you had to suffer so much because of me." I said those words to her, but, in the end, it was she who found and read my statement.

This is when we wanted to apply for the status of civil victim of war and initiate the process against war criminals. I had left that document at home, in a place where I was keeping all my papers, even though that one was filed separately. It was God's will that she found them. After she read it, she started missing school. I received a phone call from her teacher. She did not utter a word, I don't think she remembers that period that well, she seemed stunned. She neither cried nor screamed. If she would have only asked me, "mom, why haven't you told me?" If she would have blamed me, hated me, anything really, but there was no reaction. But, as I say, thank Allah and my husband. "Are you hungry, my child?" and she'd only say "uh-uh." "S. please eat." Silence. I don't remember how old she was...

We took her to a psychologist, a woman, who was assigned to us by Medica. First, the entire family had a talk, then separately, and so on. I don't know how much that helped her, but I think that my husband helped

160 Unforgetting and the Politics of Representation

her the most. I remember that my husband left the room and started crying. After his talk with the psychologist, he came out and hugged her. He said, "S., do you need another father beside me, am I not enough for you?" And it was then that she started crying, sobbing. It seems that then she let it all out. After all that, she was in therapy for a long time and since then I have been speaking with her openly. Sometimes I want to leave something out, I worry that it will hurt her, but she says, "no, mom, tell me about that at some point."

***

Alma: *I told my daughter about her origins three years ago. Until then, she didn't know. She thought she was a love child. She reacted very badly to it. She distanced herself from me. I was giving her so much, and she distanced herself. She started writing things about her SOS Children's Village mom, how much she loved her, how nobody had a mother like her and so on. However, on her last visit here, I asked her, why are you angry with me, my child. She said, I'm not angry. I guess she collected her emotions. As luck would have it, there's another child born of rape in SOS, so the two of them spend time together and talk about everything. It affected her studies. She completed her first year of university, but when she learned about that, at 24 or 25 years of age, she couldn't complete three upper year courses. She was obviously shaken by it, so she kept failing her exams. She did complete them recently, though. When she came for a visit, she was her old self. Me and her, just like it used to be. But when she came here last time, if only you could have seen that. A child gives me a kiss, and I have no idea who that is. When she started speaking, I realized it was my younger child, Arijana. I didn't recognize her. She got married recently.*

Recovery

S.:   *My husband has always been very sensitive to my needs and very considerate. He has given me his entire life, we've been married for 16 years, and in all those years all he wanted is to make me happy. Last night, and a couple of nights before that, anticipating the conversation with you, I felt uneasy. "What are you going to do," he tells me, "I know, we'll have to put up with your traumas for three nights." Because, I guess, if you don't speak about it, you forget, you push it down. When you revisit it, it stays in your head, no matter what for four days, you can't make it go away. It takes some time before you can put it back somewhere, not to be forgotten, but somewhere where it will stay. But you deal with this, you get used to it. Only talking can heal you, and we say that a scar will only grow smaller over time.*

The Vulnerable and the Brave, in Their Own Words   161

Once or twice a year, depending on funding, Sabiha[7] takes us to workshops, to Vlašić Mountain or somewhere else. You have no idea what this means to us, the women. We recharge our batteries, so to speak. But how is it for the women who haven't spoken yet? And how can we find a way to convince them to speak? The women are afraid. I think it will all be made public in the future, one thing after another. The women have seen too much. I say that about the way we had been used. Maybe the women saw all that and are now afraid to go public, as they'll be marked. The women would be strong enough, but they can't go through what we had gone through when we spoke out first…But imagine if you couldn't talk to anyone, had to put up with it, bottle it up…There are women like that, you know.

When I went in front of the commission, I was lucky, it went well, I had a good doctor. I had heard that women had difficulties with those commissions—various questions, provocations, proofs, this and that. I've been waiting for that call for a long time. She looked at those reports, glanced at me, looked at the reports again and then turned to her colleagues, "Dear God, how am I to assess this woman? Is there a rule book? What am I to say to this woman right now?" I didn't say a word. She said, "How am I to assess her wound when her wound is immeasurable? How am I to determine her degree of disability? What kind of state and legislation is this? What am I to write down about this woman?" Then, the male doctor told her, "We have to work according to this legal regulation." So, she told me, "Madam, apologies for the call, if it were up to me, I wouldn't have even invited you. You have spoken enough. Go home, we'll do our part in accordance with the law and send you everything. You'll receive the decision from social services, and the state will determine the next step. I truly don't know how to assess you." And so I went home. I am grateful. I received a report where they had also assigned us the categories. My report states something about "special category stupor." I said to myself then, this is some kind of branding, you see.

Every woman among us was wondering what the state thinks of us. Do they think that we have healed or have died? Have we lost our minds so they can now determine our degree of disability? Why are they asking for reassessment? That's not a problem, I'll go for a reassessment, but what exactly are they going to look for? Sabiha collated our statements, returned to parliament, fought very hard, and then had it addressed at the federal level. It used to be at the cantonal level, but she managed to take it to the federal level, and they even increased the payments. She went one more time to fight that we keep this right for life without further reassessments. That's where it's at now, nobody is calling us. The Federation pays us 410 convertible marks, and the canton 170.

Since the canton was affected by floods and crises, several of our monthly payments have been late. In other cantons, the two payments are combined, so their payments are on time. But what can I tell you, about 80 percent of us women live on those. There's no employment, and we work in agriculture, the women grow lavender, sew, grow greenhouse fruit, vegetables, flowers... But that isn't a steady source of income. Here today, gone tomorrow.

***

Alma: *My husband, S, is a calm man, quiet and withdrawn. With him I felt safe and secure in a way that I have never felt. When I met him, after the war, I worked for money* [as a sex worker]. *He chose me among all the rest because I was very quiet. He knows that I am a victim of war, but he never asks about my past. He was also imprisoned during the war.*

***

S.Š.: *I live in a small village, and we don't have many institutions here. I only found out about Medica two years ago, through a brochure. Since I was imprisoned in a camp during the war, I have been going to the associations of camp prisoners. There are women there and we socialize. About twice a year there are organized activities—we paint, we knit, etc. Some of this we sell, and we keep the earnings. There are organized meet ups to do something together. We do it around every six months, we get a sort of donation from abroad. Those are mainly people from abroad that buy materials for us. And we process those materials and then each person keeps earnings from what they sell. But I had not shared my story with anyone until I connected with Medica two years ago. When I got those brochures I thought, dear God, what have I been doing all this time. I wish I knew earlier that there is a nice doctor there, they really take care of women. And you can give them a call any time of day or night and tell them about your problems. If nothing else, they will listen to what you have to say and that can be a big relief. A big relief. Nowadays people are somehow withdrawn and there is no one to talk to.*

***

S.Š.: *My daughter lives with my mother. She visited me recently. She comes and dusts and helps with errands. She is attending fashion design school and has a year until graduation. Afterward she is planning to go to Germany, but we will see if she will find work somewhere around here. It*

The Vulnerable and the Brave, in Their Own Words   163

is early to tell since she has one more year until graduation. They praise her and her class supervisor says she is very good at school. We are not very close. After I remarried, she stayed with my mother. She was 17 months old at the time and we had nothing to give her. Now she comes sometimes if she needs something and I buy it for her, now when finally, we have some income. She likes to spend time with my youngest sister, her aunt, she likes to go out and is interested in makeup and dressing up while I am not interested in those things, and I prefer to be alone. I do not like gossip and women who gossip. They bore me. They want to know what is going on in my neighborhood and I do not know, nor am I interested in it.

I would like to socialize with women but there are no women my age around here. I wish I had a friend I can talk to and share my worries with. Many people do not speak to each other at all and turn their head away when meet in the street. There are unsolved issues about land division and such. My husband, too, could not stand people arguing with each other. He is now out looking for work. He said someone had to leave the house, so he did. He finds seasonal work with animals. Sometimes my son helps me since he is all grown up now and before while he was a small child, I had to help him. It is easier for me to live now. I have cats, chickens, and hens, and two cocks, so they keep me busy. I also have a greenhouse and I grow various things in it. I also have one sheep and a lamb, and three pigs—this keeps me busy. My son is my biggest comfort. Everyone else has ulterior motives. What I mean is that people will like you if you have money. That are the times we live in now over here. He is reasonable and he will mix water and sugar and drink if there is no soda around. He is not demanding and never asks for anything that I do not have to give him. He is happy with what he has.

Deconstructing the politics of victimhood

Azra: *I am glad you asked if we should work to change the way people see women survivors, not only as victims. Society puts pressure on women survivors to define themselves as victims even when they do not feel like victims. This is evident in simple things as well as in a larger sense. The thing is that society will only "recognize" you if you adopt the role of victim. If you do not adopt the role of a victim, then society does not recognize you as a survivor. There is always that expectation, I do not know, it seems as if all the things you have survived should be visible on you somehow, that you should be a slob in appearance, someone who does not take care of herself. Appearance seems to be very important in this regard, how you present yourself. So, society is putting pressure on women to fit into the role of victim, even for women who do not want to be in that role. So, I am glad that you asked that.*

Of course, it is all such a sacrifice. But everything should be seen from the perspective that everyone has their own dignity, as someone who wants to live, to keep on living. It is difficult, but this is the perspective from which all help to survivors should be offered. This perspective is about support and about justice ... That is it. That is why I am glad about this approach to research.

People in my community, at the time when I was captured, knew about what had happened. I had one unpleasant experience. When I came to Visoko after I was released, my mother went crying and begging to see if there was anything to be done, to see where my sister was, to try to do something. People who took refuge there at the same time knew what had happened to me and my sister because my mother asked for help from them. But if they knew that something like that happened to you, no one would take you into their house. My mother pleaded for someone to take me in, even people she knew very well, but no one wanted to do so. That happened to other women who had the same experience as I did. And they found out that the paramilitaries were looking for me. If people help, they will put themselves in danger.

When I first came to Visoko, we took refuge in a small house. My mother was in a line waiting for food and there was one girl who—you know how people get impatient when standing in a line, they are hungry, and they are in hiding... they were standing in line, and they started arguing who came first and who was in line first. My mother witnessed a scene where a girl was thrown out of the line and told she was a "whore" because that [rape] happened to her. My mother knew what that girl went through, and people's behavior took a toll on her. They threw her out of the food line and called her that name, telling her that she was taken away by the paramilitaries because she asked for it. That is what I mean about our society. However, those same beliefs were instilled in me, and I did not want people to know, I don't want to be looked at in this way. I also don't want people to pity me. That is why I wanted to move away. The media plays a big role in how people see survivors, of course.

That is how I ended up going from Visoko to Zenica. In general, I lost every contact with people from my city, for that reason, because those are the people whom my mother asked for help, who did not help. Then, unfortunately, some information about some cases was leaked from Medica, because of an employee who left the organization and then told her friends and acquaintances about some of the cases. One of these was mine. I was deeply disappointed because of that breach in confidentiality. I was approached by someone once asking me if those things they heard about really happened to me. I wanted to move away after that. There are people like that everywhere. I am not a fan of NGOs. In my view they operate the same way as governmental organizations. And the

The Vulnerable and the Brave, in Their Own Words 165

state here does not function properly. I am somehow disappointed. In general, women who are the loudest are always the most helped. I mean that is okay, they should be helped, each woman should be helped. I am glad, but it's always the loudest women. This means that there will be women who are left behind. The country is in a difficult situation, there is a lot of manipulation when it comes to who deserves what, and who should be paid for what in terms of their war experience. I wish I was wrong about this, but I don't think I am.

It is important to me that people don't know about me and my story around here because I do not want people to look at me through that lens. I simply don't want that. Maybe if I lived in the US, maybe I would talk about that, maybe if I lived in Germany…but even German women did not talk for so long. I know about the case of German women, I read about it and felt really sorry. I know they opened themselves up to talk only after so many years when Bosnian women started talking. Because I do not want to be seen as a victim, no matter what happened.

In 1993 Islamic religious leaders issued a fatwa that society should treat women survivors as fighters. The fatwa changed public perception a bit. But the story about the girl who was thrown out of the food line and called a "whore" because of her experience stayed with me. I still remember it.

Referring to woman survivors by numbers is also placing them in the role of victim. All the time…. I felt it on my own skin. You must appear ignorant. You can't show that you are well read, because you cannot be well read and be a victim at the same time. You must appear beaten down. I think that many women do not have awareness of how these perceptions are shaped and behave like that by default. But some of them must feel that something is very wrong, even though they might not know what that is, or have awareness of what is going on. Because when you are put in a frame by someone else, you feel that it is wrong even you do not know how to verbalize it.

Support for survivors should be provided long term, on a consistent basis so that it doesn't take ten (10) years, like it did for me to start to feel better. In most of our state-run support institutions, staff do not possess the sensitivity to listen to and hear people who survived things like this—they just offer you pills and send you home. With NGOs the support keeps changing and is not consistently offered. One day there is a group that is interested in one topic, the next day another group that is interested in another topic. I speak in general now. But it is very important to be heard, for one's voice to be heard, that there is someone who will listen, someone to ask them when they are not well and tell them not to wait.

***

166   Unforgetting and the Politics of Representation

S.:   *My daughter's teacher told me once about another woman survivor, "so what if she's been fucked during the war, what do you want, what rights?" I can't even talk about this; it will bring me to...At one point a lot was being said about civilian victims and the media used us during the elections. Everyone was using us for something. They spoke of us as numbers, the women... The worst was when a journalist would come to meet me as a civilian victim of war, as a woman who had survived all that violence. The worst is when journalists expect to see a woman who doesn't take care of herself, a woman who is pitiful, a woman who is on medication, a woman who can't utter a word, a woman who will only be begging you, saying, "give to me, I'm in need." Why won't they realize that... We live with it, but if you saw one of those women, if you came across her on the street ... It isn't written on our foreheads. The worst for me is when they point their fingers at me as if I were different. I don't have the plague. It is an ache that stays with us, but it isn't contagious. I don't have scabies, you know? That's the worst part for me, that's why there are fewer of us who choose to speak openly about their experience. I sometimes wonder why I have spoken about it, why I've said it. Is that compensation worth it, that pointing of the finger at us? The things my child went through and still goes through to this day. To this very day. One or two years ago when she came home, a neighbor visiting my mother-in-law said, "S. is pretty, we could be inlaws," I was still in the hallway when my husband's mother said, "would you really want that Ustasha bastard for your daughter-in-law?"*

     That's how it is in this village, you see. We've been marked for all life, and yet we aren't...If I hadn't told you my name, would you have recognized me? Not to mention if we were to meet by chance. But that's how it is, they imagine us to be some sort of... But I don't understand why, why do people have those ideas about us? S. says that the journalists and the media are to blame, for representing us that way. They represented us as if we are needy, asking for this or that. What I have always asked for is justice. When S. was starting school, on all doors it was clearly written that disabled veterans, fighters, and their children did not have to pay 30 convertible marks for registration, but S. had to pay. How can you prove to someone, the fact that those children of war never... I once stated it publicly for everyone to hear, in front of many people. This was in a hotel, I believe, for the 20th anniversary of Medica. There were guests from different parts of the world. Place my pain on one side of a scale and the pain of a person missing a limb on the opposite side. Is there some sort of audition in determining which one weighs more?

***

The Vulnerable and the Brave, in Their Own Words   167

Sena: *If I am perceived as a victim, then everyone should realize that I have been a victim all these 20 years. You do not have to call me victim and put me on display, but I deserve respect. It does not matter if it is not attractive this year* [to talk about women survivors]. *We have been generally neglected by Medica for a long time until a year or two ago. This is probably because a research project received funding. I do not know. Somehow everything's about money.*

The state provides small financial support to victims of war and sometimes if people know that you are receiving that amount, it is like they are jealous. Survivors normally understand. But the public does not. I mean those 200 KM do not mean a lot to me when I must pay 50 KM for only one medication, not to mention the other ones. Sometimes people see you in a different light—you do not have to work; you have a disability cheque. That is why I cut off relations with most people. Sometimes it is better to be alone than to be with whomever. I mean, my problems were not solved with that money. It barely covers the cost of my medication. When I need to see the psychiatrist once a week, that costs 200 KM per month and I cannot afford that. Also, people don't realize what it is like to be told that you cannot work, or you are not fit to drive a car because of your disability. Everyone is focused on how much money the state provides as if that is all that matters.

***

L.O.:   *After two and a half years I returned from Medica, and my mother advised me to go to municipal representative to apply for some help with finding an apartment. I did, and explained who I was, I even had a confirmation that I am a civilian victim of war which means you get a priority when you apply for an apartment. I thought everything will be okay. However, the mayor suggested to me that I should join him to spend two days at the seaside and then after that we can talk about an apartment for me. There you go ...I was very disappointed. After I returned home, I was not able to tell my mother what he suggested. I could not hurt her like that. And they were persistent, my stepfather and my mother, telling me to go to the municipal office and to ask for this and that. They are both very good parents, my stepfather, and my mother, but both are very naive about how evil people are.*

There is no division in "ours" and "theirs." There are only those who are evil and those who are not. It was hard and everyone was terrible. The SDA [Social Democratic Action] was the ruling party, and they behaved as rulers of the earth. After that I had a nervous breakdown.

***

168 Unforgetting and the Politics of Representation

Alma: *Trust me, what I hated the most about being in Medica was the fact that we were all alike, that we had nothing else to talk about, so that's why I'm glad that none of those women are near me. I'd rather not know that those women exist. Do you now understand? I know they exist, but it's easier to me to pass by S. or any other woman and pretend as if nothing happened, as if we were different people.*

***

Sena: *When I was coming back from the Hague, I had to go back to work right away, they had no understanding. They didn't even ask how it was for me there. Instead, I was asked if I felt rested. I mean, I was in the Hague twice to testify. The first time I was there for seven days. However, they were late in submitting my statement to the defense and that fell through, so I had to go back after a few months, and I gave my testimony. I found it very difficult. It was very difficult not feeling understood and feeling underestimated by my workplace in Medica. Being told that I am incapable of doing this or that and being perceived as incapable. I was capable for over ten years, why take it away from me now? Why was I not asked if I am able to do the work? Even if I was not able to do work with greater responsibilities, I would still be able to do other kind of work, something smaller. I wanted to write a letter to the director to explain this. I was writing for months, trying to tell her how I feel, but I gave up on that. I gave up because I wish I could live this little life of mine in a way so as not to look over my shoulder any longer for anyone, to have some peace.*

Of telling and remembering then, and now

L.O.:   *A lot of time has passed since the war. Instead of making it easier for me to talk about my experience, in some way it has become more difficult. After the war ended, I thought I was a free woman and that I will get support after coming here. I thought I would be accepted. I felt confident and my mother played a part in that thinking. She told me that the most important thing is that I survived, and that no one will have anything against me. In reality, there was a lot of manipulation. I gave statements, to this and that, to the police, to journalists. I was manipulated and that is the reason I do not like to talk about my past anymore and I do not trust anyone any longer. Also, I do not want to talk. Perhaps that makes me different from those who talk easily. Right now, there are many more things that I would not say, which is different from how it was at the beginning. Things I could say at the beginning, I would not say now.*

***

The Vulnerable and the Brave, in Their Own Words 169

Alma: *Am I the only one who is confined to bed and can't get over it? Some people are walking, laughing…I will take any pill so I can walk and laugh. You understand? But there's no such pill for me. I can't accept it. Neither can I forget. I can't forgive either. Because they took away my youth, they took everything from me. I couldn't even get an education. I could have gotten my education in Medica, but I wasn't psychologically ready for it, I had no energy for that. All I could think of was the war, when and where it would start again. I arrived in Medica, and I kept thinking that soon there would be more massacres. Because there was heavy fighting in Večići, Vrbanjci. I can't comprehend that they wiped out the entire male population there. How many people from my village lost their lives? I remember my brother telling me once, why are you tending those cows, let them go, can't you see a sniper is about to hit you? I had no idea what a sniper was. I see something flashing around me. … I can't, I simply can't get over it. One of the best psychologists has worked with me, but I can't. There are times when I'm scared, I'm crying and shaking, having attacks that I haven't had before. All of it comes to me in my dreams. I behave normally, at least that's what I think. I talk to people, but when the night comes, it's dreadful. I'd rather not sleep because I know what awaits me when I fall asleep. I'll either have another attack or I'll dream about the war. The only thing I don't know is where it will be this time, in Kotor Varoš or in Banja Luka…*

***

Azra: *When I came to Medica, I was not ready to talk about the details, although to some extent I was forced to because I had to provide statements for agencies that were collecting information about war crimes. And I shared some details with S. because she shared some details of her experience with me. Maybe I shared with her the most. From all the details, I shared with her the most and not with family, friends, not even with any girlfriend, absolutely nothing. Maybe I shared with her the most because she went through similar experiences. I don't know if it is important to talk about that. It is important when a person feels a connection with someone, and has a desire to share with someone, to have someone to share with. That is important. Sometimes a person does not want to share. Like in my case. Since I did not want to burden my family members because they too, they … Because my family was a support network to me. They did not reject me because of what happened. They were a support in their own capacity, as much as they knew how. People give what they know how to give. It is easier for me to know they did not go through a lot. I always hid from them that I was not well. I carried myself as if I were okay, so that they do not go through additional pain because of that. Because I know they would be in pain. It is difficult when someone during*

170   Unforgetting and the Politics of Representation

the war suffers multiple losses. A lot of things happened. Not just one thing. It is difficult for the individual who went through it all, but also for everyone. It is reflected on everyone, especially people closest to them. You want to spare them. To protect them from all of that.

***

Selma: *After being abused in the war, I went to a psychiatrist, but I never told them all of what happened. I told them I did not feel well; that I could not sleep, that I was crying, that my body was numb. My legs, my arms would get numb. I was 19 when the war started. I have been taking medications for years. Started right after that. I would not be able to function without those medications. There are still periods when I cannot get up for a whole day. I have sudden mood swings, first I am well and then I am not. Then I want to laugh and then to cry. Then I want to sleep. I do not know how to describe that state of mine. It is very changeable. And then it means a person cannot get organized, cannot function as a regular person. Cannot hold a full-time job. The first thing that I think about when I wake up in the morning, is that—what happened to me. Over my morning coffee. And then the day begins: you must have breakfast, prepare kids for school, prepare meals, do laundry, everything that needs to be done. This is how my life is passing. I cannot tell this to anyone. No one knows what is inside of my soul. No one sees my tears in the morning when I get up. Not even my children. I cannot imagine my life without medication.*

   There were other women who went through the same thing as I did, but this was not to be spoken of, not even among us. It is hard to talk about that. Let me tell you, I prepared myself very well for these conversations with you. One cries three days before and three days after. I also feel hurt when I hear someone else tell their experience. It hurts me the same as if it was me. It is like I am going through it again listening to their story. I understand. No one who did not go through the same can understand what it's like. I admire people who ask about us, who take care of us; thank God for such people. It was difficult being silent for such a long time. It has been much easier since I took it out of myself.

   My mother always asks, "What did you go through, what did they do to you?" Nothing happened. You cannot talk about that. To anyone, not even with a friend. Many women ask for their face to be covered if they talk about that. I agreed to be filmed once for a federal TV station, but my face had to be covered. So, I told it all and felt relief, opening up my soul to someone. Medica helped me a great deal. From them I learned that I am entitled to a pension. This is what I live on. That keeps me going. And I make jewelry and other objects.

***

The Vulnerable and the Brave, in Their Own Words 171

S.Š.:   *It is difficult to be alive. At least we are alive. I don't know what to say. It was not easy for any of the other women who went through a similar ordeal, but at least we got some rights of our own. I did get the status of civil victim of war last year. So, it's a little easier to live. Whatever one can do to earn a living. One keeps on thinking about what happened, it comes back whenever one works, but the work keeps you busy and occupied, it prevents you from getting lost in your thoughts. You cannot erase that experience. Each time I go to Datići I am thinking I would never be able to go back and live there even if they gave me everything. The moment I am there I see the army in front of my eyes.*

    I contacted Medica two years ago, when I was 36. I saw them on TV. I felt ashamed for what had happened to me in the war. I did not ask for it, but I felt ashamed. Then I said, I am going to ask for my rights. First, I was ashamed, and afterward I saw that I am entitled to some rights I said I am going to ask for my rights. I felt sick. I could not sleep.

    I have not spoken to my mother about it. I never wanted to tell her. She never asked. There is a lot of gossip here in the countryside, especially among women. They like to talk and even laugh at someone if they found out a story about them. When I told it to the female doctor, I also told her that I have animals and two children, and I had no desire to live nor to work. Now I go for check-ups regularly and when I come back home, I deal with animals, and I feel better. The doctor is pleasant and young. She tries to give good advice and to explain everything. She says I must fight and not give up. I cannot leave my chickens alone because if I do, a fox will come and kill them. Last year a fox strangled 17 of my chickens and I could not eat the whole day because of that. I love animals and if something happens to them, I do not feel well, and I cannot eat and I need to be left alone by everyone. So, the doctor and I talk on the phone. She calls to ask how I am and to see what is going on. We talk on a regular basis. Sometimes I call her to see how she is and such.

***

Azra: *I have not spoken to many people about my experiences. At the beginning I spoke to people in Medica, then I spoke to some other women survivors, but not for a while. Maybe I would like sometimes to give a statement, to tell people what happened to me. To tell it to someone. However, the director of Medica never offered that to me. Somehow priority was always given to other women, and that hurt me terribly.*

    When I went to see the doctor to ask for sick leave, he looked at my case and said, "What do you want? I was in the war, too, and I still go to work." He spoke about this for a long time, how he, too, was in the war.

172 Unforgetting and the Politics of Representation

I was quiet, and he gave me two days of sick leave. I am sorry, I am not sure how this sounds, I have not spoken about this in 15 years.

***

S.:　　*We are starting to languish, we will disappear. I only regret that we will not leave our mark in time. S. works hard so our stories are not forgotten. It will fall into oblivion, but maybe, God willing, someone will one day, if we live to see it… For example, my daughter., if she has any children in the future, she'll tell them about it. We will not be known, yet we have given so much, we truly have. Ahead of the next elections, someone will show up at our door, look for a story, speak for us, so that we vote for them. And then, we'll be forgotten, that's how it goes. The worst of it is when they say, "what do you want, the state has given you compensation." Once, I think it was at a workshop in Sarajevo, one of those politicians was going on and on about that compensation, so I asked him, "do you have a mother?" "I do," he said. "And a sister, a wife, a daughter? Well, imagine if one of them …" He said that he couldn't even imagine. "But why not? What kind of compensation would you give her? Could you give her 5000 convertible marks? Do you think that you will have compensated her enough?"*

Let this small voice of mine be heard somewhere

Azra:　*I hesitated before agreeing to speak to you since I have not been sharing my story anywhere for a very long time. Last time I shared it, I was a witness in court. I was hesitating for a long time since I somehow left all that behind. Not that I left it behind, it is always somewhere around, following you as a shadow. But for a long time, no one offered me a discreet opportunity to speak, like this one. So, I was hesitating, but in the end, I decided that I will. Maybe my small voice can be heard somewhere, in a book. So that is my only motive, that something is heard somewhere since for a very long time I was not asked about anything. There have always been other women who speak on behalf of this population and there are several women who agreed to speak in public, but no one thinks of women who did not agree to speak in public, women who do not want to speak in public, women who have their own lives. Often supports are directed to women who are willing to appear on TV and in other media or attend public gatherings. They may be the brave ones. But there are also the voices of other women who are not heard at all. The only thing that is heard is about the women who are willing to speak out, and how much their speaking out has helped everyone, and I understand that, since it is important for the voice to be heard, but somehow everything is concentrated around these women. And it is because of that kind of*

The Vulnerable and the Brave, in Their Own Words   173

thinking, I decided well, okay, let this small voice of mine be heard somewhere, in a body of research. And it will leave a trace and it may grab someone's attention, and it does not have to be about me, I do not think it will be very helpful, but if my small voice helps someone, some other woman, in another country, I will be glad. These are some of my motives for talking.

***

Alma: *Speaking out about my experience makes it easier for me, because somewhere in the world there will be someone who will know about my case.*

***

S.:   *My husband and I have Bosnian coffee in the morning. Sometimes we have coffee with his mother. My mother-in-law lives one floor below. She's 77, but she's relatively healthy and can still work around the house. I mean, when there's a major cleaning to be done, I'll do it for her. You know, despite everything, so much was coming from their side, you see, they had to accept the fact that someone else's child was coming into their home. They've never singled her out. When we finish paying off the loan for the bathroom renovations, if I could finish that exterior wall next to the stairs, I don't need anything else. This is enough for the two of us, I'm more than happy. That's why I'm telling you, I am well now, thank God, considering everything that had happened and what we had been through.*

***

L.O.:   *The war started shortly after I graduated from elementary school. So, I do not really have a profession. I wanted to study medicine and to become a pediatrician. I always liked that. After elementary school I started attending medical high school. I was in first year and the war started, so I never finished. I am married now and a mother of three. I do various things, agriculture mostly. I cultivate plants and I also keep bees. My husband fell very ill four years ago which means he cannot contribute financially to the household any longer. Most of that responsibility falls on me now. I do various things to earn some money and survive. Even though this situation might sound sad, I am not unhappy. Deep down I am a happy person. Even though it is difficult, and we live very modestly, and suffer at times while wondering how to make ends meet every month, I am still happy because my children are healthy and that fulfils me. Even though our little house is ruinous and old, it is full of love and fulfilment.*

174 Unforgetting and the Politics of Representation

That is why I cannot say I am a sad woman. I am cheerful and maybe it is just my spirit and something I was born with. Anyway, I am 40 years old, will be 41 in September. Sometimes when I say my age, I get surprised—I am still 29 in my head.

When I think back to my war experience, I also consider the fact that life is ever-changing and there are always new troubles, and I can say that the war made me tougher and more militant, resilient. I feel that now no one can do anything to me now. I survived what was impossible to survive and after that nothing will break me. On the other side, that experience brought me a lot of adversity too, pushed me behind, considering the fact I have a child born because of war. That did not help me to get a direction in life. When I came here, I expected that I came to a free territory. That I will be accepted. Instead, I was asked to change the name of my child, to give him up, to leave him. That created an atmosphere of mistrust. When the word "friend" is mentioned, I think I can hardly have any friends. So, I do not know. Even later when I wanted to form a new family, when I wanted to change my life somehow, everything was much harder.

Justice, redefined

L. O.:   *Preparing to go to the Hague I woke up one morning and went down to the convenience store in the building, to get some milk. I saw two uniformed police officers standing in front of the building. They followed me everywhere. They explained to me that I was a crown witness, and they have a court order to guard me. I explained to them that they were out of their mind and that we were in a small town, and everyone is staring at me because of them, and I asked them to leave me alone. That brought so much stress on me. They were standing in front of my window, in front of my door. This is such a small town; everyone knows everyone else. It is enough that they follow me down the street and everyone will ask me why. That went on for a month and a half and during that period my mother got ill, and she had to go to the hospital. I wanted to visit her, she was in the hospital in Sarajevo, but because of the policemen who followed me everywhere the doctors did not allow me to see her but instead asked for written permission and explanation from the police. They thought I was a criminal. Then letters started coming in. Threats from people who were in Fikret Abdic's unit and who were his supporters.[8] They said they will kill my child if I go to the court, they said they will kill me as well, they said I went through nothing compared to what I am about to go through ... I was receiving those letters while being guarded by the police. The police were involved, of course. Then I was attacked, beaten up, two days before I was scheduled to appear in court. And just before my picture and full name appeared in the local newspaper,* Jutarnji

(Morning). So much for being protected. I went to court, and I was supposed to face the accused and to try to identify him, so I did go, and I said I do not know him. And then I came home and after that they left me alone. I said I will never go to the court again. I do not want to. I do not believe in courts anymore. The court is a charade. It was suffering and torture at the time. Now it all might be different. But back then, people pointed finger at you publicly; it was horrible. I have horrible experiences. I do not want to have anything to do with it again. So, what if someone is sentenced to five years in prison? It does not make it any easier for me. It used to be very important to me. I really wanted all of them to be sentenced and go to jail, to pay for everything they have done. But the defense lawyers simply play games. What do I need to prove? I do not have desire to go through all that nonsense.

It is because it mattered to me that criminals are sentenced that I agreed to talk to Alexandra about the book.[9] I wanted the truth to come out and justice be served. I agreed, and we started working together, we worked for long and exhausting hours, we talked and wrote, there was a lot to be covered. Right now, I am glad that the book exists, but I don't feel well when I see someone reading it in my presence. Or even just touching it. It makes me nervous, and my palms sweat, I get sick to my stomach. The children also know about the book, but no one read it yet. There is no Bosnian translation. There is German, Swedish, Turkish, but not Bosnian. Now I am wondering how it is going to be when they read it. It is probably going to be horrible. My children know that I was…. They cannot even comprehend what that means. They cannot even imagine. My husband knows. He knows a lot but not in detail. I think I would have to take him to a psychiatric ward if I told him everything. He cannot even watch a movie with a lot of blood. I do not hide it from them, either, they know everything, but I do not want to burden them even more, so that they think about that, to imagine how it all was. I was asked about the book being translated into Bosnian and I said no. I do not know if there will come a time when they translate it without asking me.

I don't know whether the film In the Land of Blood and Honey is based on the book, for example. I met with Angelina [Jolie] at Medica, we talked, but I did not have an opportunity to ask her if the movie was done according to that book. I did not think she could understand but she seemed like a wonderful person. That surprised me. I have not seen the movie yet. I just do not want to. I know everything. I have seen the reactions; I know the script. But I never sat and watched the movie. I know that some women civil victims of war protested, and one of them [the president of one of the associations for civil victims of war] called me and told me that it was not okay. She thought that I had direct influence on the decisions. I never mentioned this to Angelina, never asked her if the movie was done according to the book nor did I tell her that I was the

176 Unforgetting and the Politics of Representation

woman from the book. There was no time, I forgot, I do not know. We talked about other things.

***

Alma: *I told my daughter to do a DNA test, so they can find him and persecute him. She no longer wishes to pursue this course of action, simply doesn't want to see that man, and there's nothing I can do. It would be easier for both of us. I'd only like him to experience what I had experienced. I'm confined to this place, so may he be confined to jail, if he's still alive... For 19 years I've needed assistance. To this day I can't stay by myself. All I want is to be able to walk again.*

Someone must be a voice for someone else who is no longer here

Azra: *Going to court to provide a testimony helped. But it has been counterproductive too. I was not well back then, and I didn't have full understanding of the legal side. At first, I refused but then relented to invitations, and went to the court in Sarajevo. I had to give all those statements again and it was stressful. I could not sleep for many nights, as my testimony date was approaching. The psychiatrist that I was seeing at the time came with me without any reimbursement, just as a friendly support. On the day of my scheduled testimony, I was waiting in a small room from where they would take us into the courtroom, and I felt sick and felt I needed to throw up again, and I did not give my testimony that day since the testifying of a previous witness took a longer time. And then again, I had to go through it all again, the next day. You know how it is, the defense is ruthless in terms of asking questions, they are trying to obstruct you in all possible ways. It can be an exhausting experience. They did everything they could to obstruct and then they planted a photograph. However, it all ended well since I did not recognize anyone in that photograph. I wonder what would have happened if I did recognize someone in that photo. Memory can play tricks on you after many years pass by. They literally planted it. Because the defense is ruthless, a person can feel bad afterward. And that is why I am saying, it is a double-edged sword. It would be good if someone told me beforehand that the defense would be ruthless, so that I could be ready for it. You know how it is when you are afraid. You spend years feeling afraid, you throw up, you don't sleep. You do not want to be there at all, and after all of that he shows you that photograph. And then they try to make you stray from your initial testimony. So, after that I was glad. I always wanted to give my testimony because of my sister. But it didn't help me psychologically.*

At least I did something. First for my sister and then for all those other people, since I survived, and they did not. Someone must be a voice

for someone else who is no longer here. If it was only about my own trauma, I may not have done it. But many people lost their lives. This motivated me to go to court. That, and the verdict. He was sentenced for life. It is rare for someone of that rank to get a life sentence. So, I was part of that, I contributed to that, but what would have happened if I had made a mistake? Say if I made a mistake having to do with that planted photograph, maybe it would have ruined it all. It is such a burden. It would have been easy to make a mistake. I feel good about the verdict even though he wasn't sentenced specifically for the rapes he committed. I wish that this was part of his sentence. I heard that if he were tried at the Hague that may have played a role in the verdict, but it didn't. But whatever is done, is done. There is no point feeling bad about it.

***

Sera: *About seven years ago I went to the Hague. I do not know how I made up my mind to do it. I did it not because I wanted revenge since I was mature enough to know that not all people are the same and that I cannot say that all Serbs are the same, or all Croats are the same. I did not want revenge. I just wanted to do something for my father and brother.*

        I testified against Milan Lukic, and he was convicted, he got a life sentence. The other one that I testified against, he took my father and brother and killed them, and he used to take me often—he got 27 years.[10] I testified against them in the Hague, and against other perpetrators in Sarajevo. It was much easier in the Hague as they had more understanding about whether you can come or not. I went to court twice and then I stopped following updates. The ICTY verdict was less significant for me personally, but more significant for my father and brother. For me, somehow, I would not be able to recognize that person any longer. I could have said that that person raped me four times, and I do not even know who he is. Why would I tell that in court? How am I going to prove it? Somehow it was more important to prove this for my father and brother, that some peace could be found. I did not insist on myself in the testimonies.

Justice is served by me being brave and strong

L.O.:   *In terms of challenges, I still have them daily. My life is strange, and each phase and year of life is different and brings new challenges. I have had to build different relationship to overcome it all. Over the years there has been a lot of nationalism, and what was important to me in all of that is that or any other kind of hatred does not penetrate my children, to keep my kids healthy and clear from that. And I worked on this through conversation and my own behavior. I think that had the most influence. Staying at Medica helped me a lot, considering their capability and appropriate educational tools to help us, to pass knowledge to us. I learned a lot. I read a lot. I put a lot of effort into acquiring knowledge. I somehow built myself up. I try to apply to myself all positive things I see around me, and I do them for a while and then that becomes naturally part of me. No one knows how to be a mother. We were not taught how to be mothers and each day brings some new experience and something new. Zoran is 21, so right now I am learning how to live with a son who is twenty-one (21). I don't know, there are no rules. I have my own group of women; we make projects and work. We have a training course in sewing. Medica donated to that project, so women are attending. There are psychological workshops too. Some women attend them. Our town is small and here women do not have the opportunity for conversation. Women here want to talk. Some of them are civilian victims of war, but many of them are in social need, those who suffer family violence and so on. We have women who are only now coming out about what happened to them.*

I think it is important to talk about our experiences if we are raising children. I have two sons. I have a daughter, and I do not want her to go through what I did, nor do I want that my sons are capable to do something like that to a woman tomorrow. We must talk about it because if we do not, then …People simply don't know what they are doing, they have no awareness and evil is always close by, and you can get lost in it easily. I think that even those people who are not evil are sometimes seduced by that. By life events. I know that in camps there were a lot of people who were saving you in a way, giving you piece of bread to eat or water to drink. It means that somewhere on a deeper level they were not evil, but they were carried away by that evil. If we were more educated, if we talked about it earlier… Maybe they would know that they cannot go around and kill people because the war will end, and you will have to pay for your deeds. I think that people thought the war would not end. I do not know what they thought. I think it should be talked about. I am not ashamed. I feel like a hero who overcame everything, who is alive and well, and proud. To me justice is served by me being brave, strong, and showing them that I am alive. There you go. That is that justice.

***

S.Š.: *My message to other women survivors is, do not forget. Try to forgive if you can. Because, we only have one life to live, but I know that I can't, because it's hard to deal with the past. After all, it is a big trauma. What can I say, I shouldn't lecture another woman.*

***

The Vulnerable and the Brave, in Their Own Words 179

Azra: *If I had a message for other women survivors, it would for them to know that whatever they feel or do not feel in any given moment, it is OK. That it is possible to carry on living. I would gladly share my own experience of living in fear and frozen for ten years, feeling persecuted, to help them understand what I mean. Many women end up in the neuropsychiatry unit and never get out, and never take themselves off the pills, they stay dependent on medication forever and that is not that good. What is important is that you can connect to your own experience, so that you are able to somehow go out of it. There is the psychiatry phase, but after that, it is possible to carry on. The past does follow you, and it is possible to continue to see a therapist. It is possible to feel happy at least once in seven days, and to aspire to greater quality of life. It is possible for the feeling of fear to go away; it is possible to have hope. I didn't have hope during those ten years. I thought that would be the end of me. But here I am. It can be done. That is what I would like to share with them from my heart. Really, from my heart.*

On peace, identity, and nationality

L.O.:   *I believe in God but not in religions. I passed that to my children even though I did not tell them that religion doesn't exist. I think God exists, someone saved me, there is a force, someone did create us, something is helping us and that is what I believe. I told my kids that when they grow up and decide to choose a religion, I will not interfere with that. However, I consider that religions brought evil and that is why I do not want my children to attend religious classes, which is what they had to do soon after the war ended. That was hard on me. Now times are different, the climate is not as nationalist as it used to be, it is not as pronounced here as it used to be. Nationalism still exists in some places, mostly in small villages much more than here, but here the population is mixed, some people returned after the war, so that we do not really have issues around that. Zoran, my son, is Bosnian, he feels like a Bosnian, he is a patriot, he is glad his roots are here. Bosnia is in his heart, his motherland, but not in a religious sense. He loves Bosnia, and I mean Bosnia and Herzegovina, to make it clear.*

     In terms of national identity, I never identified myself with any side. War came and went, and I still cannot always distinguish which first names belong to which religion, besides a few basic ones, like Mujo and Haso. Not to mention how it was before war since my grandfather was a Partisan. Even today, my stepfather supports communism, he comes from that era and still lives in it. We were not raised to be nationalist. I had no idea what the war was really about for a long time. I really did not understand it. And I did not identify with any ethnic or national side, I guess I was Yugoslavian. Before the war we never went to church or any religious institution. We never had religious education at school, so I do not really know much about it. I cannot remember that anyone ever told me I am Muslim before. I do not remember. It is the same now. I do not have affiliation. I am a human, a living being, I am a woman, an Earthling. That is what I am sure about, and I have no idea about the rest. I was born and no one asked what I wanted to be and then someone came and told me what I am and then came to kill me because of it.

Terrible. In the end, I am an Earthling and a woman and that is what it is. We, my family, we do not declare any affiliations.

Instead of religious classes what we should introduce in schools is education in women's rights. We should educate our children in women's rights.

***

Azra: *Well, it was all different before the war. I come from a family that just as most Yugoslav families, was not religious. People changed. It is hard for me to say, I was 17, I did not think about that really. It never occurred to me to wonder what nationality someone is based on their names. That was the spirit of communism and the principle of brotherhood and unity. I was not raised to make a difference among people based on their ethnic identity. After the war, of course, I declare myself as Bosniak. Even though Bosnian and Bosniak should basically be the same thing, it does bother me that some people deny the crimes. This constant denial of crimes causes me to feel Bosniak because it feels more moral and humane. After so much time I cannot understand how someone can deny the suffering of others. Overall, though, national identity is not very important to me, but it is difficult to have a meaningful dialogue in this country without making it about national or religious identity. I really don't know what to say about that. I think about national identity mostly when someone denies some things that happened. My best friend is Croatian, Catholic. We have been best friends for five years now. Being friends with her is a way for setting myself free from hatred. But then, it is not about nationality. Everything always comes down to what is someone like as a person. I was socializing with some Bosniak women too, but still, my best friend is Croatian. What makes a difference is the humanity of a person. This is how I was raised. But if you don't grow up like that, it is harder now to become like that. Even though there were some who switched, who started hating so fast. Now why that is, it is a question for another book.*

The Vulnerable and the Brave, in Their Own Words   181

There is social pressure as well. If you are an internally displaced person, and a refugee, how can you socialize with someone who belongs to the people whose representatives expelled you and made you a refugee? Do you understand? Society plays a role there. I used to get comments like that from my community. That I should not socialize with people whose representatives expelled me from my home.

***

Selma: *In my village there is one couple in a mixed marriage; he is Croat, and she is Serbian. They were imprisoned with us, and when they were released, they came back and still live there. But many other people moved away and sold their apartments. Most of our population is now Muslim. One of my neighbors is Croat, she stayed in her apartment. My very good friend is Serb, we ate, we drank together. They are not guilty for what happened to me. I do not know who did that. Maybe they came from Serbia. I hate those people who brought evil upon me. I cannot hate the whole world.*

***

Alma: *When I read the news, it's clear that in our country there's nothing to see in politics. I don't think those entities, like Republika Srpska or the Federation, should be in existence at all. We can't go forward if we aren't in it together. See, you can't and shouldn't forget the past, but you must forgive yourself and others to go on. Because we have no other way out. Where should we, Muslims, go? Wherever we end up, we are Bosnians, we are Yugoslavs, but now there's no such thing. I'll give you an example of how I think about it. At the Eurovision contest, when Marija Šerifović from Serbia performed, who do you think I voted for? For her! Those are my neighbors! I'll never be able to forget, but you can't view all people according to the deeds of bad men. I think those men were mercenaries, mercenaries from Serbia, right? They worked for money and under the influence of drugs because no normal person could have done what they did. The same goes for those from Croatia, they were paid to do what they did. They were smoking Ronhill brand cigarettes. See, even today, I can't afford to smoke Ronhill, I roll my own cigarettes. How much were they paid to commit massacres and similar crimes? It is a fact that Muslim people have suffered the greatest losses. They can deny that, but nobody can escape from it. You understand? It is difficult to live with the memory of war, so imagine how it is for those who have murdered many people. There are no more drugs, there's no more money. Nobody's paying them anymore… to stab a two-month-old baby with a bayonet, not everyone can do that. That could be done only by men who were on drugs. Can a normal person do that? To what end?*

***

S.Š.:   *Before the war the area was mixed, there were Croats and Bosniaks living there. Datići and Lalovac were mixed. Now there are all Croats in Datići. I do not really know who was here, I was 13. I only know that the men, like my father, had to dig ditches and go to fight and that the army was coming to harass them. Some people escaped; some were exchanged. A lot of people died. These things stay hidden. People will not talk. Because they may pay for it if they talk when they must go through Muslim villages. My youngest sister, she is ten years younger, got a message from a girl from her class in school that people in the village said they will rape her as well if she dares to appear over there, so she does not go there. She was in eighth grade then, and this made everyone afraid of Muslims because having to pass through their village. My mother said we need to keep quiet since we must go through Muslim villages for work. Everyone was afraid of the dark. It has been enough of war and these kinds of problems.*

    It is hard to go through something and then talk about it. I am very scared when I see what happened in Srebrenica, where people were shot with their hands tied behind their back. I am thinking that we almost had the same fate. They gathered us like that as well with the exception that they did not tie our hands, but they shot older people who were slower and could not walk as fast. People who lived nearby brought us what they had for food, but we could not eat from fear. We were sitting the whole time since there was not enough space to lie down and sleep. They did this to us because of our nationality. Before the war we went to school together, we worked together, we just had different names and last names and we had to pronounce certain words in a certain way. I do not think those people are guilty for what happened, but someone somewhere is guilty.

    Right now, I find Muslims better than Croats; Muslims are readier to help around the house and farm work. Croats will not do it. They have higher wages. Muslims are better at offering help. Before, I used to hate them a lot. But there have been times over the years when I was in trouble and needed help and Muslims have understood better when I was in trouble or was destitute. If a child is sick, a Muslim will offer to take the child to the nearby hospital while a Croat will not offer something like that. I realized that Muslims are more pleasant than Croats. I went to see the priest and talked to the priest about it all and I feel much better now. He said it was not their fault, they were just people, and it is not

The Vulnerable and the Brave, in Their Own Words 183

they who started the war. He said I cannot hate my neighbor now because he did nothing wrong. I realized he was right.

***

S.: *In the town where I live, we used to have five ethnically mixed schools. Croats, Muslims, and Serbs under one roof. Where I am from, there were both Serbs and Muslims. Now Serbs arrive by bus, escorted by police, to their commemoration ceremony. They are displaced because everything was demolished, it's all devastated. So, they fled to Modriča, Bijeljina, Doboj, fled wherever they could. Naturally, they are now coming to commemorate their own people. Many bad words are still spoken by our people.*

Our mayor went to the commemoration site there on behalf of the town. I really admire the mayor, I mean, a young man like him to come forward, wish them welcome, to express a desire for their return and a collaboration. One man from Modriča came forward and said, "this is the first time since the war that someone from this town addressed us, we are very glad, this is an opportunity for a collaboration." The people in the town, however, practically stoned the mayor for coming forward and saying those words. In the villages where we live nothing will ever change. While in Sarajevo, in Zenica, my child can live happily with everyone. I've never ever told her not to. Ever since she was a child, I've been telling her "You should always appreciate the good in everyone." I mean, how can you expect to commemorate your own losses while making it impossible for others to do the same?

On one occasion my brother-in-law told me, "If anyone should hate, then it should be you." I was taken aback, I said, "you know what, I don't hate people, I only hate evildoers. Behind that balaclava, there could have been someone with a Muslim name. Don't ever say that to me again. I don't hate, I can't hate my sister-in-law because her name is Dragica. I can't hate little Anka because of her name." He didn't say a word to me after that. The worst part is when people judge others before they have even had a chance to meet them.

The nearby town, on the other hand, is more diverse when it comes to offices in the municipal government, public services, or the hospital. You see, in the cities you'll find all three ethnicities, also in the cities like Žepče or Zenica, for example. But in the villages, it's more difficult there. There are now many who would like to go back to Tito's regime, and Wahhabis hate that. You've heard what happened this Ramadan. Wahhabis attacked a young woman because she was wearing kimono sleeves and a short skirt during Ramadan. Who gives him that right? Who gives you the right to attack a young woman you've never met?

Let's have something to eat.

184 Unforgetting and the Politics of Representation

Notes

1 The hotel is Vilina Vlas. See footnote no. 1 in Pt. III, Chapter 1.
2 S.Š. belongs to the Croat minority in her village. Ustaše [Ustashe, plural] were members of the Croatian fascist and ultranationalist organization active between 1929 and 1945. The use of the term was revived during the recent war and used as a derogatory label for anyone who was of Croat nationality without any necessary connection with the movement itself.
3 Fahreta Živojinović (née Jahić), known by her stage name Lepa [Beautiful] Brena, is a Yugoslav and Serbian pop-folk singer, actress and businesswoman. She is the best-selling female recording artist from the former Yugoslavia.
4 I have written about S's story more extensively in the following publications: "Challenging Conceptions: Children Born of Wartime Rape in Bosnia and Herzegovina," in ed. Kimberley Theidon and Dyan Mazurana, *Challenging Conceptions: Children Born of Wartime Rape and Sexual Exploitation* (Oxford University Press, 2023); "Raising Children Born of War in Bosnia: Reframing Perspectives on Mother Love Through a Mother-Daughter Case Study," in ed. Carole Zuffrey and Fiona Buchanan, *Intersections of Mothering: Feminist Accounts. Interdisciplinary Research in Motherhood Series* (Routledge, 2020), 141–155;
   "Negotiating Identities in Post-Conflict Bosnia and Herzegovina: Self, Ethnicity and Nationhood in Adolescents Born of Wartime Rape," in ed. Tamara P. Trošt and Danilo Mandić, *Changing Youth Values in Southeast Europe: Beyond Ethnicity* (Routledge, 2017), 19–38; "Raising Children Born of Wartime Rape in Post-Conflict Bosnia: Maternal Philosophy Perspective," in ed., Tatjana Takseva and Arlene Sgoutas, *Mothering Under Fire: Mothers and Mothering in Conflict Zones* (Toronto: Demeter Press, 2015), 97–120; "Mother Love, Maternal Ambivalence, and the Possibility of Empowered Mothering," *Hypatia: Journal of Feminist Philosophy* 32.1 (2016). doi: 10.1111/hypa.12310. The parts of the conversation provided here are those that, for the most part, do not appear previously.
5 Zoran is a common Serbian name. It means "dawn.".
6 Stranka Demokratske Akcije (Party for Democratic Action), a Bosniak, nationalist, conservative political party.
7 Sabiha Husić, Director of the Association Medica Zenica.
8 Fikret Abdić is a Bosnian politician and businessman who won the popular vote in the Bosnian presidential elections of 1990. Between 1993–1995, Abdić declared his opposition to the official Bosnian government, and established the Autonomous Province of Western Bosnia, a short-lived province allied with the Army of Republika Srpska. In 2002, he was convicted on charges of war crimes against Bosniaks loyal to the Bosnian government by a court in Croatia and sentenced to 20 years imprisonment, although he only served two thirds of a reduced, 15-year sentence. In June 2020 he was arrested again on suspicion of abuse of his office as Mayor.
9 The book being referenced here is Alexandra Cavelius' Leila. Ein bosnisches Mädchen, released in German only, in 2000. Also see, Tatjana Takševa and Agatha Schwartz, "Hybridity, Ethnicity and Nationhood: Legacies of Interethnic War, Wartime Rape and the Potential for Bridging the Ethnic Divide in Post-Conflict Bosnia and Herzegovina," *National Identities* (2017). doi: 10.1080/14608944.2017.1298580.
10 Milan Lukić and Sredoje Lukić were indicted on 26 October 1998. Their trial (case number IT-98-32/1) commenced on July 9, 2008. On July 20, 2009, the ICTY Trial Chamber sentenced both to life imprisonment and 30 years' imprisonment, respectively. Milan Lukić was found guilty of extermination, murder, persecutions, and

The Vulnerable and the Brave, in Their Own Words 185

other inhumane acts as crimes against humanity, and murder and cruel treatment as violations of the laws or customs of war. Lukić was convicted in relation to six distinct incidents, including the killing of five Muslim civilian men at the Drina River on or about June 7, 1992, and the killing of seven Muslim civilian men at the Varda factory in Višegrad on or about June 10, 1992. He was also found guilty of the murder of Hajra Korić and of the beatings of Muslim detainees in the Uzamnica Camp. He was also found responsible for the murder of a group of Muslim women, children, and elderly men in the house of Adem Omeragić on Pionirska Street in Višegrad on June 14, 1992, where the victims were locked into one room of the house which was then set on fire by Lukić. He was found to have shot at people trying to escape from the burning house. Milan Lukic was further found guilty of the murder of at least 60 Muslim civilians in a house in the Bikavac settlement of Višegrad on or about June 27, 1992. The Trial Chamber established that Milan Lukić was present throughout this incident, shot at the house, threw grenades into it, and subsequently set the house on fire. The affirmation of Milan Lukić's sentence is the first time the Appeals Chamber has upheld a sentence of life imprisonment. All his appeals were rejected.

Sredoje Lukić was found guilty of murder, persecutions, and other inhumane acts as crimes against humanity, and murder and cruel treatment as violations of the laws or customs of war. He was convicted in relation to the events on Pionirska Street and at the Uzamnica Camp. His sentence was subsequently reduced to 27 years. Details of the trial and transcripts can be found via web files of the UN ICTY, accessible at: https://www.icty.org/en/case/milan_lukic_sredoje_lukic#trans.

Chapter 10

Esma D., a Bosnian Woman Fighter

Not much has been written to date about women who fought in the recent Yugoslav war, but their presence was significant on all sides of the conflict in the former Yugoslavia. In Croatia, women who fought in the war are referred to as *žene braniteljice* [women defenders], and their numbers are estimated to be between 14,443 and 23,000 out of approximately 200,000 members of the Croatian army.[1] In the army of Republika Srpska, formed on May 12, 1992, it is estimated that 2–3 percent of all those who fought were women. Radmila Srdić from Prijedor has been most outspoken about her war experience, as well as after the war, relating her challenges in achieving legal recognition as a woman veteran, with the same rights and supports as men who belonged to the same army.[2]

According to data of the Army of Bosnia and Herzegovina, there were 5,360 women recruits.[3] Some of them were fighters, and some of them actively contributed to the war effort as health professionals, teachers, and other service providers. Associations of women soldiers also made active contributions as so-called patriotic volunteers who joined the Patriotic league and the Army of Bosnia and Herzegovina. Because of their courage in carrying out successful assignments, they are sometimes called "Amazon women." Some of them have been awarded medals and recognition for courage and bravery, either posthumously or while living. The order of Zlatni Ljiljan [Golden Lily], the highest war award of the BiH Army, is the honor conferred upon members of the armed forces of Bosnia and Herzegovina who "particularly stood out in armed opposition to the aggressor, who contributed to the expansion of the free parts of the Republic, who performed several acts in which their personal courage and self-sacrifice stood out and in which the aggressor was inflicted with significant losses in personnel and material resources."[4] While 1,742 individuals have received this honor since 1994, only 13 of them have been women.[5]

In spring 2022, the exhibit "Women fighters in the Army of Bosnia and Herzegovina," held in the parliament building in Sarajevo, highlighted women's contribution to armed defense. The exhibit was organized by the Archive of

DOI: 10.4324/9781003186168-14

the Bosnian Federation, the Archive of the Unsko-Sanski Kanton, Association of Women Fighters 92–95, the Museum Tešanj, and the Sarajevo municipality. The Association of Women Fighters 92–95 continues to actively advocate for the public recognition of women who fought in the war and who contributed to the war effort, and organizes regular events devoted to commemoration of those women who lost their lives. Serious inequities remain, however, as well as a gender-bias in terms of public recognition of the service provided by women in war. Esma D.'s story highlights those inequities. It also highlights the complex relationship among gender, power, and agency in the context of the recent war, the interdependence between individual and collective recovery, and one woman's active contribution to ongoing peacebuilding.

I am a woman fighter

I am the president and coordinator of the association SEKA Goražde, formed as a women-for-women project connected to SEKA Center for Education, Therapy and Democratic Development.[6] I am a woman fighter. I was on the frontlines during the war and as a result I suffered from PTSD. Because of it, I also had a stroke at 37. When I arrived to SEKA after the war, Gabriele Müller, who was a therapist here, noticed me and helped me through therapy. At that time, I did not even know what that means, nor did I know what was happening to me. Because when you are deep in trauma you do not even know that it is trauma.

People came here from all surrounding cities. There were around 60,000 people at one point in Goražde, a town that now has 24,000–25,000 inhabitants. Its population was 30,000 before the war. Working on my trauma over time, I slowly returned to normal. I wanted to get back to living life in a normal way. Because life cannot be lived in trauma, and there are always triggers that bring you back to what you went through, I learned how to deal with my triggers and all those emotions that would bubble up whenever there is a commemoration of war events, for example. I learned how to recognize the signs of being triggered and how to deal with it. My work here also helps me channel my own emotions, and it also helps other people. I help other survivors recognize their own triggers and provide support for them.

We later established a club for men former fighters suffering with PTSD. We decided to offer support and education to people who are ready to work on their own trauma and who are ready to help others. So, this work can be done with people who have a slightly higher awareness [about the nature of trauma]. We also provide education and training to volunteers. And this work gave rise to another association called Svjetlost Žene [Light of Woman], which became a gathering place for ex fighters, their wives, and children. The poor mental health of veterans affects their families as well. But it was mainly because of the veterans, so that they have a safe space where they will have someone who understands them.

188 Unforgetting and the Politics of Representation

We continue to work with a group of women victims of war who went through individual and group therapy over the years. We supported them in establishing an association Sehara Handmade Crafts.[7] They established this separate entity because there is still stigma attached to what they have survived, and the fact we live in a small community. Many of them have never told their stories to their husbands and to their children. We are working to strengthen this little organization for women victims of war.

We also help other survivors organize in a similar way, their own smaller associations, and groups across Bosnia, such as most recently one in the Bosnian Podrinje Canton,[8] to advocate for them and help them establish a business for weaving, embroidery, and agriculture. This group included some women survivors, but it was also open to other types of population since the criteria for joining were broader. So, we transformed one group of women victims of war into more groups with a more diverse population, which makes them and their experiences less visible. They met others and made friends, and they fit in very well. I think that this is our biggest success, in a way. That they would go to Foča and they would be exposed to hurtful comments from people blaming them for what happened to them and accusing them that they asked for what they got, and so on. They must go through all of that just because they receive 500–600 KM of financial support. We seized the moment with many good younger people in power and managed to provide stipends for the children of these women, as well as set up a code for women as a form of identification, so that each time they go to exercise some of their rights for themselves and their children they are not looked at strangely or exposed to insulting comments. In addition, with the help of the local Mufti and his wife we were able to set up a gynecological clinic at the Islamic Center, where they now provide regular and specialized check-ups for free. They help us a lot even though we are not connected with any religious institution.

Our door is open to all

After the war, Goražde became a majority Muslim city. There are some Croatian women who are SEKA's clients, and we do have a few Serbian women who participate in the workshops for co-living for rural areas, as well as individual and group work. We do bring in experts from Banja Luka, Modriča, Trebinje… It is much easier for those women who come as experts than for those who come to attend as participants. But SEKA is open to all people, regardless of their national identification. SEKA welcomes all people of goodwill, no matter where they come from and which population they belong to, our door is open to all.

When the war began, politically I did not support any of the sides

I served in the Yugoslav National Army (YNA) as a young girl of 19. The reason was that I was not able to finance my university studies and my parents let me decide what I wanted to do. So I went to the army, came back to Goražde, got a job, accomplished great results at work and was thinking about studying national defence. That was a big dream of mine. I socialized with a lot of people,

Esma D., a Bosnian Woman Fighter   189

had many friends from Serbia, I even took part in a great military parade of the Yugoslav National Army in 1985 that was organized in front of the President's Palace. I used to work as mechanical technician. When the war began, politically I did not support any of the sides. I grew up in a small place near Goražde where we were all raised in the Yugoslav spirit, where there were no mosques, no churches, no cathedrals, but it was one working-class area. It was wonderful to live there, full of green spaces, with a theater, folk dances, a sports hall, stadium, swimming pool. I had a nice childhood.

When the grenades started falling, friends urged me to leave Goražde, but I did not take them seriously. I could not see that a war would actually happen in Goražde. Refugees were coming from Čajniče, Foča, Višegrad, and we were still sitting in the city square sipping coffee…I was so naive. We helped those incoming people as much as we could, but still the possibility of war seemed far away. And then in May 1992 a grenade woke me up when it fell on the city. I felt angry. I wondered what I ought to do. I had been in the army before and was very good at handling weapons because of that training. I was worried at this time that someone will come and decide to do things against my will. So, I wanted to take my life into my own hands as much as I could. I lived with my mother at the time, and I felt sorry for her. I wanted to help. I decided to register with the territorial defense unit. The conversation I had there did not sit very well with me. I did not sleep for a whole night. Emotions filled me up. My soul and body were united with all people that I socialized with, people that I grew up with…So how am I going to shoot at them? Grenades continued to fall, snipers were shooting across my neighborhood, some people were already wounded. The city was being taken apart; chaos reigned. There was no water, the telephone lines were cut off. I would not wish that on anyone. And this is how I made a decision.

I have three lives

Some police officers decided to leave the city and go to the villages to be with their families, and they left their guns, so that is how I got a gun. I registered with an intervention unit. There were fourteen (14) of them and I was the fifteenth (15th). It was all of us who grew up together, we knew each other. It was so hard at the beginning, so hard. When I talk about this period, I say that I have three lives. Esma before the war. Esma during the war. And Esma after the war. And maybe this is the fourth (4th) phase, Esma in SEKA. That part of my life before the war was the best. All this in between, the war and after the war, this has been a very difficult period in my life…

So, I made a decision and went to the frontlines. I have seen all sorts of things. There were situations where I shot at people. After that experience you are not the same person as before. When you find yourself in a situation where you shoot at someone and you see a person falling because a bullet from your shotgun hit him, your life changes, you become different. War lasted three and a half years. In some instances, I felt like I had turned into a monster because of hunting down a person the same as he hunted me down, like a wild animal. Your psyche changes and you become something you never thought you could become. There are situations that require direct decisions about your own or another person's death. Also, we were hungry, there were a lot of grenades falling, and snipers shooting. We had no electricity, no medication, hospitals were full of wounded people and a lot of children died, around 150 children died in Goražde. They play and forget themselves and they activate a landmine and ...

After some time, I joined a unit that belonged to the Ministry of Internal Affairs, and we were going to the main hot spots all the time. But I managed to get assigned as a radio operator at times, and to bring food to my mother. Most of the time I was the only woman fighter alongside male fighters. As a member of the Ministry of Foreign Affairs I was called to various crime scenes, and I witnessed horrible sights. I am only able to speak about this because I worked on myself with support from an experienced psychotherapist. The two of us have been working together for ten (10) years; she raised me as her therapeutical child as it were. Gabriele dragged me from a deep, dark tunnel to a sunbathed hill with colorful flowers. That is in short what I can tell you.

I do not know how to pack all of this up and leave it on some rock over there, so that these memories become part of a life that is past, so that I can live in the here and now. The biggest challenge for me personally was when I decided to take a gun and defend myself. That was the decision after which my life changed irrevocably. My life will never be the same as it used to be. That, and the challenge of being a woman in a mass of men, to be accepted. And they really accepted me. I never had any problems from my fighters. They look at me with special kind of eyes and I received support from them. The most important for me personally is that I was able to leave the war as a human being. I never shot at unarmed people, at children, at women, I never set anyone's house on fire... I think I would not have been able to refuse help to an enemy soldier who is wounded if I saw him.

No one takes care of women in war, and women are unrecognized

Other than the one woman from Croatia and another woman from Republika Srpska, in addition to myself, there were two other women who fought on this side, and one of them died. None of us got recognition. I ended the war with a rank just above lieutenant, but this rank was never awarded to me because I am a woman; I even completed a bachelor's degree to increase the chances that my rank will be returned but this never happened. If I were a man, I would be a major at this point or something like that. All that put together probably caused PTSD and even the stroke I suffered at the age of 37. And after all that, there was declaration that women can retire after 20 years of regular service and 40 years of life, so I left military service with 29 years of work experience and 42.5 years of life. The pension that I have earned from this service is 490 KM now and I would not be able to survive on it if I did not work for additional income.

Esma D., a Bosnian Woman Fighter   191

This injustice with respect to my actual rank is entirely due to my being a woman. A similar thing happened to the other woman fighter I mentioned. She does not have a degree and she had to retire with a 400 KM pension. None of our actual war experience and service were considered. No one talks about it, or advocates on our behalf. I also happen to know that men in the service who were coast guards during the war and didn't really take part in combat ended up with pensions of 700–800 KM, 900 KM, 1,000 KM. There was a situation when a man offered me "to go out for a coffee" with him so that my rank would be returned, and I did not want that. No one takes care of women in war, and women are unrecognized.

I remember well the faces of civilian women in prisoner exchanges

In terms of civilian women, there were some who came to Goražde during the war and one of them left a baby in the hospital. That woman left because she did not want to stay in Goražde because of her family. I was present during two prisoner exchanges from Foča and Čajniče while I was in the special unit of the Ministry of Foreign Affairs. I remember well the faces of women who were exchanged. Even though the war affected all of us, and everyone was tired, I could see on their faces the enormous pain they were carrying. Fear. And pain. At the time I did not even know why I saw that pain on their faces. But when I heard stories about what was going on… there were all sorts of violence happening in Kokin Potok, on the entrance to Goražde, and no one ever answered for that. Goražde could not be captured so those things were not happening in the city—we were like an enclave that was left to its own devices.

I also know that some women attempted abortions on their own. Some doctors and hospitals were performing abortions as well, in terrible war conditions. Some of the women who gave birth to children and raised them still fear that someone will tell their children, "Your mother gets that money because of this and that." So, most children still do not know. Often, husbands do not know too. Women and men victims of war, many of them, around 30 percent or even 40 percent live at the poverty line. Despite so much financial help coming to Bosnia and Herzegovina, help that was meant for them, it all went into the wrong hands. I am not sure where it went, but it certainly did not reach those for whom it was intended. They do not have adequate psychological and health support. For many of them it is very important that their ob-gyn is a woman, not a man. Many of them would go to the doctor and he would say, "and what are victims of war? What is that?" In our organization we are also working on raising awareness among civilians, and we asked the Mufti to incorporate that in some religious rituals and to talk about it so that that topic does not continue to be taboo. So that a greater number of people realize that women who went through that are not guilty for it themselves and that support needs to be given to them.

To me, the women are golden lilies; they are the bravest women to me. They are more courageous than any fighter. To go through something like that and still be

192 Unforgetting and the Politics of Representation

living, and today face all that, with a steady series of obstacles—all praise to them.

If I had to say some something about women's rights here and now, I would say that we do have some laws that seek to provide rights for women, to protect women from domestic violence, etc. However, these are not our laws. These laws have been imported from somewhere else and don't mean much here locally, which is why it is difficult to implement them. There are no structures through which they would be implemented either. Additionally, we women need to learn to support each other, and to act in solidarity, to not accept that male nature and decisions dictate our daily lives. Men do not want us in their spheres, in public life, and so on. In theory we should be equal, but in practice this equality is being violated 70 percent of the time for women. For example, there are still cases where all property is registered under the man's name so when a wife needs to exercise individual rights, she cannot do it since everything legally belongs to the husband. There are also cases where sons are provided with land, but daughters are not... Maybe it was better in the past than it is today.[9]

Of national identity and political regimes

In terms of national identity, it seems to me that it depends on how much work someone has done on themselves, how much support they received after the war, and the degree to which one has been able to return to a somewhat normal life, as little as there may be left of it. There are cases when we are attending conferences and meeting with all nationalities, and at times if we were driving in a car, I tended to listen to Serbian music from Republika Srpska at that time, and I would ask, "Do you mind?" The response would always be, "I do not mind." So that is it.

When it comes to me personally some things were just forced on me since I now happen to live in a city where there is a clear Muslim majority. This used to be a multi-ethnic city. When I say forced on me, what I mean is that Serbs and Croats were either relocated from here by force or they left themselves. Goražde is now a 90 percent Muslim city. Lately, I started renewing friendships that I had 30 years ago. So, I talk on the phone with friends I used to socialize with while in the Yugoslav National Army, via Skype, Viber. There are people from Aleksandrovac, Banja Luka, Omiš.[10] I am still influenced by the Yugoslav spirit, the one before the war. We work a lot on that topic as well, here in SEKA, in terms of coexistence. And I do notice some animosity among members of different nationalities, but this is more due to a lack of trust, and fear. That is ultimately what you carry from your family and your upbringing. It depends how people have been raised, and how they are raising their children now. We do run camps for and with children, children from Republika Srpska, who get to spend time with children from Goražde. This is a nice little project financed by the American Embassy.

While there were things I didn't like about Yugoslavia and did not like some segments of society, being Yugoslav suited me well. Good practices from that society should be retained, such as a national and free health-care system and a good social welfare system. Even though I did not like communism as a one-party system, with restrictions over some freedoms, when I look around now, I would prefer to go into some sort of Yugoslav spirit than this democracy ... I am allowed to say what I want but I am not allowed to choose the life I want. So, before I could choose to go to Banja Luka and sleep well, to go to Belgrade and sleep well, even on the roadside bench if I wanted to, I was safe. Today I would not be safe sleeping on a bench even here in Goražde, and I don't feel free to relax, to live. The way Yugoslav society was organized, and the ways that different nationalities used to socialize contributed to variety. Those who wanted to go to a church or mosque, they could do so. We fell from one system into another one. This one is more difficult for me since it interferes with how I was raised and with attitudes that developed from that upbringing, principles I carry from my family.

Suddenly I must identify as belonging to a single national group, to go to church or a mosque to show I am human. More universal human values and morality have been lost. We took all the worst things from the West. Things that are bad and do not suit us have been imported. The State should offer equal rights for everyone, and not only to facilitate for one class of people to live as they want, and for the rest, to each his own. What I mean is that today I often feel that I do not have a state, while in old Yugoslavia I knew we had a state and that the state is going to protect me. I still do not feel well here in Bosnia and Herzegovina, and I see that a lot of youth leave. There is always some kind of tension, there is no progress, there is no going forward, or toward a sort of European path, so that it is good for everyone. The electoral system is not good enough, voters are easily bribed, people of bad morals come into power... and it is they who decide about people's destiny. People will say "you elected him." It is important to know that 60 percent of people do not vote in elections, and even those who do, a mechanism is set up so that those who are in power for a long period of time will win. We could do it again, we had a lot of means, a lot of money but did not seize the moment. There were a lot of imports into Bosnia, the world invested a lot financially, but that money went in the wrong direction.

The women I work with have no issue with national identity at all, but I know they do worry when there is a political upheaval and a threat of renewed violence. It seems that each year it gets worse. There is fear about war starting again, and that threat of violence is the hardest for them. That the same evil does not repeat itself. And the political rhetoric in Bosnia and Herzegovina is worse and worse every year. Even I find myself caught up in this fear sometimes, even though I did work on myself and turned to peace work for the past decade, and I attend all those conferences. But sometimes when you see how far it all goes, that referendum and this referendum... That is very difficult, not only for women who survived sexual violence but for all people who went through war. And along that, a constant tension exists around low living standards. Some people make ends meet with 300 KM a month. For a family of 5 this sometimes mean living on 6 KM a day. This is untenable.

194 Unforgetting and the Politics of Representation

Let us find good people now who will be brothers and sisters to all

The people of Bosnia have great potential. There are good people in Bosnia. But those good people are not seen since everything that is bad floats up to the surface and becomes visible. Some easily bribed and corrupted people are sitting in city council. People who barely graduated from elementary and high school managed to inveigle their way to a seat in city council. That is why I connect to the idea of Yugoslavia: I do not remember it for its own sake but because the state system was better. Sometimes I think the "brotherhood and unity" slogan was artificial. The war showed what kind of brotherhood and unity was had. It will take several generations for trust among people to be regained, so that we can have another kind of brotherhood and unity. Everyone calls upon brotherhood and unity within single national structures. Muslims are brothers among themselves, Serbs among themselves and Croats also among themselves. Let us find good people now who will be brothers and sisters to all, a coefficient of people who wish well to this Bosnia and Herzegovina and to all people in it, and who are committed to Bosnia and Herzegovina moving forward and not always backward.

Notes

1 Leona Slatković Harčević, "Žene u domovinskom ratu," *Braniteljski* (August 8, 2020), accessible at: https://braniteljski.hr/zene-u-domovinskom-ratu/. *Braniteljski* also published an interview with a high profile woman defender, "Žene u Domovinskom ratu: Vijoleta Antolić Vicky" (August 19, 2015), accessible at: https://braniteljski.hr/zene-u-domovinskom-ratu-vijoleta-antolic-vicky/. On Croatian women fighting in the war also see Sanja Stanić and Katarina Mravak, "Domovinski Rat: Ratna Iskustva Žena," *Polemos* 15 (2012), 1, 11–32.

2 "Žena borac u muškom svijetu," *Nezavisne Novine* (May 12, 2015), accessible at: https://www.nezavisne.com/novosti/drustvo/Zena-borac-u-muskom-svijetu/191707.

3 Ajnija Omanic, Mevlida Serdarevic, Amer Ovcina, Hajrunisa Omanic and Jasna Omanic, "Participation of Women in War in Bosnia and Herzegovina from 1992 to 1995," *Materia Socio Medica* 21.3 (2009), 175–178.

4 Purveyors of Authentic Militaria, "Bosnia and Herzegovina. A War Recognition Golden Lily Badge." 2021, accessible at: https://www.emedals.com/europe/bosnia-and-herzegovina-a-war-recognition-golden-lily-badge-iii-model-122554.

5 Sabaheta Ćutuk, cited in S.Š.U., "Žene borci Armije RBiH: Odata počast za 5.360 pripadnica oružanih snaga," Klix Intersoft (April 14, 2022), accessible at: https://www.klix.ba/vijesti/bih/zene-borci-armije-rbih-odata-pocast-za-5-360-pripadnica-oruzanih-snaga/220414108.

6 The German association SEKA Hamburg, founded in 1996 in Hamburg, provides essential financial support for the SEKA-Centre. After ten years on the Croatian Adriatic Island of Brač, the SEKA-Centre moved to Goražde in eastern Bosnia in summer 2007. The carrier organization of the centre in Goražde, Udruženje žena "SEKA" Goražde (Women's Association "SEKA" Goražde) was founded in spring 2007. The SEKA project is mainly financed by donations from foundations and organizations as well as by small and large donations from many single supporters especially from Germany. To a small extent the project is supported by the local government of municipality and District (Kanton) of Goražde. SEKA has

developed a specific peace oriented therapeutic approach focused on promoting a "culture of dialogue" between the different population groups. The association also supports women and girls and raises public awareness of gender-based discrimination and other forms of violence. More details about their work and ongoing projects can be found on their website, at: https://www.seka-hh.de/overview.html.

7 "Sehara" is a Bosnian word of Turkish origin that refers to a large wooden chest decorated with carvings, leather, and thin strips of metal, and used in the past for storing women's dowry.

8 One of ten cantons, or smaller districts, of the Federation of Bosnia and Herzegovina.

9 Esma is one of the three women fighters featured in a 2016 documentary prepared by Dragana Erjavec for TV Justice, entitled, "Žene u uniformama nekadašnjih zaraćenih strana" [Women in Uniforms of Former Warring Sides]. The other two women are Radmila Srdić, who fought on the side of the army of Republika Srpska, and Željka Ergelašev, who belonged to the Croatian Defense Counsel. The documentary is accessible via the BIRN Balkans YouTube channel, at https://youtu.be/ZFcxcc_1Hdc.

10 Aleksandrovac is a municipality in central Serbia; Banja Luka is a city in Republika Srpska, and Omiš is a town on the Dalmatian coast in Croatia.

Conclusion

The Logic of Home: Transnational Fieldnotes on Peace

What do we mean when we say 'home'? It is a virtual question because the destiny of the twenty-first century will be shaped by the possibility or the collapse of a shareable world. The question of cultural apartheid and/or cultural integration is the heart of all governments, and informs our perception of the ways in which governance and culture compel the exoduses of people (voluntary or driven) and raises complex questions of dispossession, recovery, and the reinforcement of siege mentalities... Porous borders are understood in some quarters to be areas of threat and certain chaos, and whether real or imagined, enforced separation is posited as a solution... But [it is a] major failure over time, as the occupants of casual, unmarked, and mass grave sites haunt the entire history of civilization.

Toni Morrison, "Home," Convocation Address at
Oberlin College, April 23, 2009

I came across Toni Morrison's convocation address at Oberlin College, a midsize liberal arts college and music conservatory in Ohio, US, in Maria Popova's beautiful literary blog *The Marginalian*. What Morrison meant when she said that the meaning of home represents a "virtual question" is not that this question has much to do with the virtual sphere of life introduced by digital technologies, but that it has inherent power whose relevance is near absolute from a global perspective. In post-classical Latin, the word *virtualis* relates to concepts of power or potency. Morrison herself, as an African American woman, lived her life contending with the meaning of home in a country she called her own, but one burdened by white supremacist patriarchal legacies, racism, discrimination, and growing social inequalities. Her presence at Oberlin, as the distinguished person addressing a generation of graduates, was important on multiple counts: Oberlin is the oldest coeducational college in the U S, having admitted four women in 1837 to its two-year women's program. It was also among the first educational institutions in the US to admit African Americans. Barack Obama, America's first and thus far only African American President was sworn to office in January that same year. Change was in the air. In 2009, Jóhanna Sigurðardóttir is elected as the first female prime minister of Iceland

DOI: 10.4324/9781003186168-15

earlier that year, becoming the first openly gay head of government in the modern world, Al Gore's documentary film and related album *The Inconvenient Truth* received the Best-Spoken Word Album Award at the 51st Grammy Awards that same year, and people appeared to start to care about the things that mattered.

However, change was not always for the better: by 2009 it was becoming clear that the gradual onset of the global economic recession not only created unprecedented numbers in unemployment and an economic downturn felt around the world, but also caused waves of migration. While that same year countries began to make connections between climate change and migration, and hundreds of thousands fled over land and by boat in search of safety as violence flared from Afghanistan to Iraq to Mexico this year, many governments that once welcomed migrant workers by the tens and hundreds of thousands started to rethink generous immigration policies, failing their commitments toward "immigrant integration." The year 2009 saw an exponential rise in protectionist and exclusionary politics worldwide, tightening of border protection, and migration control. This control, implicated in histories of colonialism, racism and global capitalism, was increasingly being applied to certain groups and individuals who were became designated as "illegal" and "undesirable."[1] The cultural apartheid that is at the heart of all governments, which Morrison refers to in her speech, is something that she had seen unfold in her own home country over the preceding decade, where "year after year, each annual increase in the number of border apprehensions was trumpeted by immigration officials, politicians, and pundits as proof of the ongoing alien invasion. This situation steadily solidifying a new 'Latino threat narrative' in public discourse," led to rising demands and justifications of more restrictive immigration policies, and the increasing militarization of borders.[2] Exclusionary nationalism and right-wing populist policies have been growing in countries as different from one another as Brazil, India, Hungary, and Austria, a trend that has only intensified since. These tendencies have also been visible within European contexts, where the very concept of Europe as a geopolitical space and an imaginary construct is being interrogated and critiqued from both within and without the carefully policed borders of the European Union project. From this perspective, the nationalist post-war governments of Serbia, Croatia, North-Macedonia, as well as the entity of Republika Srpska within the larger Bosnian Federation entity, rather than representing aberrations or reprehensible exemplars of deviant Balkan mentalities, appear to be curiously falling in line with what is taking place outside of their immediate geopolitical borders and in other populist movements across the rest of Europe and North America. We all have to rethink the idea of belonging from the place where we stand, since peace always begins at home.

Having been haunted by the idea of "home" and the complexities of identity and belonging since leaving Yugoslavia in the early 1990s, discovering Morrison's articulation of the global anxiety produced by what she calls "porous borders" in the context of 21st century destinies suddenly helped

198 Unforgetting and the Politics of Representation

reorder my own relationship to this research project, and to the concept of memory, unforgetting and peacebuilding as they interweave the stories of the people whose narratives I bring forward. Home, a concept embodying the possibility as well as the memory of a familiar, shareable world, and the terms on which such a world may or may not be perceived as shareable with some but not with others, is really at the heart of what it means to live in and at peace. It is also at the heart of each of the narratives in the book.

From this perspective, Esma D.'s future-oriented and aspirational redefinition of the ideology of *bratstvo i jedinstvo* is not an example of Yugonostalgia, but an active revisioning of and hope for Bosnia that is consistent with its more recent past, remembering that which was "good." The reference to the Yugoslav slogan acts as a cultural tool of remembrance and an intersubjective memory form through which she negotiates the need for continuity through time and the need to innovate for the future. Like in all the other narratives in this book, in hers, too, memories of the past are reconstructed through the present to re/define a sense of belonging, a key feature of what it means to "be well in the world," to feel *at home*. "Being well in the world" is an oblique reference to Hannah Arendt's trying "to be at home in the world." Arendt describes this concept as a dialectical, evolving process: "…an unending activity by which, in constant change and variation, we come to terms with and reconcile ourselves to reality, that is, try to be at home in the world."[3] To be at home in the world means at once to be at peace with one's own self, as well as with and within the outside world, a dimension of being that is exceptionally significant to individual and collective recovery from war-related trauma. Morrison's question, "What do we mean when we say, 'home'?" is therefore truly "virtual," namely, it is truly "essential" and "inherently powerful" for a discussion of remembrance, agency, and recovery in contemporary Bosnia, as each narrative grapples with this question and provides different answers.

From the perspective of the women who survived rape and other forms of torture in the war, coming back home is not only something that refers to the external world. For a survivor, to come back home means to find a way back to the self, and to reconstitute in a new way what it means to "be well in the world" after the self was splintered apart through unnatural, violent acts. This homecoming, therefore, represents unforgetting: recalling, restitching, and rebuilding the connections between what once was and what is now, looking back in the present moment while orienting to the future, without hatred. The contiguity between narrative and peacebuilding at the personal level is especially evident in the women's storying that makes the "unintelligible and the painful comprehensible and meaningful by contextualizing lived experience within one's larger life story."[4] Each telling deconstructs and reconstructs debilitating life narratives and reframes them in a more empowering way. Each telling functions as an active examination of all those parts of the story that no longer serve the teller well. Each retelling thus also helps the teller reintegrate painful memories into a new life history, each time told anew. From the perspective of the teller,

Conclusion 199

storying one's life help the teller to experience oneself as sufficient, as being "good enough." Personal narratives and acts of telling therefore functional, to the extent that "they assist us to integrate life events into our histories so that our story is experienced as coherent, intelligible, and meaningful."[5]

From the perspective of the children born of war rape, the fight for recognition, visibility, and acceptance in their personal lives, their communities, and within the global discourse of inclusion, diversity, and equity, entails constructing alternative narratives of emotional experience and narratives of belonging that are psychologically important to tellers as being sufficient to themselves. But these active narrative reconstructions clearly have a distinct social dimension as well, as they involve the recognition of those around them, the family, the school, the community, and all levels of policy. Their work of narrating the terms of home and peace from where they stand directly calls all others around them to bear witness to the telling. Being invited to witness the telling is in turn also a call to share responsibility for finding justice, for repairing, reframing, and healing some of the harm inflicted by the war, the violence to which they owe their very existence, and its shadow.

To the extent that "home" is a place and a form of belonging, the unforgetting of war, and narratives of suffering, recovery, and peacebuilding recorded in this book are narratives that circumscribe the shifting dimensions of home and belonging through time as well as place. Conceptually as well as practically, war represents a violent reordering of the borders of home, identity, and memory, a reordering that through conflict and suffering dislocates and rends one's sense of belonging and the meaning of home at a collective as well as a very intimate, personal level. In addition to being redrawn politically because of war or political change, as a concept that denotes the line between inside/outside, us/them, self/other, home is also defined through borders, which are also metaphorical and psychological. The borders are drawn and redrawn in the everyday interactions among people who both reinscribe them through prejudice and exclusion, and who deconstruct them, subvert them through counternarratives, individual actions, activism, and everyday gestures of solidarity and kindness. Recovery and peacebuilding, therefore, have to do with people's active reconstructing of a logic of "home," a way of constructing the possibility of "a shareable world." In this sense, post-war rebuilding is not only a state project defined exclusively through the public or official political realm, but an intimate project that depends on individual people redeveloping myriad ways of connecting different pasts to the present through time and experience, and being able to imagine a meaningful, contiguous future.

The perspectives of individuals who have been most directly involved in the war, or those who have sustained most harm through war provide a valuable lens through which to understand the complexity of peacebuilding and recovery in Bosnia. Their perspectives help us identify dimensions of agency that are often unaccounted for in discussions of Bosnia's official politics and transitional justice. They foreground individual, embodied experience as an analytical strategy to help make sense of power, gender, and agency, as well as a tool for interrogating the tensions between collective and official dimensions of nationalism, nationhood, and justice, and their manifestations in everyday interactions. Their narratives sometimes reinscribe, but also often interrogate and deconstruct what Morrison refers to as the "reinforcement of siege mentalities" within the Bosnian context, the mentality of official ethno-nationalism and the "threat of the other" propagated across various governance systems through the rigid constitutional structures of the Dayton Accord. Their stories and perspectives assert the complex lived reality of *suživost* (coexistence) both during and after the war and affirm the "porous borders" of cultural and religious identities. They emphasize and question how the notion of "home" has been politicized, weaponized, and mobilized to support oppressive political agendas and harmful scripts of prejudice.

Individual stories and perspectives also point to peace and peacebuilding as an ecology, a process that depends on complex interactions and interdependence between individuals and their cultural, social, political, and family environments. The process must be understood as relational, dynamic, and operating through multiple tensions that are at times held in a constructive balance and at other times shift the weight of the variables contained in the balance in the direction of change. In their individual complexity, people, also embedded within their own community ecosystems, bring to this interaction their own unique personal histories shaped by multiple intersections of identity: gender, class, religious denomination, level of dis/ability, political orientation, personal resilience, etc. Community ecosystems, in turn, comprise only one aspect of a larger life environment, which itself also encompasses social, cultural, economic, political, and legal frameworks that exist at the macro level.

One of the central philosophical problems relating to studying individual lives and their embeddedness and interaction with systems in the context of the life sciences has been through the lens of ecologies.[6] To look at individual lives from a social ecological perspective means to explicate the relation between diversity, stability and identity, that is, the status of "porous borders," and to interrogate the principles of what in Bosnia and the former Yugoslavia has been known as *suživost*. This relation revolves around acute questions of belonging, such as "what does it mean to live with another who may and at the same time may not be the same as me?" and, "what are the grounds for the mutual recognition of both similarity and difference and their peaceful outcome?

My own transnational and sometimes ambiguous inhabiting of the concept of home—suspended between a national identity that no longer exists geopolitically and a claim to being Canadian through naturalization and simply remaining in place for over 30 years, repositions the meaning of both "local" and "outsider" in both places. The terms of *suživost* (coexistence), the limits of national identity, and the need to clarify who is the "foreigner," the "other'" along real and imagined borders between "us" and "them," are all actively

Conclusion 201

being negotiated and debated not only in Bosnia but here in Canada, too, as well as globally. Nationalist forms of thinking, with their obsessive reckoning of who "belongs" and who does not and why, exist not only embedded in official political ideology in Bosnia, other nation-states in the Balkans, and globally, but also as a flexible discourse and social practice integral to many activities and processes present in a variety of social organizations and everyday interactions in multiple global locations.[7]

For some Bosnians, some of whom were targeted for who they were or were perceived to represent, right-wing nationalist politics of exclusion and separation based on religious denomination or nationality prior, during, and since the war simply provide a way to assert their right to life. For others those divisions justify real as well as imagined personal and/or collective grievances. For many yet, these new realities are experienced as ideologically foreign, incompatible with their own political and civic views, which were aligned with not only the official Yugoslav policy of multiculturalism, but also with a sense of regional and community loyalty. A loyalty to a friend and neighbor, which just like in the stories of people who survived the siege of Sarajevo, is rooted in the local, embodied history of place, in family, relationships with those around you, next to you, and shared living—not religion, and not nationality.

The symbolic aspects of the nation as *home* are always superimposed onto actual houses or apartments, communities, actual homes—the place where one is born, or where one lives now, and returns to every day, or once a year. Such multidirectional overlapping between the symbolic and the actual dimension of home and belonging animate all national projects. They also animate all wars, as well. The symbolic dimensions of the nation as home are what in the hands of politicians becomes weaponized and used to justify acts and policies that are ostensibly always in the service of this imagined nation. The continuities as well as disjunctions between collective and/or official discourses, and individual, private histories and experiences of home are located in the space of this multidirectional overlap. All of the people whose perspectives I bring forward in this book negotiate the nation and conceptualize national belonging in terms that are critical of the current official politics in Bosnia. In that sense, by virtue of their everyday actions and perspectives, they all participate in the cultural and social forces contributing to the gradual reshaping of the Bosnian political landscape. This reshaping, as I have argued, is multivalent and non-linear, just as it is in any complex modern society grappling with the issue of porous borders and the articulation of national identity. Narratives of nationhood never unfold or are enacted according to linear trajectories, although they are often presented as such at the normative level of ideology embodied (e.g., party-based politics).

The non-linearity of these narratives of nationhood is visible not only within Bosnia. It has been amplified globally in the context of massive transnational movements of people, goods, services, and culture across multiple borders. The consequence of movements of people across national borders is that the composition of those within national borders also changes, and the nature and borders of "home" are consequently redrawn, redefined to accommodate various forms of diverse belonging. Individual acts of remembrance, personal choices, and ways of being in the world, therefore, always have political dimensions, and are always implicated in and constitutive of politics, nationhood, memorialization, and peacebuilding. Rather than viewing nationalism as "the product of macro-structural forces," such as politics, economics, and culture in a broad sense, nationalism also operates as "the practical accomplishment of ordinary people engaging in routine activities," and studies of nationalism must increasingly focus on the ways in which nationhood is negotiated, reproduced, and in some cases undermined and subverted through the actual practices of ordinary people as they engage and enact nationhood in everyday life.[8] Manifestations of nationalist or ethno-cultural exclusionary thinking are, therefore, not the peculiar distinction of the so-called Bosnia, nor are they the single most important essentializing framework through which contemporary Bosnian politics can and should be evaluated.

The issue of "being well in the world" and of the porousness of borders is of acute relevance to many developed societies within and outside of Europe. It has been pointed out recently by US-based scholars of nationalism that "with the emergence of the radical right in Western democracies[,] it is no longer appropriate to think of nationalism and authoritarianism as problems belonging to a bygone era or to geographically distant cases," but a flexible form of thought that permeates all modern societies.[9] As a diverse set of ideas, principles, and practices that structure everyday life, nationalism is not a "a juvenile disease that one can outgrow or cure," a "marginal nuisance that periodically interrupts a natural flow of human development," but in fact a "dominant form of modern subjectivity."[10] The form of modern subjectivity that it represents exists precisely at the intersection of politics, culture, and individual belonging, that is, the domain of "home," and the drive to find its location, its walls, its boundaries. Contemporary Bosnian politics, as well as the nationalist movements and political ideology that led to the war, therefore, must always be evaluated both in their own regional specificity *and* in the context of global historical trends relating to nationalist ideas, rather than only being contextualized as a peculiar "post-socialist" aberration within Western-centric narratives of "incompleteness" and "transition."

The nation, represented as a distinct nation-state with a geopolitical global presence and form of territorial rule, is not an ideologically neutral or naturally forming entity in any context, as much as media and politicians in many neoliberal, capitalist Western nations would often represent it to be the case, seeking to render their ideology natural and invisible. Nationalist politics and populist sentiment can and do manifest in multiple ways since nationalism is a "multifaceted political ideology" which can easily coalesce with a far-right ideologies, while also being able to accommodate various moderate positions across the political spectrum.[11] Malešević has recently made the astute claim that nationalism is a habitual form of everyday social practice and a "very plastic type of modern subjectivity." The fear of the porous borders of which Morrison speaks in fact stems from the contradictory and powerful images of nationalism: as a "force of collective solidarity but also a mechanism of group aggression" against those who do not belong or are perceived as not belonging to the nation.[12] Nationalism can be embodied in the nation-state's official "elected" politics, as it is, for example, in Bosnia and Herzegovina, manifest in varying degrees across multiple political party platforms. It can also exist and be expressed in opposition to official politics, or what is perceived to be official politics. Individual and systemic racism, and anti-immigrant prejudice and discrimination are enactments of a particular type of right-wing, anti-liberal nationalism, rooted in nationalist ideas, protectionism, and exclusion, although this is never identified quite in these terms within Canada itself, where "nationalism" and "nationalist politics" remain reserved for other nation-states, frequently those perceived as "non-Western."

The narratives in the book indicate that since the signing of the Dayton Agreement a significant tension has been generated between the level of normative nationalist state narrative on the one hand, and the operational level "encountered in the features and patterns of everyday life," on the other.[13] The official political framework based on ethno-nationalism no longer—if it ever did—accurately reflects or represents the civic desires and concepts of many people in the entity of the Bosnian Federation, including those who suffered harm and great personal losses in the war. In fact, their narratives actively deconstruct and critique official nationalist politics, identifying it clearly as an ineffective hold on power by political elites who use it to exploit ordinary citizens' fear of another war especially in context of Republika Srpska's own ultra-nationalist politics and a population that has become more homogenously Serb since the war. This is not to say that the warmongering official regional politics of Republika Srpska is not a cause for concern; it is. Just as warmongering in all its manifestations is to be condemned wherever and whenever it surfaces, warmongering and hostility based on inciting fear of the "other" and the policing of the borders of the imagined home.[14]

When it comes to Bosnia, and the Federation entity specifically, from the narratives of women survivors and others whose stories I bring forward in previous chapters, the war forcefully and violently reordered the idea of "home" and homeland. Among the consequence of war, among other losses, is a loss of social context and a resulting feeling of alienation and displacement from familiar structures representing home and a sense of belonging. Displacement is possible even if one had never been physically displaced, an experience that appears to be inextricably linked to the perceived loss of sociocultural context.[15] Their narratives in fact actively reconstitute both the loss of social context because of war and represent its assertion and re-establishment. Recalling the losses of war also means recalling and identifying those aspects of life that have not been lost, that are still here, and that may be part of the future as well. Their stories frequently reveal that their lived reality during and after the war stood and continues to stand in contrast to the official nationalist politics of war, as well as the three-way cleavage among the three constituent peoples recognized by the constitution: Bosniaks, Serbs, and Croats that was ossified through the Dayton Agreement. The stories also reveal that many people in Bosnia have not been served well by the institutionalized emphasis on nationality as a main marker of identity. Having in many cases a first-hand knowledge of an alternative, of peaceful coexistence in a multicultural secular system that emphasized strong civic values and the care of the state to develop strong networks of social support and welfare, means that they can clearly identify the shortcomings of the current model and ideology.

Given that "the nation" is not only a political project but also a cognitive, affective, and discursive category deployed in everyday practice,[16] the discursive space opened by this tension may not only lead to a weakening of the official nationalist agenda, at least in the Federation entity, but to a broader ideological and civic realignment of values. The same process of realignment of values and political orientations applies to any national context where the tension between the normative and operative levels of ideology becomes too great, and therefore warrants change. This statement is neither optimistic nor pessimistic when it comes to Bosnia. It is simply based on lessons from Bosnia's historical reality. Based on a long historical view, the process of change and realignment is neither linear nor confined to a specific time frame. Rather than being explained in terms of axiomatic Balkan turmoil, these changes in the Bosnia and Herzegovina are a matter of self-determination, citizenship, and minority rights, problems associated with religious and other forms of autonomy, the changing role of domestic and international institutions in response to the pressures of a globalized, transnational cultural, and political arena, just as they are everywhere else.

The nation accomplishes its symbolic role of "home" only to the extent that it can successfully hold in balance and functionally align, at least for a period, the normative with the operative level of ideology. Forms of nationalist politics in Bosnia, in Canada, in France, Hungary, the UK, and elsewhere, do not belong to "a doctrine whose pinnacle was long in the past and whose decline was inevitable," or a phenomenon that can be ascribed to "belated" or "incomplete" trajectory toward the accomplishment of a settled democratic nation. Nationalism is in fact the "most popular operative ideology" that has been the "dominant mode of political legitimacy and collective subjectivity in the modern era," for the last 200 years, one only made more visible by unregulated economic globalization, the transnational movement of people, and the consequent sharp rise in economic inequalities globally.[17]

Conclusion 205

To be meaningful and to avoid falling into the Balkanist discourse or other forms of "Othering," all discussions of sustainable peacebuilding must begin within a self-referential perspective, and analysis grounded in the awareness that principles of peace and justice equally pertain to each society where difference is being actively negotiated. In a dynamic and fiercely interconnected global world, peace processes, the accompanying political restructuring and re/building of civil society are only nominally more relevant or applicable to so-called post-conflict societies, such as Bosnia. A narrow and reductive focus on peace and conflict and binary framing of peace processes in terms of victims and perpetrators stifles meaningful reconceptualizing of what it takes to create a peaceful and just society, in Bosnia, as well as here in Canada, and everywhere else where the logics of "home" are being actively negotiated.

Moreover, the "post-conflict" designation is becoming increasingly imprecise and debatable within Bosnia itself, as well as in how it is applied to the country externally, as it is unclear what period must elapse since the armed conflict for it to lose its nominal significance. Continuing to conceive of Bosnia with a focus on its status as a "post-conflict" society, both internally and from the outside, continues to reinscribe dominant discourses about the country within the context of international relations, and deflects much-needed attention from a variety of peace actions and processes that unfold through the lived experiences of people within it.

Peace is a complex process and a dimension of life encompassing not only the absence of open warfare and armed conflict but also identity, meaning, a sense of belonging, and the experience of well-being beyond lifestyle and purchasing power. In terms of the process of justice within Bosnia and Herzegovina, and from the perspective of survivors of rape and other forms of torture, positive peace cannot be fully achieved until they have received adequate support and recognition across all entities and levels. Within Bosnia and Herzegovina and other former Yugoslav states, "achieving a state of positive peace depends on accepting collective moral responsibility for harms caused by each side in the war."[18] The voices of women survivors of war rape and other forms of war torture and the children born because of war, in particular, are key to understanding the ecology of peace in Bosnian society. As those who directly experienced the violence of war and live with its consequences daily, they are well positioned as key voices in peace processes calling for accountability, broadening conceptions of justice, pointing to what it means to live with others and looking to the future while remembering the past. Their perspectives and lived experiences, arising from their specific positionality within Bosnia and in relation to the war, represent the most ethically meaningful place from which to continue to build sustainable peace across all levels of society.

Notes

1 Nicholas De Genova, "Migrant 'Illegality' and Deportability in Everyday Life", *Annual Review of Anthropology* 31 (2002): 419–47.
2 Douglass S. Massey, "Creating the Exclusionist Society: From the War on Poverty to the War on Immigrants," *Ethnic Racial Studies* 43.1 (2020), 18–37. doi: 10.1080/01419870.2019.1667504, n.p.
3 Hannah Arendt, "Understanding and Politics (The Difficulties of Understanding)," In ed. J. Kohn, *Essays in Understanding 1930–1954* (New York, NY: Harcourt, Brace and Company, 1994), 307–327, 307–308.
4 Christine E. Kiesinger, "My Father's Shoes: The Therapeutic Value of Narrative Reframing," In ed. Arthur P. Bochner and Carolyn Ellis, *Ethnographically Speaking: Autoethnography, Literature, and Aesthetics* (Walnut Creek: Rowman & Littlefield Publishers Inc., 2002), 95–113, 107.
5 Kiesinger, "My Father's Shoes: The Therapeutic Value of Narrative Reframing," 107.
6 See Introduction in this book, note 21.
7 Siniša Malešević, "The Many Faces of Nationalism," *Nationalities Papers* (2023), 1–10. doi:10.1017/nps.2022.114, p. 2.
8 Jon E. Fox and Cynthia Miller-Idriss, "Everyday Nationhood," *Ethnicities* 8.4 (2008), 536–563, 537. doi: 10.1177/1468796808088925.
9 Bart Bonikowski, "Ethno-Nationalist Populism and the Mobilization of Collective Resentment," *The British Journal of Sociology*, 61.1 (2017). doi.org/10.1111/1468-4446.12325, n.p.
10 Siniša Malešević, *Grounded Nationalisms: A Sociological Analysis* (Cambridge University Press, 2019), 3–4.
11 Malešević, "The Many Faces of Nationalism," 2.
12 Malešević, "The Many Faces of Nationalism," 2; cit. Tom Nairn, *Faces of Nationalism: Janus Revisited*, 2005.
13 Malešević, *Grounded Nationalisms*, 78.
14 For different types of warmongering politics currently being relied upon in western neoliberal capitalist economies see the Mar 23, 2022 Editor's note of the *Global Times,* "Warmongering US," accessible at: lobaltimes.cn/page/202203/1256639.shtml. Also, see, Caitlin A. Johnstone, "Modern U.S. warmongering is scaring Henry Kissinger,"*MROnline*, Aug 16, 2022, accessible at: https://mronline.org/2022/08/16/modern-u-s-warmongering-is-scaring-henry-kissinger/; Richard Sanders, "Fuelling Wars, Supplying the Warmongers.
   Canadian gov't heavily subsidizing our military companies," *Canadian Centre for Policy Alternatives*, Mar 1, 2010, accessible at, https://policyalternatives.ca/publications/monitor/fuelling-wars-supplying-warmongers; "Canadian Foreign Affairs Minister Called 'Warmonger,' Town Hall Cut Short," *teleSUR*, Sep 23, 2022, accessible at: https://www.telesurenglish.net/news/Protesters-Cut-Short-Canadian-Foreign-Affairs-Minister-Town-Hall-20190923-0011.html; Simon Jenkins, "Truss's Warmongering Rhetoric Is Empty, Antagonistic – And Wildly Dangerous," *The Guardian*, Aug 26, 2022, accessible at: https://www.theguardian.com/commentisfree/2022/aug/26/liz-truss-warmongering-dangerous-craving-theatre-conflict; "Our Warmongering Politicians Disgrace the Memory of the War Dead," *Morning Star*, n.d. accessed on Dec 8, 2022 from https://morningstaronline.co.uk/article/e/our-warmongering-politicians-disgrace-memory-war-dead.
15 Sandina Begić, "Imagine Being Alone: Making Sense of Life in Contemporary Bosnia and Herzegovina by Remembering the Past," In ed. O. Simić, Z. Volčič and

C. Philpot, *Peace Psychology in the Balkans*. Peace Psychology Book Series. (Boston, MA: Springer, 2012). https://doi.org/10.1007/978-1-4614-1948-8_8.
16 Bart Bonikowski, "Three Lessons of Contemporary Populism in Europe and the United States," *The Brown Journal of World Affairs*, XXIII.I (2016), 9–24.
17 Malešević, *Grounded Nationalisms: A Sociological Analysis* (Cambridge University Press, 2019), 3–4.
18 S. Čehajić-Clancy, "Coming to Terms with the Past Marked by Collective Crimes: Collective Moral Responsibility and Reconciliation." In ed. O. Simić, Z. Volčič, and C. Philpot, *Peace Psychology in the Balkans*. Peace Psychology Book Series. (Boston, MA: Springer, 2012), 235. https://doi.org/10.1007/978-1-4614-1948-8_14.

Index

Pages followed by "n" refer to notes

Abdić, Fikret 144, 174
Alexievich, Svetlana 1, 18, 89, 133
Anglosphere 5, 8–9, 49
the Association of Women Victims of War 86, 122, 188
Association Forgotten Children of War x, xi, 17, 43, 46, 53, 98–100, 102–105, 108

Balkan Insight 97
Balkans 8, 15, 33, 37, 53, 77, 86, 94, 104, 197, 201, 204
Balkanism 8, 16, 48, 52; Balkanist forms of thought and representation 17; harmful Balkanist stereotypes 51; the Balkanist discourse 205
Banja Luka 3, 62, 125, 169, 188, 192–193
Belgrade 2–3, 86, 100, 193; the Serbian Youth Initiative for Human Rights (YIHR) in Belgrade 107
Beširević, Selma 51, 83
Bosniak (includes: *Bošnjak, Bošnjaci*) 11, 48, 51, 59–61, 66, 73–74, 126, 135, 143, 145, 155, 180, 182, 204
Bosniak women 11, 13, 30, 37, 41, 54, 93
Bosnian: culture 15–16, 53–54, 64, 66–68, 72–77, 83, 91, 93, 103; Federation (includes: Federation of Bosnia and Herzegovina) 11–12, 48, 50, 55, 64, 74–76, 91, 98, 106, 186–187; future 60, 96, 107–108, 116, 120, 127, 129, 149, 179, 193–194, 198; history 49–50, 94, 204; identity 8–11, 19, 48, 54, 61, 65–66, 73–74, 76, 86, 94–96, 104, 108–109, 116,

125, 127, 129, 140, 145, 180, 182, 204; politics 12, 16–17, 48, 52–53, 66, 73, 76, 86, 104, 107, 127–128, 136, 191, 193, 199, 201, 205
Bosnian Serbs 3; Bosnian Serb militias 63
Bosnian war 1–3, 7–9, 12–13, 17–18, 30, 61, 63–64, 71, 93–95, 97, 205
Bratstvo i jedinstvo (includes: "brotherhood and unity") 58, 71–72, 96, 180, 194, 198
Brčko District 11, 48, 106
'Brotherhood and unity' *see Bratstvo i jedinstvo*
Broz, Josip *see* Tito

Čajić, Jelena 106
Chetniks (includes: *četnici, četnik*) 59–60, 66, 93–94, 119, 128, 157
child of war 17, 31, 40–42, 51, 53–54, 91–96, 98–109, 113, 120, 122, 129, 137, 155–156, 160, 174, 199, 205
Civilian Victims of War (including: *civilna žrtva rata*) 10, 12–13, 41–42, 99, 102, 106, 114, 118, 125, 159, 162, 166–167, 171, 175, 178; *see also* victims of war

Damon, Lejla 96
Dayton Peace Agreement 3, 7, 9–11, 16, 30, 48–49, 59, 64–65, 72, 75, 95, 109, 122, 156, 200
Delić, Amra 43, 98
Dodik, Milorad 76, 126–128

FAMA 64, 68–69

Gegić, Šemsudin 92–95, 97
Goražde 93, 97, 128–129, 187–193;
  SEKA Goražde 136, 187–189, 192
Grbavica 64, 95, 137, 155

Hodges, Natalie 1–2, 10
the Hague 136, 168, 174, 177
Halilović, Jasminko 43

the Institute for Research of Crimes
  against Humanity and International
  Law 97
International Criminal Tribunal for the
  Former Yugoslavia (ICTY) 7, 10, 13,
  30, 132n2, 136, 177, 184
the International Organization for
  Migration, Mission in Bosnia and
  Herzegovina 99
Izetbegović, Alija 3, 59, 78n5, 128
Izetbegović, Bakir 126, 128

Jugoslovenstvo see Yugoslavism
Jusić, Ajna x, xi, 17, 43, 46, 99–108

Kovačević, Milomir *see* 'Strašni'

Medica (includes: Medica Zenica) 11,
  122–123, 151, 154–155, 158, 162,
  167–168, 170–171, 177–178
Milošević, Slobodan 2–3
The "Mothers of Srebrenica" *see*
  Srebrenica
Muhić, Alen 92, 97–98, 129
The Museum of War Childhood 43, 99

NGOs in Bosnia 11–13, 106, 136, 164–165

Omeragić, Merima 51, 83
Omerović, Armin 98
Omerčausević, Mirna 100

Partisans 119, 179
peace 15, 30, 32, 40, 48–50, 52, 74, 100, 102,
  104, 107, 136, 140, 177, 197–199, 205
peacebuilding xi, 7–8, 15–16, 19, 31, 33,
  40, 64, 66, 71, 74, 76, 104–105, 107,
  109, 187, 198–200, 205
PTSD 137, 187, 190

rape 2, 11, 30, 33, 37–38, 40, 42–43, 54,
  84, 87, 91, 93–94, 96–103, 107,
  116–120, 135–137, 139, 148, 150,
  154–156, 159, 164, 177, 182, 198, 205

Republika Srpska 11–13, 48, 61, 76, 86,
  97, 103–104, 107–108, 125–126, 129,
  157, 181, 186, 190, 192, 197, 203

Sarajevo 59–68, 73, 75, 77, 83–84, 87, 94,
  103, 105, 116, 120, 125–127, 138,
  145–147, 151, 172, 174, 176–177, 183,
  186, 201
SEKA Goražde 136, 187–189, 192
Serbian Youth Initiative for Human
  Rights (YIHR) 100, 107
sexual/sexualized violence 1, 7, 10–12, 16,
  18, 30, 36–37, 40–41, 43, 94–96, 99,
  102, 104, 106–107, 119–120, 140, 193
Social Democratic Action (SDA) Party
  128, 158, 167; SDA [Stranka
  Demokratske Akcije, "Party of
  Democratic Action"] 127
Srebrenica 126, 136, 151, 182; *Mothers of
  Srebrenica* 84, 136
'Strašni' Milomir Kovačević 66–68
Subašić, Munira xi, 136

Tito 58–59, 61, 68, 71–74, 77, 85, 128;
  Titoist 5
Todorova, Maria, *Imagining the Balkans*
  8
trauma 16, 18, 29, 32, 36, 38–41, 48, 54,
  65, 85, 97, 100–102, 106–107,
  136–137, 139, 152, 158, 187
Tudjman, Franjo 3, 5
Tuzla 98, 101, 128

UNPROFOR 99, 154
Ustaše [ustashe] 59, 66, 87, 93–94, 147,
  159, 166

victims of war 12–13, 86, 103, 167, 188,
  191; *see also* Civilian Victims of War

women survivors 10, 33, 38, 41, 43, 50,
  91, 95, 103, 108, 117, 120–121, 130,
  137, 152, 163, 165, 167, 171, 178–179,
  188, 193, 198, 203, 205

Yugonostalgia 5, 52, 85, 193, 198
Yugoslav 11, 145, 180–181, 186, 192;
  former Yugoslav countries 3, 8–9, 30,
  53, 74, 91; former Yugoslav
  nationalities 54, 68, 71; the former
  Yugoslav republic 11, 48, 68; the
  official Yugoslav policy of
  multiculturalism 4, 201; post-Yugoslav

states 52, 104, 107–108, 205; pre-Yugoslav, Yugoslav, and post-Yugoslav Bosnian identities 74; the Yugoslav citizen 2, 73; the Yugoslav constitution of 1974 73; Yugoslav National Army 2, 145, 188–189, 192; Yugoslav national iconography 72; the Yugoslav Navy 68, 71; Yugoslav passport 2–3; Yugoslav Peoples Army 63; the Yugoslav People's Liberation War (1941–45) 71; Yugoslav Republic of Macedonia 4, 77; Yugoslav socialism 5, 8, 15, 73–74, 105; the Yugoslav spirit 189, 193; the Yugoslav state 52, 96

Yugoslavia 2, 4, 10, 28, 52, 60–61, 68–69, 72, 77, 86, 128, 192–194, 197; disintegration of Yugoslavia 5, 7, 9, 52, 54, 66, 72; the former Yugoslavia 9, 11, 49, 51, 79n20, 85, 96, 101, 107, 186, 200; the League of Communists of Yugoslavia 71–72, 96; socialist Yugoslavia 53–54, 71, 73; Tito's Yugoslavia 73, 85, 128

Yugoslavism 74; ideology of Yugoslavism 72; *Jugoslovenstvo* (Yugoslavism) 73–74

Yugosphere xii, 5, 8–9, 17, 19, 49, 53, 55, 67–68, 73, 83

Milton Keynes UK
Ingram Content Group UK Ltd.
UKHW031330071224
451979UK00005B/71